Developing International Business in the Context of Culture and Ethics in Transformation

European University Studies
Europäische Hochschulschriften
Publications Universitaires Européennes

Series V
Economics and Management

Reihe V Série V
Volks- und Betriebswirtschaft
Sciences économiques, gestion d'entreprise

Vol./Bd. 2899

PETER LANG
Frankfurt am Main · Berlin · Bern · Bruxelles · New York · Oxford · Wien

Ingmar Wienen

Developing International Business in the Context of Culture and Ethics in Transformation

The Example of China

PETER LANG
Europäischer Verlag der Wissenschaften

Die Deutsche Bibliothek - CIP-Einheitsaufnahme

Wienen, Ingmar:

Developing international business in the context of culture and ethics in transformation : the example of China / Ingmar Wienen. - Frankfurt am Main ; Berlin ; Bern ; Bruxelles ; New York ; Oxford ; Wien : Lang, 2002
(European university studies : Ser. 5, Economics and management ; Vol. 2899)
Zugl.: Washington, Internat. Univ., Diss., 2002
ISBN 3-631-39533-7

Gedruckt auf alterungsbeständigem,
säurefreiem Papier.

ISSN 0531-7339
ISBN 3-631-39533-7
US-ISBN 0-8204-5985-2

Printed in Germany 1 2 3 4 5 7

www.peterlang.de

TABLE OF CONTENTS

I. INTRODUCTION

The central question of this study is how to develop business activities that match a developing foreign culture. In an era of globalization, this question is becoming ever more important.

The example of China has been chosen, because the country is perceived as being far away, having a difficult language and a strange culture. The country does not take a central position in the minds of many people in the West. Recent history has left their traces, so that common associations with "China" still include crowds of people wearing dark Mao suits while riding bicycles. Chinese culture is widely associated with eating rice with chopsticks and the production of silk. In this sense, a reason for the choice of China is that from a Western perspective, China is probably the most „**different**" country on earth; if one can find a method to bridge that gap, than other cases will probably be relatively easy to solve.

Another reason consisted of the challenge China provides due to the deep **transformation** from a centrally planned to a market economy that the country is undergoing at the moment. Before writing this book, I had come to the conclusion that most of the common associations with "China" had to do with prejudice. I wanted to live in China in order to understand something about the country, its history and culture, that have developed with so little interaction with the West. I also wanted to understand what this idea of emerging markets in Asia was all about, and I thought that China would be a good example.

Finally, other than the extra large challenges, China represents also an enormous potential reward due to the sheer size of the country. I had witnessed the transformation of Eastern Europe, and more closely the integration of the two German states, and I wanted to experience what changes are taking part in China, were any change would have a different **magnitude** due to the enormous size of the country. My main question was: how can one build a sustainable business in China?

The process of writing this book was closely linked to my personal discovery of the China of today, which I think can only be understood in its historical context. Therefore, after a summary of prior research and my own view on the work that has been done so far, I explain the numerous sources in China that have been used to give as authentic an overview as possible. Following the methodology, I give an account of the history and culture of the country. Other important aspects receive equal attention, such as the legal, the political and the education system. But the study has also included subjects more directly linked to business activities: the definition of economic regions, the changes in the national economic model and their impact on the Chinese people, and finally business practices in China.

Based on those findings, I am presenting a guide for doing business in a foreign culture, addressing the process of building business step by step: from preparing for market entry and understanding government policy and relevant laws, to investigating the environment and starting the operation. I am also providing some insights in areas that are especially important in China: Human Resource Management and relationship building, including personal and public relations. I have evaluated this model in the case of China, and in the last part of this study, I am presenting a number of conclusions.

Now that this book will be published, I have a strong feeling that it is work in progress, because the situation in China is developing every year, or better: every day. I would encourage everyone to take this research just as an analysis of today; more research is needed to keep up with the pace of development in this great country.

This study would not have been possible without the support of a number of friends and family. My special gratitude goes to HongLing Wang, who has been my personal guide in finding my way in China.

II. PRIOR RESEARCH

A lot has been written about international management and intercultural management; this study is far from being the first of its kind. This section analyses a number of specific examples of prior research that is close to this work, grouped by types of study.

A. INTERCULTURAL STUDIES

Hofstede has published comprehensive research on the interdependence of culture, organizations and management. He has developed five categories that allow to classify nations, organizations and companies (Hofstede 1993):

1) the degree of integration of individuals in groups,

2) the differences between social roles of men and women,

3) ways to deal with inequality,

4) lack of tolerance of the unknown and

5) long-term versus short-term satisfaction of needs.

This is basis for advising on how to cope with a given culture which he sees as important within business.

Trompenaars has tried to provide solutions on how to integrate local cultures and the international environment, or how to gain an international dimension in companies that do business on an international level. He would not agree that there are cultural stereotypes. He argues that a culture may well have some dominating characteristics. However, there is a cultural identity of each individual person and company which enables it to adapt to a wide range of contexts. Trompenaars (1994) suggests a set of seven cultural dimensions.

Usunier has shown the impact of culture in a more closely defined area: marketing in an international context. Not unlike Hofstede, Usunier (1992a, 61-66) describes a range of "sources" of culture, including nationality, religion and family.

He shows that as a consequence of dealing with different cultures, products may need to be modified, negotiations reviewed or partners to be searched.

Hermel has studied the reality of management at a European and international level, focusing on the aspect of human resource management. His results demonstrate clearly, that within Europe there are large differences (Hermel 1993).

An important overview of comparative research on management cultures in the German speaking world has been published by **von Keller** (1982). He has defined culture as all shared implicit and explicit rules for behavior that are passed from one generation to the next. In his research he favors a qualitative approach, given the weaknesses of quantitative intercultural research.

Dülfer has published a major work that deals with the potential long-term implications of international management. He argues that companies will become increasingly global and therefore have to understand international business customs. Similar to Hofstede, Dülfer (1997, 318-359) looks at the ethical standards influenced by culture.

In summary, work done before on international management and intercultural management have shown the importance of cultural and ethical factors in doing business. It is recognized by several researchers that international business is influenced by the interaction of different cultures. However, they have not given sufficient guidance on how these factors have to be taken into account in the business process. Furthermore, they provide limited insight in the specific situation in China today.

B. STUDIES ON BUSINESS IN CHINA

One of the most prominent writers on business in China, **Brahm**, has provided a practical guide, covering possible forms of investment as well as operational and financial issues. Brahm (1996) also addresses more specific subjects such as intellectual property.

He has the merit of putting his advice in perspective, linking current Chinese business attitudes to the historical strategists Zhu Ge Liang (Brahm 1998) and Sun Tzu (Brahm 1997). He has also compiled an outlook on the future of China (Brahm 2001).

Grünebaum has contributed in a similar if more condensed way, outlining the path from an initial business contact to the setting up of a Joint Venture. He provides a number of case studies from which lessons can be learnt (Grünebaum 1995).

Thomm has reflected on his own experience. He touches upon issues covering negotiation, financial management and marketing. He has complemented his practical guide with a little language course (Thomm 2000).

A comprehensive study on Sino-German Joint Ventures has been presented by **Schuchardt**. He analysis the Critical Success Factors of Joint Ventures as well as their interactions. Schuchardt (1994) provides advice on strategic goals, the choice of partners and forms of cooperation.

Looking at business context in China in the broader perspective, there are numerous studies available, out of which two will be mentioned here as an example:

- **Bond** has published a handbook of Chinese Psychology, addressing numerous key aspects related to business: Chinese communication processes, personal relationships, decision-making as well as understanding Chinese people as consumers. Bond (1996) has also included the subject of employee motivation and attitudes in the Chinese workforce.

- **Feuchtwang** describes official and local cults, and gives insight in Taoism. Most importantly, he describes the relation between politics and religion (Feuchtwang 2001).

In conclusion, work done before on doing business in China in particular too often concentrates on how to quickly make a profit, without much reflection about or attention to the culture, ethics or the current state of the society. More reflective publications often provide only limited advice on how to deal with the problems that are being analysed.

III. METHODOLOGY

Research can be understood as the interpretation of signs in order to formulate general laws. In order to verify theses laws, it is essential to refer to an explicit research method.

This research method consists of all practices and operations which the researcher uses to make observations, and of the rules by which theses observations can be modified and interpreted in order to asses their meaning as clues. Research can easily become an activity influenced by numerous prejudices, if it is not carefully reflected upon (Alasuutari 1995).

After the analysis of prior research, I have aimed to overcome its weaknesses. Of the various possible strategies for doing this (guided by literature etc.) I choose to carry out fieldwork, i.e. participating observation. The method of participating observation has been identified as most suitable for the following reasons:

- it allows to gain first hand information about the object of study, the Chinese business environment;
- it makes it possible to trace back observations to theories that have already been established in prior research;
- it allows for the formulating of new theories.

Hypothesis is that that there is a limited number of Critical Success Factors to be taken into account in order to develop international business in the context of culture and ethics in transformation.

The period of my observations was from September 1999 to August 2001, a total of 24 months. During that time, I have taken on different roles: Initially, I have taken part in a post-graduate, post-experience training programme in China, set up for young managers from the European Union. The EU-China Managers Training Programme consists of Mandarin Chinese and business studies, enabling participants to gain a first, if still rather theoretical, understanding of the business environment. After completion of the programme, I have, as a Human Resources Advisor, contributed to the starting up of one of the largest Joint Ventures between a Chinese State Owned Enterprise (SOE) and a European Multinational Corporation (MNC).

Any researcher has to ask himself the question, whether he himself or the methods he is using are changing the object he is studying. I think, that the ever more intense presence of Western business people, students and scholars in China is not only a side effect of the country's efforts to open up and to reform its systems. It has a rather profound effect in that this presence is actually increasing the drive for modernization: not only require Western people certain facilities to enjoy a comfortable life, they also expose Chinese to modern ideas about subjects ranging from business to family life.

IV. DATA AND INFORMATION

In this part of the study, I provide an overview of China's history and culture, following which I provide data and information on the legal, the political and the education system. This is followed by the definition of economic regions, the changes in the national economic model and their impact on the Chinese people, and finally business practices in China.

A. BRIEF INTRODUCTION TO CHINESE HISTORY

1. ORIGINS OF CHINESE CIVILISATION (-21ST CENTURY BC)

a) Archaeological findings

The origins of the Chinese civilization can be traced back to five thousand years ago. A large quantity of archaeological findings have proven that as early as 3,000 BC, Chinese civilization had entered into a preliminary period. The use of metal, the appearance of cities, the differentiation between rich and poor as well as the formation of etiquette were signs of the early Chinese civilization (Cao FuLin 1994, 39). The ancient Chinese liberated themselves from purely obeying the rule of nature; they began to use and improve their environment. Cognitive abilities towards nature laid the foundation for the Chinese civilization to grow, and to hand knowledge down from generation to generation.

According to the archaeological findings, human beings inhabited China already in the "Old Stone Age" around 680,000 BC. The Old Stone Age (2,000,000 BC-50,000 BC) is a period during which people used clipped stones as tools to cut and to go hunting. Four ancient skulls of the ancestors of today's Chinese were found near present-day Beijing, together with stone tools, bone tools and the remains of usage of fire. But this is only the prehistoric phase of the Chinese civilization. What really can be called "Chinese civilization" began during the late period of the "New Stone Age" (18,000 BC-2,000 BC) about 7,000 BC (Cao FuLin 1994, 23). The New Stone Age is defined as the time when people used polished stones as working tools. The Yellow River was the center of this civilization.

The Yellow River is the second longest river in China. It originates from BaYanKeLa mountain, QinHai province. It flows past nine provinces - QinHai, SiChuan, GanSu, NingXia, NeiMengGu, ShanXi, ShánXi, HeNan, ShanDong - and finally flows into BoHai sea from KenLi, a county in ShanDong. The total length of the Yellow River is 5,464 kilometers, and the drainage area is 7,524,000 square kilometers.

The soil of the Yellow River region is rich, smooth and prosperous; therefore it is suitable for the utilization of stone, wood and bronze tools of the prehistoric age. Furthermore, it is fit for the growth of the crops planted in ancient times. In consequence, the agricultural production reached a higher level in Yellow River earlier than other regions. Naturally, the Yellow River became the center of politics and of economy. That is the reason why modern Chinese believe that Yellow River is the cradle of the Chinese civilization (Zheng Ping 1998, 43).

Archaeologist found pottery with red and black pictures on it and proved it belonged to the people of 5,000-3,000 BC. Among the pottery, there was a small pot with one small pole in the bottom of it. It is assumed to be the utensil people used to preserve fire. The archaeologists also found ash and wheat in the pit, which was said to be the place that people used to preserve wheat (Zhi Yuan 1998, 38). In other sites to the south of Yellow River, the remains of silk and thread were found. There are several ruins along the banks of the Yellow River (Zhu YouXin 1999, 54). Archaeologist found bronze tools, utensils which belonged to a period around 3,500-2,050 BC. The ruins of houses demonstrated that ancient Chinese had the technique to build houses to protect themselves from the bad nature environment.

The scales of tombs, and the objects buried in them, vary greatly which proves that as early as 3,000 BC, differences in standard of living could be found, probably resulting from private property existing at that time. There were exquisite jade articles in some tombs, and nothing in most of the others. Furthermore, archaeologists found several people buried in one tomb, some of them decapitated – and some others looked as if they had been buried alive. One explanation is that they were the slaves of the person who was buried honorably: their owner could dispose of them at his liking (Shen QiYe 1997, 29). Therefore, one may conclude that even people could become someone's private property at that time.

b) The legend of the origins of the Chinese Nation

Other than archaeological findings, there are a lot of legends about the origins of the Chinese Nation. Chinese like calling themselves the decedents of "the sons and the daughters of *Yan* and *Huang*" (Chen JinChuan 1998, 9) who were the leaders of two different tribes in 3,000 BC. In ancient times, a tribe was formed by a group of people who were of the same nationality, and it was named after the name of the leader, who would bear the title of "emperor". So the two tribes were called *YanDi* nationality and *HuangDi* nationality. "*Di*" is Chinese and refers to emperor.

The *Huang* nationality originated from the loess plateau in the what is now the northern part of ShanXi province. With the development of the tribe's power, the HuangDi nationality extended and moved consistently towards the south, and then crossed the Yellow River to the south of ShanXi. Finally, it settled in ZhuLu, HeBei province. In the process of moving towards the east, their productive power raised to a higher level; animal husbandry and plantation developed unceasingly. In this way, they managed to become a powerful tribe group. In the meantime, culture developed greatly and possessed a leading position compared with the surrounding tribes. As a consequence, the culture of Huang had great influences upon later generations. Over time, HuangDi nationality became the orthodox representative of Chinese culture.

The *Yan* nationality originated earlier than HuangDi nationality, in the Northwest of the loess plateau. After extension and moving towards the east, it settled in ShanDong province. It was the second most powerful tribe next to the HuangDi nationality. Facing challenges by other nationalities, the two tribes united to defeat the other tribes, and to gradually build up a stable status in central China. Later, the two tribes started fighting with each other, ending with the defeat of Yan. As a consequence, the two tribes merged into one and become a predecessor of *HuaXia* nationality (Wei XingDong 1998, 10).

The origination of *HuaXia* nationality was the result of a merging process among several nationalities. The HuaXia nationality was formed mainly by two tribe groups. One tribe group was the Yan and Huang nationalities, and the other tribe group was composed of LiangHao (ShaoHao, TaiHao) nationalities and some other small tribes. These two tribe groups fought against each other in the lower reach of Yellow River, north and south to the regions YanShang and HeJi, and finally merged into *Xia*, *Shang* and *Zhou* nationalities. These three nationalities developed for more than one thousand years and merged together, thus becoming the embryonic form of the HuaXia nationality. "Spring and Autumn Period" and "Warring State Period" witnessed the final stage of formation of the HuaXia nationality, which originated from the integration of

HuaXia nationality and many other new nationality components (Qi Tao 1999, 516).

HuaXia nationality is the predecessor of the *Han* nationality; therefore the Han nationality always respected the YanDi and HuangDi as their earliest ancestor. Thus, the concept of the sons and daughters of Yan and Huang is deeply rooted in the heart of Chinese people and is handed down until today.

2. FOUNDING AND TRANSITION OF THE EARLY STAGE (21ST CENTURY-221 BC)

a) Xia, Shang and Zhou Dynasties

The three dynasties Xia (21st century BC-16th century BC), Shang (16th century BC-11th century BC) and Zhou (11th century BC-8th century BC) were the period during which the Chinese nation came into being and was formed. *Xia* was the first country developed independently in Chinese history (Gu JianHua 1998, 109). To say it developed independently means that the economy development and the formation of the political system of Xia were developed by itself, without learning or drawing support from other nationalities, and without their interference. The coming into being of Xia went through a natural developing process. Xia kept the tradition of the original tribes, but the country was better organized in political terms than any of the earlier tribes. A system of heritage was founded during the Xia Dynasty, and it was very strict. Throne and private property could be inherited for generations; power and status were taken as the private property of people, which could not be violated (Yin ChengLin 1994, 17). *Shang* and *Zhou* strengthened the state system and set up a comparatively more centralized state power than Xia Dynasty. The concept of a country's territory achieved a lot of progress. That is to say that every country had a clear dividing line or boundary. The relationship between central and local government was one between subject and subordinate, thus laying the foundation for the idea that the imperial court was the only legitimate one. Shang was the first dynasty in China to have written records. China has always been a multi-nationality country. During the history of Xia, Shang and Zhou, the struggle of the different nationalities and the trade between them promoted the development of the Chinese civilization.

b) Spring and Autumn Dynasty

Spring and Autumn Dynasty (770 BC- 249 BC) witnessed the formation of feudalism step by step (Lei YiQun 1999, 56). In *economic* terms, ironware and cattle were used to cultivated the land. Private ownership of land began developing, and a new productive relationship came into being. Here the term "new productive relationship" refers to the relationship of the landlord class and the peasant class: the peasants rented land from the landlords, worked on the land and gave a large part of the return to the landlords (Yin ChengLin 1994, 45). In *political* terms, royal court declined: dukes or princes under the emperor competed to seize power; they were the representatives of a new and rising landlord class.

The Warring States (475 BC-221 BC) saw the establishment of the feudal system. The landlord class who had already seized power conducted reforms within their territory. Their reform measures included charging tax according to the quality of land. In this way, the farmers' initiative was encouraged and the national revenue grew. A census register system was set up, thus the control and management of the country was strengthened. The state took advantage of natural resources to develop agriculture, fishing and other industries; the army was reformed to let the soldiers produce and train during times of peace, and fight when warfare were aroused. Through such reform, the feudal land ownership and productive relationship established, and the feudal centralized political system was formed preliminarily. Another feature of that period was that the productive powers were liberated due to the substitution of feudal system to the slavery system. As the consequence of such progress, the feudal economy developed rapidly, and a prosperous state appeared in the fields of ideology and culture (Lei YiQun 1999, 56).

3. FEUDAL SOCIETY HISTORY (221 BC-1919 AD)

a) Common features of feudal society

The Chinese feudal society had more than 2,000 years of history. During these 2,000 years, China changed its master a dozen times. But no matter who governed the country, the relationship of "exploit and be exploited" between the landlord class and the peasant class never changed. The dynasties share some identical features: almost all of them tried their best to build a centralized state power, and almost all of them were overthrown by a peasant uprising.

b) Qin Dynasty (221BC-207BC)

During the Warring State Period, the different countries staged large-scale annexation wars. Because the reforms of Qin were more thorough than the reforms in other countries, the state power strengthened and finally finished the task of unifying the whole country. During a period of nine years before it came into power, from 230 BC-221 BC, Qin destroyed six countries: Wei, Han, Zhao, Chu, Yan and Qi. Qin then established the first multi-nationality unified country in Chinese history. Although it existed only for fourteen years, its influence on Chinese history has been far-reaching. The Qin Dynasty formed a set of centralized governing state organs and conducted a series of measurements in politics, economy and culture to strengthen the unification of the country. The founding of Qin Dynasty was inseparable from the first emperor of Qin who is regarded as one of the outstanding landlord class politicians in feudal society (Ke JianZhong 1998, 13). Qin ShiHuang (the first emperor of Qin) was only 29 years old when he founded the Qin Dynasty. The achievements of Qin proved that he was a brilliant emperor, but at the same time, he was a tyrant in Chinese history.

The cruel rule of Qin was embodied in two aspects. The first aspect is the tax legislation. The tax of Qin was very heavy, it was said to be 20 times more than before. The rent paid in labor was said to be 30 times more than in earlier times. For example, it took 700,000 men to build Ebang Palace - a palace of the Qin and Li Shan tomb, which was the tomb of Qin ShiHuang. A part of this tomb is the famous Terracotta Army, close to Xi'an, in ShánXi. The Terracotta Army lies 1.5 kilometers to the east of the grave mound. The wood and clay figures of warriors and horses would safeguard the tomb just like when Qin ShiHuang was alive. These figures are of the same size as real men and horses. It is a miniature representation of Qin's strong army: there are 130 chariots, 616 pottery horses, and more than 8,000 soldiers (Yuan XingPei 1998, 181-182). It is not difficult to imagine that the tomb was a great project that has been built by people's blood and sweat. In addition to this, Qin ShiHuang sent men to build the Great Wall and main roads. He recruited young men to defend the boundary of the country, and to do a lot of other labors. According to the statistics, there were 2,000,000 forced laborers at that time, accounting for 10 per cent of the total population. Thus the number of people engaged in production reduced to a large extent, leading to miserable living conditions of the people.

Apart from the above mentioned heavy tax and labor rent, the criminal law of Qin was very cruel: organs were cut, people were oil boiled alive or split alive by five horses, to name but a few. Furthermore, one of the laws regulated that if one man violated the law, his relatives would be punished as well. It is safe to say that the law of Qin was cruel and out of proportion when it comes to punishment. The jails were full, and new prisoners sometimes caused traffic jams on their way to jail (Jian BoZhan 1983, 65). Under such high pressure of living, the people of Qin often revolted and eventually topped over the rule of Qin.

c) XiHan (207 BC-25 AD)

After the extinction of Qin Dynasty, Liu Bang set up the Han Dynasty and settled its capital in XiAn. It was referred as "XiHan" in Chinese history. XiHan adopted the principle of "govern by doing nothing against nature" (An ZuoZhang 1986, 135), and ensured its citizens a peaceful environment to develop the economy. The policy of "govern by doing nothing against nature" was a kind of method that the ruler sorted to cozen the civilians: give them enough to eat and let them lead a decent life, but do not let them think. In this way, the common people could be governed by knowing nothing and seeking for nothing. Those who do have intelligence would be ruled by killing their leader and threatening the rest to have the same fate if they would dare to utter any differing opinions. Therefore, the so-called "doing nothing" was only a clever way to govern the people by essentially fooling and threatening. XiHan also enforced a series of reforms in order to strengthen its centralized power and defeat any invaders. The trade relations with the surrounding nationalities and with foreign countries further away prospered during Han, bringing about the first golden age in Chinese feudal society.

In the course of the XiHan Dynasty, the famous "Silk Road" (An ZuoZhang 1986, 150) was opened. The emperor of XiHan sent Zhang Jian to XiYu (a region inhabited by minority nationalities) in 138 BC, trying to build an alliance with the minority nationalities there. The minority nationalities also had the desire to build relations with XiHan. Thus they built up political, military and trade relations soon. The advanced techniques of XiHan, such as iron casting and land cultivation, were introduced into XiYu. The silk fabrics and ironware were welcomed by the people of XiYu. In exchange, the people of XiHan learnt how to plant grapes and some other plants.

Since the beginning of the contacts with XiYu, the trade relations with central Asia, West Asia, North Africa and Europe developed. Chinese silk and silk fabrics were transported from ChangAn towards the west, passed through HeXi corridor (a narrow and long district to the west of the Yellow River) and then divided into south and north routes. One south route went through YuMenGuan which is in the west of today's GanSu province, along the KunLun mountain to ShaChe, which is situated in XinJiang province, across CongLing to DaYuan, KangJu, and continued to Southwest and then reached AnXi, finally reached west Asia, North Africa and the Roman Empire. The name for these trade routes, "Silk Road", was given by the famous German geographer von Richthofen (Zhao RuQing 1999, 1). He did so because he found silk a typical Chinese product that was transported on that road. China was known as Silk Country.

By the end of XiHan, land annexation became more and more severe. For example, the prime minister of YuanDi, whose name was KuangHeng, owned 300,000 *mu* land, but he was not satisfied and encroached 40,000 mu of public land. Other than officials, landlords possessed large quantities of land. On the other hand, many peasants did not have land to cultivate. Consequently, they became servants of the landlords, thus leading to a serious social problem – the servant problem. Under the rule of YuanDi, there were more than 10,000 servants in the imperial court alone; this was only a small portion of the total number. The largest portion of servants concentrated on landlords, nobles and rich people's homes. These servants were severely exploited by their owners; the contradictions between them intensified gradually (Jia BoZan 1983, 294). The land and servant problem deteriorated in the last period of XiHan, and eventually led to serious social crisis. In the end, the feudal government could not be maintained and was substituted by DongHan.

d) DongHan (25 AD-220 AD)

The productive techniques developed rapidly, but in the meantime, the social contradictions became extremely sharp in the course of the DongHan Dynasty. The first prepared, organized and programmatic peasant uprising, the HuangJi Uprising, occurred during DongHan. The "HuangJi Uprising" (Yao FuLin 1994, 262) was named after the yellow scarf on the head of the peasant soldiers. The leader of the uprising, ZhangJiao, distributed his ideas when curing illnesses of the people. More and more people believed in him; he managed to gather almost half million people around him. He divided his soldiers into 36 branches; big branches had more than 10,000 people, small branches 7,000. The leaders of each of the branches were commanded by Zhang himself.

The uprising was defeated after nine months of fierce fight. But it set an example for latter peasant uprisings. Furthermore, the fact that it took advantage of religion to organize its followers exerted deep influences on the later dynasties. It was a reflection of the deep contradictions which existed between the different classes and nationalities. It seemed that the state power was laying in the hand of the government, but in fact, local forces were not controlled by the central government. The development of big landlord country estates could prove this point strongly. After the middle stage of DongHan, the relatives of the emperor and the eunuchs commanded the government affairs, leading DongHan to corruption and extinction.

e) WeiJin and NanBei Dynasties (220 AD-581 AD)

The dynasties of WeiJin and NanBei can be divided into three periods. The first period lasted from the Warfare Period at the end of DongHan to the unification of XiJin. The second period can be defined between the extinction of XiJin and the establishment of the sixteen countries of DongJin. From the establishment of Song by LiuYu (the emperor of Song) and BeiWei to the unification of Sui was the third period which is called South and North Dynasty. During the second and third period, the whole country was in a confrontation state, with the northern and southern part opposing each other. The northern part experienced three cycles of disruption and unification since the extinction of XiJin. The southern part went through a total of five dynasties: DongJin, Song, Qi, Liang and Chen.

After the destruction of Sui by Chen, the whole country was unified (Zhu DaWei 1998, 1-2). Except for 36 years of short integration of LiangJin, the feudal countries were in a state of disorder. Integration and stability gave way to fighting and separation; the economy was destroyed, the society stopped developing, and even retrogressed. But big separation mixed with partial unification, large-scale economic destruction mixed with partial and temporary development. During this period, an unprecedented unification of nationalities emerged nationwide. Common living regions, a common economic situation, and the common struggle against the heads of the government they shared pushed people from various nationalities together, thus forming close relations. Therefore, the dynasties WeiJin and NanBei were an important stage to re-establish a unified multi-nationality country of China.

f) Sui Dynasty (581 AD-618 AD)

Sui Dynasty had a short history of 38 years, with a prosperous state as its feature. The establishment of Sui ended the separation situation of China which had lasted for 270 years during the dynasties of WeiJin and NanBei. The imperial examination system was created during Sui Dynasty; officials were selected among those who got good marks (Yin ChengLin 1994, 232). The emperor of Sui enforced a series of political and economic reforms, such as checking permanent registered residence, rectification of taxes, equal distribution of land, labor rent reform and reform of the political governing organs. The Sui people worked hard and creatively. All of this laid the foundation for the social and economic development of the prosperous Tang Dynasty. The political organs, laws, military rules and taxes system played important roles for building up the social system of the later society.

g) Tang Dynasty (618 AD-907 AD)

Tang was the golden age in Chinese feudal society; it exerted great influences on historical development of China. The Tang Dynasty can be divided into two parts with 755 AD as the dividing line. State unification, social stability, strong state power, prosperous economy, close nationality relations as well as trade and cultural exchange with foreign countries were the features of the first part. The second part saw the declining of the prosperous state. Thereupon, towns were separated from the state, eunuchs seized power in the government, domestic troubles and foreign invasion happened continuously, social contradictions sharpened. The final result was the peasant uprising which overthrew the rule of Tang (Lei YiQun 1999, 304).

h) WuDai, SongLiaoXiaJin (907 AD-1234 AD)

The feudal productive relations developed further, the inner contradictions within the ruling class intensified. On the other hand, the economy, culture and scientific technology developed continuously and occupied a dominant status in the world. In the course of the BeiSong Dynasty, Wang AnShi accepted the order of the emperor, enforcing a reform policy (Pan ShuZhi 2000, 220). He focused the reform on financial matters and the reorganization of the army, as well as on intellectual education. In the beginning, the reform achieved some temporary merit, but stopped producing effects shortly afterwards due to the shortcomings of the reform policy itself. It could solve some problems of the society, but the deep contradictions could not be solved by the moderate reform measurements. During this period, Liang, Xia and Jin minority nationalities contributed greatly to the exploration of Chinese boundary regions.

i) Yuan Dynasty (1206 AD-1368 AD)

In 1211, the king of the Mongolians led his army to invade China, and twenty years before the end of the thirteenth century, they destroyed Song, Lao, XiXia and Jin, which were the four countries in China. The Han nationality for the first time was controlled totally by another nationality, while Yuan was the first united regime founded by a minority nationality (MeiGu). The establishment of Yuan gave an end to the four hundred years dissension of nationalities since the later period of the Tang Dynasty; brought stable living and productive environment for varied nationalities. Yuan helped to found the scale of Chinese territory and strengthen the governing to the boundary areas. But Mongolians adopted a discriminating policy towards the other nationalities in order to uphold their special rights. They divided the people into four classes (Ge Jian-Xiong 1999, 30):

- the first class was Mongolians;
- the second class was SeMu (ZhongYa, XiXia, HuiHui nationalities);

- the third class is HanRen (especially Han, QiDan, NiuZheng ruled by Jin);
- the fourth class was NanRen (the Han nationality and minority nationalities in west and south part).

The differences between the classes were visible in every aspects of life. In politics, the real power lay in the hands of Mongolian and SeMu. HanRen could be assistants, NanRen rarely entered into government. In the military field, the Mongolian army was the major force, the generals of the army had to be Mongolians. According to laws, if Mongolians killed HanRen or NanRen, they would not be punished to death, in the inverse case, however, the HanRen or NanRen would receive the death sentence in order to compensate the life of the Mongolian being killed. Furthermore, the nobles of the Mongolians colluded with the nobles of the other nationalities and oppressed the peoples of different nationalities together. The social contradictions were increasing continuously, thus speeding up the extinction of Yuan Dynasty.

j) Ming Dynasty (1368 AD-1644 AD)

Ming Dynasty marked the decline of the prosperous feudal society. In the early period of Ming, the state power was strong, the authority of the emperor strengthened and the economy recovered rapidly. In the middle period of Ming, eunuchs seized the power, politics corrupted, land annexation prevailed, peasant upraised unceasingly. During this period, the commodity economy developed, the bourgeoisie productive relationship come into being in its infant stage. The bourgeoisie productive relationship emerged from handicraft industry in the beginning of the 16th and 17th century. With the development of a commercial economy, the manual operation factories appeared. In those factories, the division of work was elaborate, the scale was relatively larger. Many handicrafts men worked for one factory and got their pay according their respective turnout (Fan ShuZhi 2000, 329). In the later period of Ming, the parties of courts competed bitterly, the people were exploited severely, thus politics became darker and darker. The cruel rule of Ming caused the dissatisfaction of common people towards the ruling class. The fate of Ming, just like the fate of early dynasties, ended with the peasant uprising which topped over Ming.

k) Qing Dynasty (1644 AD-1911 AD)

The Manchus, today a minority nationality, just like the Mongolians, conquered China and established the Qing Dynasty. Qing has been the last imperial court in Chinese history. The Qing government unified the whole territory of China including Inner Mongolian, Northeast, Mongolia, Tibet,

QingHai, XinJiang and TaiWan in fifteen years. The territory developed by Qing was four times larger than the territory of Ming. The Ming Dynasty had 3,530,000 square kilometers, the territory of Qing however was 13,006,000 square kilometers (Bai Yang 1998, 397). The early stage of Qing saw economic development and social stability as a result of the reform policy of the Qing government. In the later stage of Qing however, corruption prevailed, and the people could not live a decent life. As a consequence, national power was in vain, giving foreign countries the opportunity to invade China. Against this background, the "First Opium War" broke out (Wang LiWen 1999, 16-18).

> *The First Opium war broke out in June 1840. The two belligerent countries were China and the United Kingdom. The blasting fuse of the war was that the Qing government destroyed opium that was to be sold into China by the United Kingdom. Looking at it from the Chinese point of view, the intended sale of opium was an excuse of the British government to open China's door for trade: at that time, the Qing government stuck to the close-door policy that put the United Kingdom in an unfavorable trade status. The attraction of Chinese richness however was irresistible. Therefore, when the government of the United Kingdom saw the failure of their trade attempts, perceived as opium invasion policy by the Chinese, it decided to wage a military intervention to realize their hostile ambition.*
>
> *The war lasted for two years, with the defeat of China as a result. The backward Qing government was forced to sign an unequal treaty called "NanJin Treaty", which was the first of a series of unequal treaties in Chinese modern history. From then on, the Qing government signed more unequal treaties with Western countries including Belgium, Denmark, France, Germany, Holland, Italy, Norway, Portugal, Russia, Spain, Sweden and the United States. These countries looked at the profits they could get from China and asked to enjoy the same rights, and the Qing government had no choice but to agree. As a consequence, the Qing government lost a large part of its sovereignty, while remaining nominally independent. The society continued to be feudalistic.*

The period from 1840-1919 is called the "Old Democratic Revolution Period" in Chinese history (Cheng ShiYing 1997, 3). The leaders of the revolution were members of the landlord class, bourgeoisie class and peasant class of the Qin Dynasty. The aim of the revolution was to advocate democracy and science in China under the rule of the feudal emperor. This implied that the Old Democratic Revolution neglected the incompatibility of democracy and feudal autocracy. For example, the reform-orientated part of the landlord class advocated to learn from Western countries and to perform reform under the ruling of an emperor. That means, the prerequisite of their reform was to admit that the emperor enjoyed superior power over the other classes; they did not intend to overthrow the governing of the feudal kingdom. To the contrary, the emperor represented the highest class enjoying special rights; the existence of such a class would certainly ensure the existence of other "special rights" classes. Everyone knows that special rights and democracy are contradicting concepts. Therefore, the conclusion could be drawn that the Old Democratic Revolution was not thorough enough and its failure was foreseeable.

4. THE HISTORY OF THE REPUBLIC OF CHINA (1919-1949)

a) The founding of the Republic of China

As the ruling of Qing weakened during the last half of the nineteenth century and the first half of the twentieth century, China fell under the control of warring factions and Western forces. The period of the warlords created chaos for most Chinese. In 1911, the Qing Dynasty was overthrown by Sun Yat-sen (Sun ZhongShan), who attempted to establish a more democratic society than that of the Old Democratic Revolution Period. The major goals of the revolution were to develop an industrialized economy and to establish a central government that would unify China. The guidelines of the revolution were (Luo ZhengKai 1999, 30):

1) the Chinese nation seeks liberation by itself;

2) all nationalities are equal within the territory of China;

3) all power belongs to the people;

4) peasants have land to cultivate and

5) capital should be accumulated.

On the New Year of 1912, Sun Yat-sen took his oath of the office and became the president of the NanJing provisional government. At that time, Western countries had great rights in interference with the internal affairs of China. These countries refused to recognize the provisional government and to provide loans to the new government. They thought Yuan ShiKai who was the leader of BeiYang warlord, which was the most powerful army at that time, was the ideal candidate for the post of president. Due to the pressure of the outside world and the weakness of the revolution party, Sun Yat-sen proclaimed resignation on 1st April, 1912. The resignation of Sun indicated the failure of the revolution because Yuan stood on the opposite side of revolution. Furthermore, the government did not ensure people a peaceful living environment: in the coming years, the country experienced successive warfare between the warlords. According to statistics, there were 457,000 soldiers in 1914, and in 1919 the number increased to 1, 380,000, which means it roughly tripled within 5 years. The government put 4/5th of its revenue into the expenses of the army. As a consequence of such turmoil, the people's life was miserable. From 1914 to 1918, the number of farming households declined to 15,640,000, or 4,000,000 per year on average (Shi YuanQin 1999, 329).

b) New culture movement period

One of the most important events in this period was the "May Fourth Movement" (Yang XianCai 1993, 164). May Fourth Movement was defined as a patriotic movement, which marks the beginning of the New Bourgeoisie Democratic Revolution period. The direct cause of the movement was the failure of the negotiations during the "Paris Peace Conference" in 1919. As one of the allied countries of the First World War, China hoped to get its rights to and the land of QingDao back, which was a colony of Germany and later occupied by Japan. But the meeting was controlled by the United States, the United Kingdom and Japan; in the end China got nothing back at all. It was regarded as a humiliation by the whole people, especially the intellectuals and students.

On 3rd May, 1919, thousands of students from the universities of Beijing gathered in Peking University and appealed to the representatives of the meeting to refuse to sign the agreement. The counter-revolutionary warlord government threatened to suppress any gatherings of students. The indignant students gathered in TianAnMen Square, made speeches, distributed leaflets and appealed for punishing the pro-Japanese officials. The students' movement spread nation-wide very soon and was supported by a large number of people. In June, the student's movement developed into a large-scale movement with a workers strike, shopkeepers strike and students strike as a feature. Under the pressure of the strong patriotic emotions of the Chinese people, the warlord government was forced to dismiss the pro-Japanese officials and refused to sign the agreement, as QingDao was not returned to China.

After the death of Sun, Chiang KaiShek (Jiang JieShi) became the president of China in 1925, but his party, GuoMinDang, was not able to control all of China (Cheng ShiYing 1997, 51). Western powers and Japan gained more and more control over China's port cities and the economy. By the 1930ies, there were 33 areas, called concessions, in China controlled by Western powers and subjected to Western laws rather than to Chinese law. Consequently, the Chinese were forced to obey foreign laws in their richest urban areas, such as the city-ports of ShangHai and GuangDong (Canton). More than half of all the industrial workers were employed in foreign-owned firms, and Westerners essentially controlled China's export economy. This condition is considered as a national shame and is still remembered.

Many recent laws and policies governing the activities of foreign firms and foreign trade reflect this historical abhorrent and fear of foreign economic dominance. Taking the trade protectionism as an example, during the period prior to the WTO entry, China has been charging high tariffs on some agricultural products (50%-100%) (Yu YongDing 1999, 10), cars as high as 80%-120% (Yu YongDing 1999, 384), petrochemicals 17% (Yu YongDing 1999, 19) to protect its infant industries.

There are also many non-tariff barriers, such as foreign exchange control, import quota system, import license systems and so on. In the aspect of market entrance, the finance and telecommunication markets are still controlled by the Chinese government and in a very low degree open to the outside world. As to foreign investment, the government has made various specific regulations on which field foreigners are allowed to invest, and in which field they are not allowed.

The field of cooperation was limited to export-orientated, tech-centralized industries. – These laws and regulations reflect the contradictions of Chinese economic policies. On the one hand, they want to attract foreign capital to promote the economic growth, on the other hand, numerous regulations are in effect to limit the foreign involvement to avoid the dominance of foreign economic elements.

In the 1930ies, the Chinese communist party under Mao ZeDong emerged as another competing force in the then unstable China. Numerous warlords continued to challenge the legitimacy of the central government, and foreign powers still controlled the economically significant port cities and the economy in general. Then, in 1937, the Japanese invaded China and soon controlled large areas, including the resource-rich region of Manchuria (Jon Alston 1997, 3).

Japan waged its invasion war to China in July of 1937, with the purpose of taking China as a colony. The cruel war killed millions of Chinese people, which was a tragedy beyond comparison in the human world. After eight years arduous struggle, the Chinese people drove the invader out eventually. The Japanese government was forced to declare unconditional surrender to the United States in August of 1945.

There were three major forces competing to control China: the GuoMinDang under Chiang KaiShek, the Communist Party, and the Japanese. In addition, local warlords controlled large tracts of isolated areas, while the economy along the coast was dominated by Western powers. China continued to be a battle field during and following the Second World War. The struggle for controlling China continued until Chiang KaiShek was driven off the mainland by Mao and the Communist Party in 1949. At that time, China's economy had been almost completely destroyed.

5. THE HISTORY OF THE PEOPLE'S REPUBLIC OF CHINA (1949-PRESENT)

a) The major events up to the Cultural Revolution

The People's Republic of China was founded on 1st October, 1949. It was the first socialist country in Chinese history. The newly founded republic had many internal and external affairs to deal with; the Korea War was one of the most urgent affairs.

On 25th June, 1950, the Korea War broke out. The United States took advantage of this opportunity, proclaimed to provide support to the South Korean government. Maintaining world peace was seen as an American excuse to invade Taiwan, Korea, Vietnam and the Philippines by the Chinese government (Chen MingXian 1997, 28).

The Chinese government resisted to what it saw as American invasion policy: China's central government decided to sent troops to Korea and to help the Korean people fight against the invader. After three years intensive fighting between the two sides, a cease-fire was signed on 27th July, 1953.

As far as internal affairs were concerned, the Chinese people began to rebuild China along socialist lines, led by the Communist Party. Civil order was established, and the economy began to develop. China adopted a close-door policy except for accepting support and aid from the Soviet Union – then the " brother" of China – which ended in 1960. The difference in the ideology of Communist Party of the Soviet Union and of China began in 1956. Some arguments of the Soviet Union were regarded as "serious mistake in principle" (He Xin 1997, 193). In terms of relationship between the two countries, the Soviet Union wanted to control China, and tried to intensify the difference between the two communist parties to the level of two countries. In June 1959, the Soviet Union refused to perform the new national defense technique agreement signed in October 1957. In November 1960, the Communist Party of the Soviet Union distributed a letter of 60,000 words, affronting the Chinese Communist Party. Furthermore, the government of the Soviet Union took a series of actions which damaged the relationship between the two parties, such as asking China to return loans prematurely while China was facing economic difficulties. This kind of deterioration of relationship continued until 1966, then it broke completely. Chinese leaders ignored the West; China became a closed society.

In 1958, Mao initiated the "Great Leap Forward Movement" (Liu GuoXin 1995, 182) to speed up the process of industrialization. There were slogans commonly shouted at that time, such as "catch up with America in 10-15 years"; "the courage of man determines the output of the land". In correspondence with these slogans, the government drew up some impractical plans which were not proper for the economic situation of China at that time. In order to fulfill those plans at least nominally, the local governments provided false information to the central government, boasting their achievements, such as "One *mu* 10,000 *jin* wheat" and so on.[1] Instead of punishing their cheating, the central government praised their boasting behaviors. This promoted the general "boasting mood" to prevail in society. Needless to say, this kind of mood did harm to a state which had been backward compared with other countries. The facts proved that the guidelines of the Great Leap Forward were wrong, and by 1960 the economy was in near-collapse.

b) Cultural Revolution

The economy began to rebuilt slowly until 1966, when Mao initiated the Cultural Revolution (Yan XianCai 1999, 377-387).

[1] One mu is equal to 666.7 square kilometres and one jin is equal to half kilograms.

The "Cultural Revolution" began with the political prosecution to some important government leaders, who were forced to stop working and to do self-examination. Then, in May 1966, the central political bureau of the Communist Party summoned a conference, in which a substantial number of arguments were raised, such as: a large number of bourgeoisie representative and counter-revolutionary persons sneaked into the party, government, the army and cultural activities; the power was seized by them. Therefore, it would be necessary to set up a "Cultural Revolutionary" panel to get rid of those people. School masters and teachers were the first to be attacked among the large number of so-called "bourgeois". The students stopped studying and went around the country, criticizing and fighting against what they called "feudalism, revisionism and capitalism". Society was in chaos; fighting, robbing and confiscating of private property of families were the common practices of that time. People holding diverging ideas fought against each other, disregarding if they were friends or family members. Railways were damaged and many enterprises stopped production. The whole country was in turmoil.

There were two groups competing with each other in the "Cultural Revolution" to command the state and party power: one was led by JiangQi, Mao's wife, the other group was led by Lin Biao, the vice-chairman at that time. But Lin Biao's plot of usurping the state power was detected by Mao, therefore Lin Biao decided to wage a counter-revolutionary coup d'état as soon as possible. So on 7th September, 1971, Lin Biao issued an order to his son to murder Mao in ShangHai and stage a coup d'état in Beijing (An ZuoZhang 1986, 386). His son Lin LiGuo issued that order to his fellow party members. They even made four detailed plans about how to murder Mao. But the plot failed and Lin Biao had to flee by plane to Mongolia on13th September, 1971. Li Biao and the other eight members on the plane died when the plane crashed on its way. After the event, Mao partly realized that perhaps there were mistakes in the "Cultural Revolution" policy, but he still was not aware completely. He summoned to carry the "Cultural Revolution" through to the end.

This decision gave the "Gang of Four", namely his wife JiangQing, together with Zhang ChunQiao, Yao WenYuan and Wang HongWen, an opportunity to command the state power and continue their plot. *Jiang Qi*, was the group's leader. In order to be "the female emperor of China", she tried her best to persecute the cadres of the central and local government, the army and the Communist Party. Liu ShaoQi, the vice-chairman of China, and Zhang LiZhi, the minister of the coal industry ministry, were two among a large number of people who were prosecuted to death by the "Gang of Four". *Zhang ChunQiao* was the second important figure in "Gang of Four". He rose in rebellion and grasped the power of the local government, created trouble and riot. *Yao WenYuan* was the active participant of the group; he was in charge of propaganda and used public opinion to prosecute innocent people. *Wang Hong-Wen* prosecuted premier Zhou EnLai, Deng XiaoPing and Chen Yi. He set up faction armed forces based in ShangHai. The four of them were members of the Standing Committee of the central political commission. Mao was aware of their ambitions and pointed out that Jiang Qing had the ambitions of commanding the state‘s power, and prevented the "Gang of Four" forming a government.

Consequently, in January 1975, Zhou EnLai was elected premier and Deng XiaoPing vice-premier. After being elected, Deng put all his efforts into rectifying the guiding ideology, convening a series of regulations to solve the problems in industry, agriculture, transportation and science. After a few months of rectification, the situation improved gradually. But Mao could not bear that Deng corrected the mistakes of the "Cultural Revolution" and waged another movement aimed at criticizing Deng. Premier Zhou, who was loved by people, passed away on 8th January, 1976, which aggregated the indignation of people towards the "Gang of Four". Chairman Mao passed away in the same year and the "Gang of Four" intensified their efforts to usurp state power. At that crucial moment, under the leadership of the central political bureau, with Li XianNian, Ye JianYing and Hua GuoFeng at the core of the bureau, the "Gang of Four" was crushed, and an end was brought to the ten years of "Cultural Revolution" (Jin Chong Ji 1999, 303).

The "Cultural Revolution" period was a special period in the history of the People's Republic of China. Its major feature was making class struggle the highest priority. This idea proved to be wrong, because it eventually led to disorder and backwardness while completely neglecting economic construction. Therefore, "Cultural Revolution" was by no means a political revolution, economic revolution or cultural revolution in its real sense. It was a long period of disaster that damaged the progress of the society (You Lin 1998, 98).

c) Reform and opening-up

When the Cultural Revolution ended in 1976 after Mao's death, China experienced an economic crisis. The nation had lost its economic momentum, and a whole generation of Chinese was poorly educated, since most schools and universities had been closed for a decade. In 1976, a new era slowly emerged, as economic reforms were instituted. The reforms of the 1970ies centered around a limited acceptance of some forms of capitalism and an open-door policy towards Western knowledge and investments. The overall reform of China concentrated on politics and the economy with "one center and two basic principles" as the guiding principle of the reform (Bao Yue 1998, 226). "One center" refers to taking economic construction as central task, "two basic principles" refers to persisting in reform and opening-up, and to persist in four basic points. These four basic points refer to persisting 1) the socialist road; 2) the people's political rule of the country; 3) the Communist Party's leadership and 4) with Marxism-Leninism and with the thoughts of Mao. It indicates that after so many years of political struggle, the Chinese government eventually put the economic construction in a central position; this was a major step-change in ideology.

Today, China is a country with ever more open ideas, wanting to absorb the essence of good ideas from abroad, while discarding the ideas that are not suitable for the development of China. China has found the motivation to go forward. In this way, China achieved a great deal since the official opening to the outside world in 1979: The discretionary income of the average city citizen was 343 Yuan in 1978, but 5,160 Yuan per capita per year in 1993. The net income of the rural citizen was 133 Yuan in 1978, but 2091 Yuan per capita per year in 1993. In real terms, the average growth rate of GDP has been 9.8 % from 1978 to 1997 (Lu Zheng 1999, 92). It is estimated that China will make rapid progress if it keeps the current growth rate in the future.

B. HISTORICAL OVERVIEW OF THE CHINESE CULTURE

1. PHILOSOPHICAL GROUNDING

Before one can actually plunge into the depth of Chinese culture, one should understand that the Chinese traditional culture was heavily influenced by Confucianism, Taoism and Buddhism. Confucianism clearly stands in the center. Therefore, understanding Confucianism, Taoism and Buddhism is the first approach to understanding Chinese traditional culture.

a) Confucianism

(1) Creation period

The development of Confucianism can be divided into three stages, while each stage can be further divided into sub-stages.

The ideas of Confucianism were created by Confucius at the end of the Spring and Autumn Period (500 BC) and evolved with the progress of the times. Though the theoretical forms of Confucianism changed continuously, its basic characters have never changed (Zhang LiWen 1998, 23). Some of the ideas it propagated still contribute to the modern Chinese concept of morality.

> *During the Cultural Revolution period, Confucianism was severely criticized and condemned as "old culture" that should be abandoned completely. Confucianism was condemned as a backward idea that handicapped the progress of society. But as a part of the cultural heritage of China, if it is understood and applied well in the context of a modern society, it still has its progressive meaning.*
>
> *Thus, when studying Confucianism, it is entirely necessary to adopt an objective attitude and to conduct the study from a historical and developing perspective. An evaluation should be given about what part of Confucianism can contribute to the social development and which parts are really "old" and not suitable for modern society. A totally negative attitude seems to be wrong.*

The first stage is the creation of Confucianism. Confucius (Kong Zi, 551 BC-479 BC), who was a citizen of Lu Guo which was a small country in the Spring and Autumn Period, created Confucianism (Cheng ZhiLiang 1996, 4). Confucius was from a poor family; his father died when Confucius was still very young. He worked as an accountant and shepherd before he began giving private lectures to his students. Confucius was the first in Chinese history to set up a private school. He showed his sincere consideration to the common people, and he did not chose his students according to their social status or family background. During his education practices of nearly fifty years, Confucius had almost three thousands students, and many of them became famous politicians and educators.

The idea of destiny could be seen in Confucius's works, but the idea often contradicted itself. For example, Confucius worked very hard and often did things that could not be understood by common people. He refused to be an official because he thought that their main activity was to flatter the people who are in power, but he hoped the feudal landlord could give him an opportunity to realize his ideas aimed at reforming the evils of the society. Confucius did not believe in the so-called destiny, but he illustrated in his works "life and death are decided by God; richness or poverty are decided by God as well" (Jin YuanPu 1999, 258). In summary, the destiny idea of Confucius was full of contradictions, when compared to his action.

Confucius emphasized etiquette – "*Li*" – in his philosophy: "do not see without etiquette, do not listen without etiquette, do not speak without etiquette, do not move without etiquette" (Liu GuoDang 1998, 5). *Li* was revered as the behavior standard of all people. This set of strict etiquette rules played an active role in society, because it helped to regulate the social order effectively. But it is undeniable that the idea restrained the people's creative ideas. The etiquette regulates people in a tight ring, and people are only allowed to do everything according to *Li*; otherwise, they would be condemned by public opinion. In such a social environment, obedience is the only thing that people were taught, therefore people did not have the awareness to create something. – "*Yue*" was another aspect of Confucius's idea. *Yue* means music in Chinese, but here *Yue* is not limited to music. The deep connotation of "*Yue*" was to use music as an instrument to stimulate and express the people's emotions and thus to form relationships of harmonious and fraternal love. "*LiYue*" stands for a gentle philosophy, which was not only a basic method for individuals to cultivate their ideas and complete their characters, but also a principle of national politics.

The core of Confucius's idea was "*Ren*" (Zhang LiWen 1998, 29). Here "*Ren*" is not only limited to benevolence and kindheartedness, but includes all excellent moralities. If a person can be called "*Ren*", then he is a complete man. Confucius thought if all the people could reach the morality level set by "*Ren*", there would be no contradictions in society. Therefore, *Ren* as the core of Confucius idea aimed at regulating the people's behavior by giving them a set of strict rules to abide, thus leading to a strict ruling of their country.

Mencius (MeiZi, 298 BC-238 BC) was another representative character of Confucianism. Mencius was respected as the second sage next to Confucius. The idea of "policy of benevolence" (Shang GuoJun 1998, 47) which developed from Confucius' idea of "rule by morality" marked a great progress of Confucianism. Mencius' idea advocated little tax on people so that the civilians live a stable and comparatively sufficient life. Mencius embraced the same idea as Confucius in governing the country. Mencius ethics-political ideas further developed the historic idea which emphasized that people are the essence of the country. He pointed out that people are the most important element, the country is the second and the ruler ranks third.

Another important philosophy of Mencius was the theory of "man's nature is good at birth" (Jin YuanPu 1999, 264). He assumed that human beings had the feeling of sympathy, shame, respect and the ability to judge right and wrong at the moment they were born. In one simple sentence, the morality of human beings is born. Men are born good, if they could maintain such good characters, they would enjoy great spiritual happiness. The philosophy of

Mencius emphasized the subjective initiation of human beings, which was a progress of the "destiny" philosophy upheld by ancient Chinese people.

Xun Zi (298 BC-238 BC) was an outstanding representative of Confucianism whose ideas were more radical than those of Confucius and Mencius. He advocated "grand ceremonies" and "rule by law" which had great difference from the idea of Confucius and Mencius. The idea of "man and heaven are different, man could conquer heaven" (Shang GuoJun 1998, 84) denied the power of heaven totally. It is a scientific judgment of the relationship between man and heaven. He illustrated that heaven was unconscious and aimless natural world, and that man had the ability to recognize the objective world. The philosophy of Xun Zi was one of the philosophers leading most clearly to an active attitude towards life in Chinese philosophy. It was he who for the first time pointed out that it was man that ruled the world, not heaven, which was an unknown force beyond the real world.

Xun Zi put forward a concept completely opposite to Mencius, who thought that man's nature was evil at birth. Xun Zi took the material world as its theoretical foundation from which he drew the conclusion: the social dissension was the indispensable result of man's desire for material enjoyment.

(2) Reform period

The second stage of Confucianism is its first reform during the Han Dynasty. Confucianism was reformed by Dong ZhongShun during the Han Dynasty in accordance with the unification of the ideas of the rules. Dong ZhongShun (179 BC-106 BC) was the first master of scriptures in Chinese philosophical history. The ruler of the Han Dynasty adopted his proposal of "ban all the philosophical schools but Confucianism" in order to strengthen the centralized power (Zhang LiWen 1998, 46). In general, Dong's Confucianism was full of theological flavor. Its aim was to paralyze the people's mind and uphold the governing of the state.

The core of Dong's ethics was "three cardinal guides and five constant virtues" (Yang ChaoMing 2000, 99), that is, to begin with the "guides":

ruler guides subjects – father guides son – husband guides wife

This is what the "three cardinal guides" stand for:

- "Ruler guides subjects" emphasizes the absolute power of the emperor over the state. The whole country is the private property of the emperor, the citizens are the servants of the emperor. The citizens should respect the emperor as the "son of the heaven", and the will of the emperor is seen as the law that should be obeyed without any hesitation.

- "Father guides son" means that the father is the governing person of a big family formed by blood relationship. The son must show filial obedience to his father. The family's property belongs to the father, and he enjoys the right to allocate and distribute it. The members of the family must follow the will of the father and his judgment unconditionally.

- "Husband guides wife" refers to the rule that a husband has the right to control and possess his wife. The wife must subject to her husband, and the wife has no right to inherit property, no right to go to school or take part in social activities. All the rights that she enjoys is to stay at home, doing housework, raising children and looking after her husband's parents. The rule also asks the wife to be loyal to her husband even after the death of her husband. That means she could not marry another man if her husband died while her husband could marry several women at a time even when she was alive.

Five characteristics were regarded as the basic good virtues that everyone should have:

benevolence – righteousness – propriety – wisdom – fidelity

This is what the "five constant virtues" stand for:

- "Benevolence" (*ren*) has three meanings: firstly, the individual is striving to become stronger and to try to help others; in the meantime and in this way, everyone can achieve progress in general. Secondly, *ren* can be regarded as respecting others. Thirdly, *ren* takes oneself as the standing point to emphasize the motivation in morality (Zheng XiaoJiang 1998, 57).

- "Righteousness" (*yi*) refers to the rules of social interaction between people. It emphasizes that one should treat the others fairly. One should adopt a set of right principles when it comes to deal with relationships with others. *Yi* comes into being when one is *ren*.

- "Propriety" (*li*) refers to the ability to apply etiquette. Abiding etiquette and establishing order in society is the core of propriety.

- "Wisdom" (*zhi*) refers to the ability to distinguish between right and wrong. Wisdom is a prediction to the developing trend of something. One should have the ability to predict happiness and disaster, gain and loss. One should understand the beginning, process and result of a thing (Zheng XiaoJiang 1998, 420).

- "Fidelity" (*xin*) means one should keep his promises, and help the others sincerely. It emphasizes the responsible attitude of a person. If one does not care what one has said and even goes against his own words in action, then one is not a human being but an animal. *Xin* asks people not to say big words and not to promise what one can not fulfill (Zheng XiaoJiang 1998, 136).

This set of ethics restricted people in a rigid frame. People had to adhere to the principles strictly, otherwise they would be condemned and punished by the laws or the public opinion. For example, husbands had absolute authority over their wives; wives had to obey every order of their husbands. Otherwise, a wife would be beaten or even dismissed by her husband.

This unequal status of the family members regulated by the ethics still exerts influence on modern society. In rural areas, the male patriarch is the major worker of the family; therefore he possesses a leading position, and the female members of the family are in a subordinate position. This unequal status is embodied in the birth control concept of farmers: most farmers would adopt family planning on condition that a son was born. Man is not only the major working force but also the person who passes down his family; most farmers stick to this idea. This double responsibility forms the higher status of the male patriarch in China's rural areas. –

In urban families, either the mother is the principal decision-maker or father; their status never can be equal. In most families whose income are only salaries, "wife guides husband" is a widespread phenomenon. In some families, the one who earns more money will be the subject of the family.

The "three cardinal guides and five constant virtues" intended to divide people into several groups (emperor, citizens, fathers of a family, family members, husband and wife) and give each group a set of rules to obey. It stands on an opposite direction of the modern ideas of equality and freedom.

(3) The appearance of LiXue

The third stage of Confucianism was marked by LiXue, a new school coming into existence during the dynasties of Song and Ming. LiXue was a combination of Confucianism, Buddhism and Taoism, with Confucianism as the major content. Zhu Xi (1130 AD-1200 AD) has been praised as the third important representative of Confucianism after Confucius and Mencius. In Zhu's philosophy, "the course of nature" (TianLi) enjoyed the highest position (Zou YongXian 1993, 73). He emphasized it was not only the essence of the universe that dominated everything, but also the origin of social morality standards. All the principles of feudal ethics and regulations were revealed through "*Li*". In Zhu's view there was no beginning and no end in the universe; the universe went around forever. This is a progress of man's understanding of the world. Zhu's view of the character of man was neutral. He thought man's nature was good, but the real sages were few.

Zhu's philosophical view was composed of two parts. Firstly, the man who is in power determined the prosperity or decline of the society. Man is the motive power to push the history to develop, but he limits the man to a rather narrow concept which referred only to authorities. This reflected the limitation in Zhu's idea on one hand; it also reflected the reality of the society, that is, rulers were the men governing the state, not the people. – Secondly, history was seen as retrogressive, but the retrogression was not consistent but moving in circles. Zhu's "*LiXue*" was a criterion for the intellectuals to form their judgment; its position of absolute authority was unshakable, for the rulers supported it. In feudal society, if the rulers said one thing was right, then no one dared to say it was wrong, therefore, with the support of the ruler, no one dared to create a theory to compete with *LiXue* (Wu NaiGong 1999, 236).

The scholars of successive dynasties reformed Confucianism. During the process of reform, it combined different ideas, thus reaching its contents and completing its theory. At last, it developed into the major contents of Chinese national spirits and mainstream of Chinese traditional culture. Confucianism has exerted far-reaching influences upon the personality, the way of thinking, the value tendency and the social psychology of the Chinese people.

b) Buddhism

Chinese Buddhist culture is another important component of Chinese culture. It is a part of the Chinese philosophy which exerted great influences upon the long history of Chinese feudal society. As a religion, Buddhism had significant influences upon the culture and folk customs of various nationalities.

According to historical records, Indian Buddhism was introduced into China by the end of XiHan (Lou YuLie 1998, 4). Under the reign of emperor MingDi (58 AD-75 AD), the court recognized Buddhism as a religion. MingDi asked to build the first Buddhist temple of China in LuoYang. From the last year of the Eastern Han Dynasty until the Liang Dynasty (502 AD-557 AD), Buddhist scriptures were gradually translated from Sanskrit into Chinese. The translation of scriptures enabled the Chinese people to read the texts of the holy scriptures, thus laying the foundation for the propagation of Buddhism.

The propagation of Buddhism in China has always been engaged in two fields. One field was the study of scriptures; the aim of such study was to seek for a philosophy to reach the ultimate target of life. The other field was to practice Buddhism in order to free oneself from the suffering of reality and to reach a splendid state. Chinese Buddhism is different from Indian Buddhism: it absorbed some ideas of Confucianism and Taoism, and gradually developed into a form of Buddhism that was complying with the Chinese culture. The *Chan* sect (ChanZong) was a remarkable symbol of the integration of Confucianism and Taoism into Buddhism (Li Xia 1996, 33). The *Chan* sect emphasized the understanding ability of the individual, teaching: Know yourself and then free yourself from all bounds and eventually became Buddha. Buddha is nowhere, it stands in your heart, and the heart is Buddha.

One of the two basic essences of Buddhism are "bitterness and emptiness", while Chinese Buddhism emphasized "emptiness" (Lai YongHai 1999, 16). The world, the pride and shame, the wine and money and even oneself are not really existing; all of them are false appearances in a dream. Therefore, there is nothing in the world, there is nothing to be worried about and pain has no grounds. Buddhism required the followers to abandon all the emotions and desires in order to seek for the liberation of spirits. Chinese Buddhism had unique understanding for smoothness and hardship. According to Buddhism, hardship was just an emotion when one was not satisfied with the circumstance. Without desire, without the motivation to run after reputation and benefits, there would be no adversity, so adversity could be smoothness as well. This kind of life philosophy was taken by those people who underwent hardships all their life as an excuse to comfort the spirits.

The fact that most Chinese are able to adapt to difficult circumstances is a reflection of the influence of Buddhism. The positive part of the character is steadiness and perseverance, while the negative part of it lies in lack of initiative, a spirit which is necessary to promote social progress. Buddhism has stopped to be worshipped by Chinese for some time, but is coming back on a small foot eventually. It is undeniable that as a kind of culture, it has penetrated people's mind deeply, and it may influence future generations.

In general, Buddhism acts as a religion for people wishing to alleviate pains and to keep balance of spirits. From the perspective of modern value concepts, the ideas of Buddhism are passive and might be criticized.

c) Taoism

The Taoist school is a school considering "*Dao*" as the highest philosophical sphere and ultimate solicitude. Here, "*Dao*" refers to a kind of phenomenon and general principle, which passes through universe and human beings. Lao Zi said that *Dao* could not be expressed by language; *Dao* did not change forever; *Dao* was shapeless (Li Xia 1996, 120). Lao Zi was one of the representatives of Taoist school, respected as the master of ancient simple dialectics. He revealed the transition and unification of the opposite part of the things profoundly. The "*Dao*" of Lao Zi has three kinds of connotations:

- The first illustrates the unification of "not existing" and "existing". Taking "*Dao*" as an example, "*Dao*" possess no form, no sound and no taste, but it exists in everything by its affection on human being's action; thus it could be seen that "not existing" and "existing" are unified.
- The second connotations of "*Dao*" refers to the unification of "eternal" and "change". "Eternal" is used to describe a comparative concept but for absolute. It could be explained as: everything in the world keeps its characters comparatively under certain conditions, but because of the interaction of things, this kind of comparatively stable characteristics could change during some developing period.
- The third spirit of "*Dao*" embodies in the unification of "non-action" and "self-transition". As everything is connected with each other, things could change naturally by the interaction between them without the interference of man. The idea of Lao Zi had an active part, it confirmed the connection of things. But he did not distill his connection concept to a higher level of causality. That is just the limitation of his philosophy.

Zhuang Zi developed the idea of Lao Zi further. He explained *Dao* as the "general principles of the universe that is unchangeable and endless" (Zhou GaoDe 1999, 22). Zhuang Zi revered being quiet and doing nothing against nature as the highest behavioral standard. He emphasized the absolute freedom of spirits and the way to keep in good health, thus forming a free and unfettered independent life style. Zhuang Zi thought if one wanted to reach the state of freedom, one must restrain and cultivate oneself from inside and outside. To restrain from the outside is to resist the attraction of various desires, such as material enjoyment, reputation and status, knowledge and judgment ability. Zhuang sharply criticized those who run after reputation and status. In his opinion, reputation and status are worth nothing.

Therefore, to run after them was regarded by Zhuang Zi as wasting energy and distorting the beautiful human nature with material enjoyment. Zhuang Zi had his unique view: he said that if a person seeks material enjoyment, he would be like a bird in a birdcage or tiger in a cage, having lost his leisure completely. Zhuang Zi asked the people to give up the study of knowledge for keeping the naive characters: life is short, knowledge is endless, so it is impossible to command all the knowledge; not to say knowledge is the root of all evils. Zhuang Zi discouraged people to form a definite judgment. He said that if a man did not take judgment serious, he could get his comfort throughout his life. The surmounting spirit also reflected in his concept about life and death: "do not laugh because you have life and do not worry just for you would die" (Jin YuanPu 1999, 324). From the above illustration it can be seen that Taoism is a passive life philosophy; it could pose a barrier in the way of social progress.

2. CHINESE TRADITIONAL CULTURE (-1840)

a) Development stages of Chinese traditional culture

Chinese traditional culture could be described as broad and profound. Its philosophies are full of wisdom, which exert far-reaching influences upon the modern world. The rich ancient books and records, especially the unique Chinese character system, are entering into the modern world through the use of the computer. The deep thought over the relations between man and nature has a positive influence on the modern conditions. The rich and generous ethics enlighten the modern industrial society. Its art and literature attract the attention of the world due to its Eastern artistic concept.

Chinese traditional culture underwent a winding developing process. From ancient civilization to modern cultural practice, it strides across 5,000 years of history. It was a process of developing, reforming, breaking and progressing of the material culture as well as of the spiritual culture. In the process, the Chinese nation created its unique cultural system and cultural forms. This process could be divided into four stages.

(1) Embryonic period: From the origination of human beings to Qin (Before 221 BC)

This period could be further divided into two parts. The first period was the period before the Shang and the Zhou Dynasty. The major achievements of this period was the invention of working tools, the utilization of fire, the transition from a hunting and gathering economy to an agricultural economy (Zhou Dao-Sheng 1999, 5). The emergency of private ownership was also one of the features of this period. It was also during this time that people started to write down words using characters.

The Shang and the Zhou Dynasty (11th century BC-8th century BC) marked the beginning of the second period. The use of bronze became the symbol of the production tools and of culture. The authority of Heaven was commonly recognized as the absolute power governing the activities of man. From the Spring and Autumn Period until the time of the Warring States, the great thinkers as Confucius, Lao Zi and Zhuang Zi built their philosophical systems (Zhou DaoSheng 1999, 5). These thinkers and the schools they created, i.e. Confucianism, Taoism and Legalist schools, have had a consistent influence on China's ideology, politics and culture.

(2) Foundation of Chinese culture: Qin, Han, SanGuo, Jin, NanBei, Sui (221 BC-618 AD)

The achievements of this period include the unification of characters, standardization of infrastructure, issuing of a single currency and standardization of measurements. New Confucianism, scripture schools and metaphysics dominated the philosophy of the period (Zhou DaoSheng 1999, 6).

(3) Prosperous periods: Tang, Song and Yuan Dynasties (618 AD-1368 AD)

The poems of the Tang Dynasty (618-907) and the *Ci* of the Song Dynasty have always been praised as the treasures of Chinese traditional culture. *Ci* actually describes a song form, characterized by lines of unequal length. The rich contents, the purity of the art form and the large numbers of the poems and *Ci* made it a peak period of Chinese culture (Shou Yong 1999, 7). The competition of Confucianism and Buddhism and the results of it, the emergence of a Confucian school of idealistic philosophy, are the main features of the culture of that period.

(4) Period of decline: Ming Dynasty and early Qing Dynasty (1368 AD-1840 AD)

The dynasties Ming and Qing were the last period of the feudalistic society. The appearance of new production relations, which means the relationship between capitalist and worker, and the invasion of Western culture brought the traditional culture into a transition period.

The ideas of the enlightenment emphasized democracy and the value of the person, resisted the dominance of monarchy and criticized the deceitful style of study. From reform schools that existed in the landlord class to the techniques of Western countries, from the bureaucratic reformist to the revolutionist, the Westernisation of the Chinese society became more and more radical.

b) The features of traditional Chinese culture

Traditional Chinese culture belongs to the group of "continental culture". The geographical situation limited the Chinese economy form to a self-sufficient small-scale peasant economy, for it matured in the isolated East-Asian continent. The multi-mountain environment caused the isolation of Chinese culture from other cultures. The self-reliance character of the Chinese culture was due to this reason (Zhou DaoSheng 1999, 22).

(1) Agriculture culture

From the perspective of the relation of culture and production mode, the Chinese culture belongs to agriculture cultures (Jin YuanPu 1999, 120): Chinese people hold the idea that agriculture is the foundation of the development of the country throughout feudal history. The policy of emphasizing agriculture and restraining commerce was the psychological reflection of the Chinese agriculture culture. The possession of land became a criterion to judge a person's position and fortune. In correspondence with the agriculture economy, Chinese people had been working in the fields, leading a simple life, but they always kept an optimistic attitude towards life. Judging from a modern value perspective, that is an optimism that was satisfied with poor and low conditions; anyway, it is worth sympathizing with. People did not hold too many extravagant hopes to life. On the contrary, they always did self-examination. This activity was different from what later was called "self-examination" by Mao during the Cultural Revolution. It is much more simple and out of the will of the people, and not forced by anyone. Its aim was to see if people were satisfied and following God's will. This kind of attitude had a direct, inner link with the self-sufficient natural economy. It was a kind of conservative life philosophy that contradicted with the modern society. It could not motivate people to go forward but paralyzed their spirits.

(2) Ethnic political culture

Ancient China did not have independent political subjects or a theory system which focused on the study of politics. But it had varied political ideas and theories. The ancient political theories were influenced by the ethical traditional culture, which mixed with ethical theory and formed a unique ethics – political culture theory. "If you want to rule the country, you must regulate the family first; if you want to regulate the family, you must cultivate yourself first" (Tian GuangLin 1999, 42) was the political theory of the ancient times. It was full of the ethical color of the Chinese traditional culture. The core of Chinese traditional culture embodied in seeking for good, which was governed by politics. Cultivating, regulating, governing and ruling were the guiding principles of the Chinese culture. The perfection of one's morality was the first choice of a person. The human being had the same status as heaven and earth. The idea that human beings are the soul of all things put people on a relatively high position in the universe. Nevertheless, Chinese traditional culture did not respect personal values and personal development, but blend the individual and beauty, human beings, nature and society. It emphasized the responsibilities of every individual towards the country, society and religion. Therefore, Chinese traditional culture was a kind of political ethics culture targeting at seeking for rule.

(3) Confucianism as orthodox school

Chinese traditional culture respected all orthodox schools and excluded heterodoxy schools. The respect to the orthodox school could be explained as holding one idea as the only legitimate truth and letting people to abide and imitate. Excluding heterodoxy schools could be explained as repelling and criticizing the ideas that were not in conformity with the orthodox idea. Confucianism had been worshipped as the orthodox school among all academic schools. As orthodox school, Confucianism penetrated all cultural spheres, whether it is history, philosophy, education, science, art or law. Confucianism restrained the development of science to some extent due to its repelling character. In the practicing process, Confucianism restrained the development of religions due to its orthodox status (Jin YuanPu 1999, 128).

It is an irrevocable fact, that religion has never exerted a deep influence in China. In a sense, religion in China could never compare with the Judaeo-Christian or the Muslim tradition in Europe and the Muslim World (Wienen 1999, 31). On account of the orthodox position of Confucianism, it not only gained the attention and active support of the rulers of almost all the dynasties, but also gained the worship and obedience of the common people. Furthermore, under the influences of other religions, people worshipped Confucianism just like a religion. In the political practices, the orthodox status of Confucianism also forced the rulers to compete with each other in order to prove that their regime was legitimate. In this sense, the argument of orthodox and unorthodox was not only an academic problem, but a political problem as well. Confucianism's doctrine were put into law to govern the people.

c) The key ideas of the Chinese traditional culture

The Chinese traditional culture underwent a long development period, which was not only rich and varied, but also full of attractive ideas and abundant connotations. These attractive ideas and abundant connotations were the key concepts of Chinese traditional culture. It goes without saying that these fundamental believes – concerning the outlook on the world and the vision of life of Chinese people – promoted the development of Chinese traditional culture. In summary, the Chinese nation's ideal could be described as follows:

(1) Be vigorous, be promising and make unremitting efforts to improve yourself.
(*Gang jian you wei, zi qiang bu xi.*)

This idea has always motivated the Chinese nation to strive upwards. It can be found in many masterpieces of Confucius and Mencius (Mei Zi). With the struggle between Confucianism and Taoism which advocated the idea of "Do not be the first person to do anything; seek for silence; doing nothing is doing something" the idea developed itself (Tian GuangLin 1999, 75).

(2) Humanism (*Ren Ben Zhu Yi*)

This idea could be further developed as: people are the essence. That means, people were more important than the state or the monarch. "Think highly of people rather than of ghosts and Gods", that is, people's life was put in the priority position in comparison with the ghosts and Gods. Confirm that the individual has the desire to complete himself. Here, the individual was put in an ethical relationship web, abiding the ethics of the society was everyone's duty (Tian GuangLin 1999, 70).

(3) Heaven and people were integrated (*Tian Ren He Yi*)

Heaven meant unknown power in nature. The development of heaven and the development of people interacted with each other; people should adjust and regulate their behavior according to the changes of nature. Looking at Chinese history, one may conclude that the idea restricted politics. In the meantime, it also influenced the social life. Therefore, the idea was a vital component of Chinese traditional culture (Tian GuangLin 1999, 74).

(4) Rule by etiquette (*Li Zhi*)

The so-called "*Li*" refers to the etiquette that was followed when people or states interacted with each other. "*Li Zhi*" means ruling by etiquette. Here, "*Li*" was raised to the status of a social idea and then promulgated and promoted. "*Li Zhi*" was a ladder system in its essence, a tool to govern the country and the people. It played an active role in the feudal society (Jin YuanPu 1999, 160).

3. TRANSFORMATION FROM TRADITIONAL TO MODERN CULTURE (1840-1919)

From the first opium war (1840) to the May Fourth movement in 1919, Chinese traditional culture changed in its essence.

The transformation brought about the disintegration of the traditional culture and the establishment of new Chinese culture. During the process of transformation, the reality of Chinese was the inner reason that caused its development; the impact of outside culture was an indispensable factor that imposed influences on it. The Chinese society of that period was unstable and backward compared to the Western countries. Some knowledgeable people produced the idea to learn about advanced civilization from the outside world. Democratic ideas and Western science were embodied for the first time in Chinese cultural history.

The transformation of Chinese traditional culture was embodied in five aspects:

a) The traditional value concept weakened.

The traditional value concept paid more attention to reputation than to benefits. The concept motivated people to maximize their personal power by obtaining government posts, rather than putting their efforts into raising the power of the state. The concept had already become a barrier for social development in the late Qing Dynasty. Therefore, to get rid of the old concept and to set up the new practical value concept was an imperative trend (Jin YuanPu 1999, 601).

b) The "self-centered" culture concept was broken.

China had always been an isolated society before the 19th century; "we are the best" was a self-centered concept that existed in China for thousands of years. But the defeat in the Opium War broke this vision completely. Chinese people began to self-criticize and realized the gap between themselves and foreign countries. The changes in the concepts opened the door, and new goods and ideas flew into China. It could be regarded as the beginning of Chinese awareness of "open the eyes and observe the world" (Jin YuanPu 1999, 349).

c) The scientific concept became a component of Chinese culture.

The advanced scientific technology and knowledge of the Western countries were introduced by some Chinese intellectuals (Lian YongJie 1999, 349). There were mathematicians who translated many works on mathematics; railway engineers designed and built the first important railways in Chinese history; airplane designers constructed modern planes. In this way, the scientific system of the modern China was set up step by step. Science entered Chinese culture for the first time.

d) Industry and commerce were emphasized.

Chinese traditional culture emphasized agriculture and repelled commerce. While the Chinese people were still satisfied with the "self-sufficient" agriculture economy, the industrial revolution had already begun heatedly in Western countries. Chinese people began to become aware of the fact that widespread poverty and backwardness were the reasons why their state was oppressed. With this idea being around, Chinese commerce and industry began to develop (Jin YuanPu 1999, 604).

e) New fields of study emerged.

The social and national crisis made the representatives of bureaucracy, namely Liang QiChao, Kang YouWei and Yan Fu became aware of the fact that the old study style was too impractical and contributed nothing to the development of the country. In order to save the country from crisis, they devoted themselves to the study of the most outstanding problems concerning government policy and people's daily life.

The modern Chinese history is a history of wars, with turbulence as its major feature. Therefore, the complicated social situation should be taken into consideration when analyzing the transformation of culture. A lot of new ideas and scientific technologies were introduced into China at that period, but domestic troubles, foreign invasion and the flaws that existed in the transformation itself made the progress rather slow in comparison with Japan during the same period.

> *Japan began to enforce reform in 1868. The leading idea of the reform could be illustrated as: absorbing advanced scientific knowledge, including new ideas and political systems, combining it with Japan's heritage. The Japanese adopted this extensive criterion on the absorption of new things: they did not put their national morality as the center, but have given the same status to their own morality and to the foreign ideas. Thus, they have been more open and complete than Chinese when absorbing new things (Li XiangHai 1999, 68).*
>
> *By comparison, Chinese reform ideas had their limitation, focusing only on the scientific knowledge "as far as it can be used in China", while maintaining that the Chinese political system and ideology should not be changed.*
>
> *The difference of the reform idea made China and Japan go to two totally different roads eventually. On the one hand, Japan became a capitalist country and a dominant regional power after less than twenty years of reform, while remaining an empire. On the other hand, China overthrew the Qing Dynasty and continued its fight for sovereignty and economic and scientific advancement (Zhao DeYu, 1998, 49).*

The progress of the society is determined by many factors. Culture, as a feature of a society, could be regarded as cause that affects progress. On the other hand, social progress could promote the development of culture. That means, culture and social progress interact with each other. Therefore the conclusion could be drawn like this: the social reform is the foundation of the transformation of Chinese traditional culture to modern culture, and it is the inevitable outcome of social development (Jin YuanPu 1999, 605).

4. CONTEMPORARY CHINESE CULTURE (1919-NOW)

Contemporary Chinese culture underwent three developing stages.

a) Culture of the New Democratic Revolution Period (1919-1949)

The first stage ranges from 1919-1949 and is called "New Democratic Revolution Period". During this period, China was attacked by both economic and political crisis. In the political field, the warlords fought for years in order to command state political power. The invasion by Japan in 1937 threw Chinese people into disaster. Under such political circumstances, economic progress was impossible. National industry stopped developing, and the rural economy depressed. The Chinese culture of this period was embodied in philosophy, literature and scientific fields respectively.

In the field of *philosophy*, historic materialism was propagated by Li Da-Zhao (1889-1927) and some other progressive scholars. In their philosophic works, they stated that the motivating power of social development were the people, that history was created by people rather than a sage. – Mao ZeDong (1893-1976) was another philosopher of that time. His "comment on practice" and "comment on contradictions" gave an illustration of the relationship of knowledge and practice. He pointed out that practice is the source of knowledge; practice is the impetus of the development of knowledge; practice is the aim of the knowledge; practice is the only criterion to judge the correctness of knowledge (An ZuoZhang 1986, 1104). In fact, the philosophy of the New Democratic Revolution Period was the theoretical foundation of the revolution. Under the guidance of these theories, the Chinese revolution found its direction and its way.

In correspondence with the features of the time, the *literature* of that period focused on criticizing the social reality, appealing for revolution to change the current situation. In other words, it is a kind of literature that is full of the revolution spirits. Resisting oppression and seeking for liberation is the subject of this literature. The representatives of the world of literature of that time are Lu Xun, Guo MoRuo and Mao Dun. The works of Lun Xun gave a clear description of the realities of the Chinese society of that period. For example, in "biography of *AQ*" he depicted a backward peasant image *AQ*. *AQ* used the "spirit win" method to alleviate his pain and to satisfy his resistance and revenge psychology to the landlord class. Guo MoRuo was a poet and playwright who wrote many poems and plays to express his patriotic emotions and summoned people to participate in the revolution. "Zi Ye" was the masterpiece of Mao Dun which exposed the contradictions between different bourgeois, as well as other social contradictions.

In the sphere of *science*, many scientists contributed their research achievements to the development of the subjects. The study of geologist Li SiGuang on stratigraphy, the fourth century glacier (that is a glacial epoch in the history of the development of globe) and geomechanics laid the foundation for the further study of the geological science, which is an achievement belonging to the world. Zhu KeZhen was a meteorologist and geologist who founded the geography department in Southeast University, which was the first in China. He established the first observatory station of China in NanJing in 1927. He drew the first weather map of China in 1930, while before that time meteorological undertakings were dominated by foreign experts. There were also some achievements in chemical industry, bridge building and studies of physics. Taking the complicated social environment into consideration, it can be perceived that the Chinese scientists conquered many difficulties in acquiring those achievements.

b) *The Socialist Revolution and its Cultural Revolution (1949-1979)*

The second period lasted from 1949 to 1979, which was the Socialist Revolution Period. The People's Republic of China was founded on the 1st October, 1949. Under the leadership of the Communist Party, Chinese people began to set up state power organs, turned private ownership into state ownership. Economic construction was put in an important position in the socialist construction. But as the new state powers were only just set up and the new leaders did not command much experience in running the country, certain mistakes were made in the process of construction, which lead to retrogression rather than progression.

One can argue that the Cultural Revolution (1966-1976) was the biggest mistake of that period. The revolution emphasized the contradictions between the different social groups and took class struggle as the main principle of the socialist construction. The development of culture of this period encountered great obstruction (Lian YongJie 1999, 365). A large number of intellectuals were put into prison and eventually killed; truth and false were reversed. Therefore, ideological confusion dominated that period.

A series of movement was launched, which destroyed many treasures of Chinese culture. "Destroy the four old things – old ideas, old culture, old customs and old habits" was one of them. The "Red Guards" which were formed by middle school students went into the streets, put up "*Da Zi Bao*" – propaganda papers – and held speeches in the streets by the summon of the Cultural Revolution Committee. Many intellectuals were classified as "devil" and were beaten and insulted, their families were searched by the Red Guards, and property was confiscated. From 23rd August to 8th September, 1966, the Red Guards searched 84,222 households in ShangHai alone, among them 1,231 were high-level intellectuals and teachers (Zhang ShuQing 1992, 152).

During the movement, many temples and pavilions, which were of high artistic value, were destroyed. Many historical tombs, ancient memorial archways, statues of God or Buddha were smashed into pieces. According to statistics, 4,922 ancient historic remains were smashed in Beijing alone. The famous Confucius Temple, the Confucius Mansion and the Confucius Forest of Steles suffered serious damage. 6,388 pieces of classical books and pictures, horizontally inscribed boards, antique couplets, ancient bronze utensils, China and steles were put into fire or destroyed; 1,000,000 volumes of valuable data was thrown into fire; 1,000 steles were pulled down and smashed (Zhang ShunQing 1992, 168). Except for the serious damage to traditional culture, there were many other things which were regarded as "old customs". Women were not allowed to have long hair or wear colorful dresses at that time. Although one may find it difficult to understand today, it is a fact that everything was destroyed that was thought to be "old". As a consequence, splendid cultural remains were destroyed, which caused great loss to China and to the world.

c) Opening up of China (1979-now)

The third period started in 1979 and continues until now. After one and a half centuries of struggle and several generations untiring efforts, Chinese traditional culture saw its hope and marched towards the world. Chinese culture is encountering the world and finding scientific and practical ideas.

Heated cultural discussions have prevailed in the 1980ies and continue till now (Tian GuangLin 1999, 317). The subjects of the discussions extend to many spheres, including the study of Chinese traditional culture and its effects on modern culture; culture and politics, culture and economic development; culture and science; cultural construction and construction of a socialist civilization; culture and education. Some scholars focus on studying regional culture, such as: "JinChu culture"; "WuYue culture"; "YouYan culture" and "GuangDong culture" and so on. The discussions contributed a lot to the development of the contemporary culture. Many scholars pointed out that the discussion was to meet the needs of further reform and opening-up policy of China. It was an echo to the ideological and academic world of the times. After the third plenary of the 13th session of the Communist Party in December 1978, China entered into a new era that took the economic reform and the political reform as its center.

The rapid development in the economy brought about changes in people's psychology, ideological modes and value concepts. These changes promoted the reform, opening-up and the process of modernization. In the meantime, serious problems appeared with the deepening of the reform. People often contradicted consciously or unconsciously (Wang XinTing 1997, 281). This phenomenon handicapped the modernization development. Among all the resistance, one may think that the most powerful one comes from the reformists themselves; it may be a limitation in their mind. In other words, it possibly comes from the shortcomings in the national cultural structure. The old value concept advocated by traditional culture did not conform to the demands of reform, therefore a new value concept needed to be erected. Thus, to conduct a discussion about culture is totally necessary, if it focuses on reality, analyzing the deep-rooted cautious attitude to reform in China, such as conservatism and lack of creativity. It is indispensable to think over the nation's traditional culture and to promote the reform consciously, overcoming the potential barriers in people's mind.

The current cultural structure is composed of three parts: dominant ideological culture, elitist culture and mass culture (Jin YuanPu 1999, 692).

- The dominant ideological culture of China is the socialist culture, guided by doctrines of Marxism-Leninism, former chairman Mao's thought and the theory of Deng XiaoPing. Its purpose is to help people establish a socialist value concept. Collectivism embodies its value tendency.

- Elitist culture is created by intellectuals, and prevails among the intellectuals. Elitist culture has special rational characters and value tendencies. Elitist culture reflects the level of a nation's culture development. In today's China, facing the powerful dominant culture and the prevailing popular culture, the elitist culture retreats to some extent.

- The mass culture belongs to common people, which is a new type of culture based on the rapid development of the media and the construction of a market economy, becoming the center of social life. Television, radio, newspapers and the Internet are the prevailing channels of the popular culture.

The rising of the popular culture is in accordance with the principle of the market economy. Nevertheless, it raised great challenges to the dominant and elitist culture, although the elitist culture have prevailed for thousands of years. The contradictions between them provide opportunities for further development. Developing in the light of contradictions, unifying amongst opposites is the developing direction of contemporary Chinese culture.

C. BROAD DESCRIPTION OF THE CHINESE LEGAL SYSTEM

1. HISTORICAL DEVELOPMENT OF THE CHINESE LEGAL SYSTEM

China is a country with one of the longest histories in the world. Nevertheless, the concept of law and the notion of the "rule of law" never took a central position in the Chinese society until the late 1970ies, when the People's Republic of China decided to rebuild and modernize its socialist legal system (Wang ChengGuang 1997, 7). After two decades of development, Chinese law has achieved a great deal, but it is still far from being perfect. New problems have emerged during the transition period of Chinese reform. This is an inevitable phenomenon, because there is no development without problems. Considering these problems from the historical perspective, it is not difficult to find the impact and influence of traditional law on contemporary law. Therefore, it is necessary, before diving into the rules and concrete field of laws, to have a bird's eye view of the history, characteristics and structure of the Chinese law.

a) The traditional legal system

The long history of Chinese law is divided into two parts, that is, the part of the *traditional law* – ranging from the Law of Yu which prevailed in Xia Dynasty to the codes of the Qing Dynasty – and the part of the *modern legal system* starting from the legal reform in the late Qing Dynasty around 1840 to the present time.

(1) Slavery system

Chinese *traditional law* can be further divided into the law of slavery society and the law of feudal society. The establishment of the Xia Dynasty marked China's entrance into slavery society; since then the concept of law emerged in the society. The historical book "Zuo Zhuan", which states "there was disordered politics" refers to the struggle of common people against owner of slaves, and the "Law of Yu" refers to law of the Xia Dynasty (Zheng Qin 1999, 10). In the 16th century BC, the Shang nationality destroyed Xia and established the Shang Dynasty. The emperor of Shang governed the country by religious superstition. Whenever a penalty was to be made, they would say it was the order of heaven.

Compared with the law of the two previous dynasties, the law of Western Zhou was much more sophisticated. Western Zhou had professional officers in charge of the drawing up and enforcement of law, and Western Zhou abandoned the superstitious law system of Shang, substituting it by the "Five listening" trial method. "Five listening" refers to look at the suspected person and listen to his words, thus judging if he was guilty (Zheng Qin 1999, 45). Western Zhou witnessed the establishment of a set of written laws, which was called "the penalty code of Liu" (Xiong XianJue 1999, 9).

(2) Feudal society

The law of feudal society started with the establishment of Eastern Zhou Dynasty and lasted to the late Qing Dynasty (1840). The Eastern Zhou Dynasty is further divided into Spring and Autumn Period on the one hand and the Warring State Period on the other. It witnessed the decline of the slavery system and successive wars of small kingdoms, which caused enormous social unrest and upheavals. The newly arising feudal lords and the populace had no political powers or privileges in the patriarchal and aristocratic system. Under the appeal of those people for social reform, the former secret law was replaced by publicly displayed legal document. During the Warring State Period, more profound changes in the law took place, such as the development of Shang Yang in 361 BC (Zheng Qin 1998, 61). As the first unified state in Chinese history, Qin upheld the legalistic school and vehemently prohibited the ideas and books of Confucianism and other schools, by burning all other scholarly books and executing the disciples of Confucius. This extreme approach of the legalist school which advocated cruel and excessive punishment of those who dared to show even the slightest resentment caused great dissatisfaction of the people, and the cruel rule of Qin eventually led to the collapse of the short-lived Qin Dynasty.

Drawing lessons from the collapse of Qin, the ruler of the Han Dynasty that replaced Qin adopted different laws in the hope of winning the support from the people. Advocated by Dong ZhongSu (179 BC-104 BC), who was an ardent disciple of Confucianism, Han banned the legalistic school and other schools, by elevating Confucianism to the position of the official orthodoxy of the country. From then on, Confucian concepts and ideas were promoted to be the dominant orthodoxy, which permeated through all legal rules and codes as the underpinning spirit of traditional Chinese law, throughout the entire feudal society (Huai XiaoFeng 1998, 75). The *Han Code* formed a solid foundation for later dynasties: the subsequent *Tang Code* – established during one of the most perilous periods in Chinese history – and the *Qing Code* – established the during last dynasty – are considered the most representative pieces of traditional Chinese law.

The traditional law, started more than 4,000 years ago, fortified by Confucianism in the Han Dynasty, persisted until the beginning of the 20th century. This long-lasting legal system was different from common law and civil law, and to a great extent opposite to the concepts of modern law. It has several characters that distinguish itself from the modern law systems

(3) The characteristics of traditional Chinese law

There are many extraordinary features in Chinese traditional law. *One* is the combination of *Li* (etiquette) and *Fa* (law) (Zhan JiFan 1997, 28). There were two schools competing with each other to possess governing positions: one was Confucianism, which advocated *Li*, the other was the legalist school, which advocated *Fa*. – For a period *Fa* held precedence over the Confucian model. On the other hand, *Li* was a social phenomenon of ancient China; it originated rather early and went through the whole ancient society. Since *Li* could function as the governing power of people's mind, it was used as an important tool to govern. *Li* influenced every aspect of social life, regulated interpersonal relationships and the relationship of the individual people with the country as a whole.

But eventually, *Li* and *Fa* became integrated; the legalist school that advocated a clear distinction between morality and law became submerged by Confucianism, which did not distinguish between the two. The imperial legal codes that existed from the time of Han through the Qing Dynasty repented the "legalization" of *Li* in the form of *Fa* –positive law; in other words, law was "confucianized". Fa came to include the ethical precepts and rules as encompassed by *Li* (Peter 1997, 18). The combination of *Li* and *Fa* went through a long historical development; it was determined by the patriarchal ethical characters of the society. *Li* and *Fa* were complementary with each other, and their combination could meet the requirements of the country to realize long-term governing and stability.

The *second* feature of traditional Chinese law is the connection and communication of the course of heaven, the law of the country and the human feelings (Zhang JinFang 1999, 51). The "Course of Heaven" refers to three cardinals as advocated by Dong ZhongShu. The patriarchal politics and the hierarchy system were permanent and could not be violated under the protection of the Course of Heaven. The Course of Heaven was legalized by the law of the country: "if you go against law, then you go against heaven". In the meantime, the feudal governor advocated law, and the ethical human feelings were in harmony with each other. In order to avoid the contradiction between law and human feelings, the governors tried to legalize human feelings and duties. The national law stood in the center of the three — between the Course of Heaven and human feelings; the three were harmonious and unified.

The traditional law recognized and protected the unequal status of persons. It was the feature of the times that social status had apparently more importance than legal rules. "Equality before the law" was never accepted as a legal principle and as a legal practice; therefore, inequality is a feature of the traditional law (Zhang JinFang 1997, 56).

The traditional legal system was not founded on a democratic system, but on a totalitarian one. In correspondence with it, "rule of man" was emphasized, whereas the concept of "rule of law" was neglected. Even the legalist school, which advocated the importance of law, also emphasized the central function of a wise and able emperor (Xin ChunYing 1999, 3). There was argument of "rule of man" or "rule of law" in Chinese legal history, but the focus of the argument was: which would be the foundation for ruling the country. Law as a superior power, a concept developed in Western countries, has never been recognized in China. In connecting with the legal culture, ancient China did not distinguish between legislative power, executive power and judicial power; these three powers were integrated and were commanded by the emperor. The emperor was authorized by heaven to draw up laws; his words were laws, and the law could stop being enforced by a single sentence of him.

The traditional law is constructed on the basis of a monolithic and comprehensive code that contains all types of rules, with criminal laws as the backbone of the entire system. It is no exaggeration to say that traditional law had the same nature as criminal law as it depends on criminal punishment to structure the system. As criminal law was highlighted, civil law received little attention. In ancient times, the major codes were penalty codes, penalty and law were synonyms (Zhang JinFan 1997, 136). The penalties were very cruel, and the litigation system was comprehensive when dealing with criminal cases. Therefore, the traditional law took criminal law as the backbone of the entire system. The law was viewed as a cruel instrument of suppression by both the ruling class and the common people. That lead to a hostile attitude towards litigation in the Chinese society, which still exists to some extent.

In the traditional legal system, there was no separate judicial branch. The administrative officials exercised both executive power and judicial power. The typical format of a trial was a process of inquisition, backed by physical torture, to obtain a confession. This irrational practice of law is not able to establish impartiality but rather prejudice against parties to litigate. In the process of adjudication, a single party performed as both prosecutor and judge. This may be a partial explanation for the deep-rooted distrust of the Chinese people towards law.

There were no professional people engaged in the legal system. To start litigation or to be sued by the government or another person meant to be left at the discretion of officials, without any legal assistance. The lack of a systematic legal education system contributed to the absence of a distinct legal profession and the lack of qualified legal officials (Zhang JinFan 1997, 277). Although there was a tradition of learning from officials, legal education by dedicated institutions has never occurred in traditional law. In addition, Confucianism advocated “no litigation”, therefore, the number of litigations became a criterion to judge the merits of a local officer. In order to reduce litigation, morality education was used as one tool; the other tool was mediation. The mediators could be local officials or the members of the wider family. Some mediations were compulsory. The rights of litigants were often neglected; this caused the weak awareness of Chinese when it comes to litigation. The social environment did not provide conditions for the emergence of a legal profession.

The emphasis of law was on the protection of government powers and societal interest rather than on the protection of individual rights and private interests. To a great extent, private interests and rights have never been the concern of Chinese law. This historical feature has been ingrained in Chinese legal culture and continues to influence the current development of the legal system.

Despite of the flaws existing in traditional law, it also has its positive contributions and values to the modern legal system. The mixed system of codification and precedents, an emphasis on the educational function of law, the experience of legal practice, and the stabilizing function of law in maintaining social harmony were the strengths that are worth learning from. Nevertheless, compared with its perceived backwardness, the strengths and values may be seen as relatively few. Furthermore, one could argue that it posed an obstacle in the historical course of transition towards modernization. Therefore, discarding the old and building a new legal system is an urgent task of modern legal professionals in China.

b) The modern Chinese legal system

The *modern legal system* in China began with the legal reform in the late Qing Dynasty. In 1840, China’s gate was broken by the armies of Western powers. The Chinese who lived in an unenlightened world realized for the first time that China had been left behind by the Western countries which had previously been perceived as under-developed by the Chinese. Therefore, conducting political and legal reform became the destination of advanced Chinese bureaucrats. In 1898, “Constitutional reform and modernization” marked the beginning of law reform (Huai XiaoFeng 1998, 431). The leading person in the movement were Kang YouWei and Liang QiChao. They thought that division of the power would lead to prosperity of a country and strengthen its position towards other countries; if China was to be powerful, it had to adopt the same system as Western countries. However, the reform party was not able to not conquer the conservative party. In the end, the advocates of reform were arrested and six of them were executed (Xin ChunYing 1999, 6).

It is safe to say that the reform failed due to the incompatibility of the newly designed legal system with the old social structure. Under the tutelage of Japanese and European advisors, beginning in 1904, the Qing regime made a bilateral attempt to modernize its codes. The leading figure behind this efforts was Shen JiaBian, the ministry for law reform, whose work, together with that of the Imperial law drafting commission, lead to the promulgation of a European-style Judicature Act in 1907, an imperial Constitution in 1908 and the drafts of a commercial law, civil law, as well as criminal and criminal procedure laws (Peter 1997, 20). However, with the extinction of the Qing Dynasty, these laws ended in the dustbin of history. Nevertheless, they exerted a significant impact on later reform attempts.

Later on, the national government continued the course of legal development by copying Western patterns on a broader basis. But these laws again were never effectively implemented throughout the country because the national government failed to unify the country. – The legal reform scheme, though failed, had great contribution in ending the old traditional system (Zheng Qin 1998, 279). The new legal regime had distinctive differences with the old one, because it was based on totally different social and economic structures. In this sense, it may be asserted that there is no inherent connection between the traditional Chinese law and the modern legal regime in China. But, it is undeniable that the traditional legal culture has persisted obstinately, and it will influence the modern legal system for a long time (Wang ChengGuang 1997, 10).

c) The development of the legal system after 1949

The legal system of the People's Republic of China was established in 1949 upon the founding of the People's Republic of China. The new legal system was established on a different political, economic and ideological bases, that was entirely different from the traditional legal system. The construction of the legal system underwent four stages.

(1) Stage of legal groundwork

The stage of legal groundwork lasted from 1949-1956. During this period, the newly founded People's Republic of China faced many problems and tasks, such as recovering from the war-demolished economy, strengthening the new regime, reforming the capitalist ownership, constructing a socialist system and the Korea War. One striking feature of the period was that social reforms and movements were constantly launched throughout the country. In order to meet the needs of such a situation, the People's Republic of China promulgated the first Constitution in 1954. From 1954 to 1957, as many as 731 pieces of laws, orders and administrative regulations were promulgated by the China People's Congress and its Standing Committee and the State Council (Xin ChunYing 1999, 14). Many basic legal institutions were established, such as the judicial structure, the procuratorial structure, the government structure and the legal profession as such. Although this period witnessed some great achievements, its questionable aspects can not be ignored: the idea prevailed that government policy was superior to law; thus violation of law was a common practice of that period.

(2) Decline and suspension of the legal system

The second period started from 1956 and ended in 1966. During this period, the government policy that concentrated on economic reform was slowly replaced by class struggle. The movement caused serious consequences, that was, democracy gave way to personal autocracy, rule of law was substituted by rule of man. In the legal field, the "anti-rightist movement" proved neglecting law; numerous lawyers were condemned as rightist (Cai DingJian 1999, 82). The concepts of legality, equality before the law and the independence of the judiciary were labeled as bourgeois ideas and discarded completely. In 1959, the Ministry of Jurisdiction and the State Legal Affairs Bureau were canceled, and as a chain reaction, the jurisdiction bureaus in the provinces, autonomous regions and the municipalities directly under the control of the central government were canceled as well. The so-called anti-rightist movement was staged on a broad basis. The National People's Congress virtually suspended its legislative function. Law was regarded as nothing compared with the policy of the Communist Party and of the state. Until 1966, the year of the beginning of the "Cultural Revolution", Chinese society was fully equipped with the conditions for revolution; that is to say, there was no restriction to personal will. There was no legal control over any act of infringement (Cai DingJian 1999, 105).

(3) Destruction of the legal system

During ten years of "Cultural Revolution", the law was abolished and the legal apparatus completely abandoned. At that time, political order substituted the legal order. From 1966 to 1976, the legislative organ, the National People's Congress did not meet regularly. In 1975, the fourth National People's Congress revised the Constitution: there were only 30 articles in it; and almost no meaningful legal principles to challenge and stop the action of the political authorities. Law was degraded to an attachment of politics. The best way to safeguard oneself was to participate in the revolution and not to became its target (Xin ChunYing 1999, 17). It is no exaggeration to say that the country was in chaos, and that the development of the society was suspended.

(4) Legal reconstruction and reform

After the nightmare of the "Cultural Revolution", China began to engage in unprecedented legal reconstruction work. Law was regarded as the most efficient and institutionalized means to safeguard people's rights, social stability and economic development of the state. The ideological changes paved the way for the fourth stage of the development of the legal system (Gong PeiXiang 1999, 314). The social reform in the political and economic fields laid the foundation for legal reconstruction and reform. In the *political* field, economic construction has replaced class struggle as the basic task of the state; democracy and the protection of the citizen's rights have been emphasized by the party and the government; decentralization has been introduced into the power structure; and the governmental organs have been streamlined around the People's Congress system. In the *economic* field, the policy of structural reform and opening-up to the outside world has been introduced and implemented; the rigid planned economy has been abandoned and replaced by a "*socialist market economy with Chinese characteristics*"; private ownership has been allowed and protected; foreign investment and foreign trade have been encouraged and promoted (Gong PeiXiang 1999, 298). Corresponding to such a scenario, the legal system has been redesigned. The achievements of this stage are analyzed in the following parts.

The awareness of the government and the populace raised to a certain standard. "Governing the country by law" is the idea advocated by government (Gong PeiXiang 1999, 445). In relating with this idea, debates have been conducted over the issues of the nature of law; the dichotomy between party policy and law; the division between private law and public law. Many ideas discussed by the legal scholars have been incorporated into the laws and regulations, such as the Constitution, which was revised totally in 1982, civil law, administration law and procedure law.

Since 1979, China has embarked on a large-scale legislative work. Since 1979, the State Council, ministries, commissions and other branches of the government have promulgated more than 100 administrative regulations. The National People's Congress and it's Standing Committee promulgated more than 300 laws and related decisions. The thirty provinces, autonomous regions and the cities directly under the control of central government promulgated or ratified more than 4,500 regional regulations. The regional ministries and people's governments promulgated about 30,000 pieces of regulations (Shao BingRen 1998, 1). The ever-expanding number of laws and regulations embraces almost every aspect of society.

A legal structure has been established throughout the country. It includes the system of the People's Courts and the system of the People's Procurators –

these two are the judicial branches established by the People's Congress. In the meantime, various government law enforcement organs such as public security organs, tax bureaus, administrative reconsideration offices and arbitration committees have been set up (Cai DingJian 1999, 59).

The legal profession has been restored. Law firms have been set up; the forms are varying from the cooperation to state sponsorship. According to the 1998 law statistics, there were 8,946 law offices in all, 51,008 professional lawyers, and 17,958 part time lawyers and a total of 10,966 specially invited lawyers (Wang ZhongFang 1999, 1039). Legal education has also flourished during those years; it helped to educate a large number of legal professionals.

2. STRUCTURE OF LAWS, RULES AND REGULATIONS

The legislative system of China is a top-down system with several levels, which means that the National People's Congress as the highest state organ has the unitary legislative power over the entire nation, and it delegates certain legislative powers to local People's Congresses and the central and the local governments. The sources of legal rules are as following:

a) Constitution (XianFa)

The subsisting Constitution was promulgated on 4th December, 1982, and it has been subsequently amended in 1988 and 1993. In a broad sense, it includes the statement of the Constitution and the election law, as well as organic laws of the People's Congress, of the State Council, of the local governments, of the People's Courts and of the People's Procurators. Although the Constitution is regarded as the prevalent law in the country, it can not be quoted in judicial verdicts and administrative decisions as a direct legal ground for solving concrete disputes and problems. It is a therefore out of direct touch with daily legal practice and operation, and it is regarded as being of a general and vague nature (Wang ChengGuang 1997, 18).

b) Law (FaLu)

All legal documents promulgated by the National People's Congress and its committees belong to the category of documents which comprehends laws, decisions and ratified international treaties (Liu JinHua 1998, 45). Law could be further divided into two sub-categories: one is basic laws, which have a general impact throughout the nation, such as criminal law and marriage law; the rest are non-basic laws, which have a wide impact in specific areas only, such as patent law and trademark law.

Law is the backbone and principle of Chinese legal system. The Constitution does not define the fields which should be regulated by law. However, according to the related articles in Constitution and the practice, the following affairs should be governed by law (Yu MinSheng 1997, 438-439):

- organization and authorities of the state organs and the basic procedures of exercising power;
- basic rights and duties of citizens;
- system and principles on civil and commercial affairs, the state's economic administration, the state's administrative administration, labor and social insurance, natural resources and environmental protection;
- system and principle of litigation;
- legal standards of criminal matters;
- basis system of diplomacy and national defense;
- issues belonging to the authority of the National People's Congress and its Standing Committee, such as military service.

According to Constitution, the effect of law is second to the Constitution, but above the other legal matters. In addition, the law formulated by the National People's Congress is higher than the law formulated by its Standing Committee.

c) Administrative regulations (XingZheng FaGui)

This refers to the legal documents issued by the State Council. As the central administration of the country, the State Council has the power to enact rules concerning important issues of the country, provided they do not contravene the Constitution or any laws. On most occasions, they are detailed rules for implementing laws; on other occasions, they are experimental regulations (Liu JinHua 1998, 45).

d) Administrative rules (XingZheng GuiZhang)

This category includes regulatory rules issued by the ministries, commissions and departments of the State Council (Li BuYun 1998, 187). From a practical perspective, this set of rules is very important, for it provides detailed procedures, standards and requirements for practitioners. For example, rules issued by the Ministry of Foreign Trade and Economic Cooperation

(MOFTEC) are most useful for practical issues regarding foreign investment and foreign affairs.

e) Local regulations (DiFang FaGui)

Local regulations are enacted by local People's Congresses and their respective Standing Committees. Their effects are confined within their respective geographical territories.

Local regulations do not produce the same effect as administrative regulations, but they are more effective than local administrative rules, because local regulations are formulated by local state power organs, while the local administrative rules are formulated by its executive organs (Chen WangLi 1998, 43).

f) Local administrative rules (DiFang XinZheng GuiZhang)

This category includes regulatory rules issued by provincial, city and county governments and their administrative branches. They are detailed rules for implementing national laws and regulations as well as local regulations in their respective areas (Li BuYu 1998, 250).

g) Autonomous regulations and special regulations (DiFang ZiZhi TiaoLi he DanXin TiaoLi)

According to the Constitution, the People's Congresses and their respective Standing Committees of Autonomous Areas of all levels have the power to enact autonomous regulations and special regulations which may not contravene the Constitution, but may adopt flexible and different rules according to special local conditions and customs.

h) Autonomous rules (DiFang ZiZhi GuiZhang)

Although there are no specific provisions defining the legislative powers of the autonomous government, in practice they have similar power to the local governments to provide rules regulating affairs and matters that are part of their daily administration.

i) Regulations by Special Economic Zones (JingJi TeQu FaGui)

The Special Economic Zones' economic structure is different from other places in terms of preferential treatment for foreign business and powers of enacting more radical measures of reform and experiments. Authorized by the National People's Congress, the Special Economic Zones have the power of enacting Special Economic Zone's regulations which institutionalize the economic practices in these areas.

j) Judicial interpretation (SiFa JieShi)

Judicial interpretation consists of detailed rules for implementing law and regulations, of judicial guidance to resolve issues encountered in the process of application of law, and of answers to special questions raised by lower courts and procurators by the Supreme People's Court and the Supreme People's Procurator. According to law, the Supreme People's Court and the Supreme People's Procurators have the power to issue judicial interpretation on questions concerning specific application of laws and regulations in judicial proceedings (Li BuYu 1998, 344).

k) HongKong Basic Law and Macao Basic Law (XiangGang JiBenFa he AuMen JiBenFa)

These two kinds of Basic Laws occupy a special position in the legal system of the People's Republic of China. It is proper to see it below the Constitution and above other national laws, due to the special position of HongKong and Macao (Li BuYu 1998, 276).

In the process of adjudication, laws and regulations have greater effects than rules. According to the administrative litigation law, People's Courts must conduct adjudication according to administrative regulations and local regulations, but may take administrative rules and local rules as reference. – In this sense, courts may decide whether a rule is enforceable or not in the process of a litigation on the grounds of contradicting higher legal rules. From a practical perspective, administrative rules and local regulations are more useful, in the sense that they provide more detailed guidelines and procedures on concrete legal issues. The problem is that these rules and regulations are not published in a systematic way. Therefore, it is difficult to find proper and applicable rules in legal practice.

As mentioned before: one point that should not be overlooked is that the policy of the Communist Party has significant impact on law, although it is not formally a part of the legal system.

3. OVERVIEW OF TODAY'S JUDICIAL SYSTEM

In China, "judicial system" does not only refer to courts, but also to procuratorial organs, public security organs, judicial administrative organs, law offices and notary organs as well as to the arbitration system (Xiong XianJue

1999, 24-28). Each one of them functions under the responsibility clarified by the Constitution. It may be explained as follows:

a) Trial organs

The People's Courts exercise independent power in accordance with law. The courts are divided into four levels: the supreme courts, high courts, middle courts and lower courts. At all levels, the courts have criminal tribunals and administrative tribunals. Apart from the People's Courts, there are special courts such as martial courts, maritime courts and railway transportation courts. The Supreme Court is the highest trial organ, and its judgment is final. It supervises the work of all local courts and special courts (Li BuYu 1999, 100).

b) Procurators' system

People's Procurators are the state organs which supervise the implementation of law. It also has four levels which exercise independent rights in accordance with law. They are in charge of authorizing arrests and imprisonment in criminal cases as well as supervising the activities of other judicial organs (Xiong XianJue 1999, 89-92).

c) Public security organs and state security organs

The public security organs are in charge of detection, investigation, arrest and preliminary trial in criminal cases and security work. Public security organs are part of the government functional departments at four levels, namely: the ministry of public security under the State Council; public security administrations in the provinces, municipalities and regions; bureau's; and district divisions in the counties or city administrative regions (Li BuYu 1999, 109).

d) Judicial administrative organs

The judicial administrative organs are in charge of the legal education of cadres; publicizing the legal system; work undertaken by lawyers and notaries; mediation in disputes; prisons and reformation of criminals through forced labor and re-education; foreign affairs in the judicial field; and research on policy and theoretical studies (Li BuYu 1999, 111).

e) Law offices

The all-China association of lawyers has come into existence in July 1986. The basic duty of a Chinese lawyer is to render legal help to state organs, institutions, social groups and citizens in properly enforcing the law to protect the interest and legitimate rights of groups and individual citizens (Xiong Xian-Jue 1999, 184-187).

f) Notary organs

Notary offices are the state notary organs under the direction of the judicial administrative organs. On commission from clients, they provide testimonials and authenticate legal documents and facts of legal significance in accordance with the law (Xiong XianJue 1999, 301-302).

g) Arbitration system

China's arbitration is included in the law of civil procedure of the People's Republic of China. The law stipulates that, with respect to disputes arising from foreign economic trade and maritime affairs, if the parties concerned have a written agreement, they have the choice not file a lawsuit in People's Courts. Furthermore, when a case has been arbitrated, as the objective of arbitration, the People's Courts may adopt measures for the presentation of a lawsuit at the request of one of the parties. The People's Courts may authorize a ruling to be executed by the other party (Gan JunQi 1998, 65). China has enacted detailed arbitration rules of procedure, which have many points in common with those of the civil code countries of Europe. An interesting feature of arbitration in China is the combination of arbitration with conciliation. In other words, the arbitration may conduct conciliation during the process of arbitration.

4. IMPORTANT LEGISLATION SINCE THE OPENNING UP OF CHINA IN 1979

Since the open-up policy was adopted, the legislative work of China has achieved great progress. In order to regulate market operation, numerous laws concerning the market, market behavior and market order have been promulgated. Here is a brief introduction of the relevant laws:

- "*The Law of People's Republic of China on State Owned Enterprises*" – The law was passed on 13th April, 1988. It is the first basic law concerning the operation of the State Owned Enterprises since the founding of the People's Republic of China, which made a regulation to the general principle, the setting up, the change and the suspension of these enterprises. It also provides a clear definition on the rights and duties of the enterprises; the relations of managers and staff; the relations of government and enterprises; and the legal responsibilities of the enterprises.
- "*The Company Law of the People's Republic of China*" – The law was promulgated on 19th December, 1993. It stipulates the setting

up, regulations, organizational structure, rights and duties and the behavior of companies, including limited-liability companies and state-owed companies.

- "*The Law of Commercial Banking of the People's Republic of China*" – The law was passed on 10th May, 1995. In the market economy, finance plays an increasingly important role, therefore, deepening the reform of the financial system is inevitable.

There are also some other laws and administrative regulations related to the subject of market economy, such as the laws of the People's Republic of China on: "China-foreign cooperative enterprises" (1979), the "Bankruptcy of Enterprises" (1986), "Wholly Foreign Owned Enterprises" (1986), "China-foreign Equity Joint Venture enterprises" (1988) and "Provision regulations of the People's Republic of China on private enterprises" (1988).

In the process of establishing a socialist market economy, the subjects that perform productive and managing activities have to do this according to law. Therefore, certain laws are needed to regulate the behavior of the subjects. It includes the following laws of the People's Republic of China: Trademark Law (1982), Patent Law (1984), Economic Contracts involving Foreign Interest (1985), Economic Contracts (1987), Technical Contracts (1987), Copyright Law (1990), Maritime Law (1993), Guaranty Law (1995), Insurance Law (1995), and Provisions of Civil Law of the People's Republic of China" (1987).

The laws dealing with the market order are designed to guarantee the players an open, fair and competitive market environment. It contributes a lot to the circulation and the establishment of the multi-direction key element market. Here is a selection: Products Quality Law (1993), Anti-Improper Competition Law (1993), and The Law of the People's Republic of China on Protection of Consumer's Right (1993).

5. PROBLEMS IN THE LEGAL SYSTEM OF THE PEOPLE'S REPUBLIC OF CHINA

After two decades of reconstruction, China's legal system enters into a more steady developing phase. But it is important to look into the critical side of the system. One may find some problems due to the contradictions between the rapid social reform and a backward social structure. These problems and deep-rooted contradictions sometimes may create certain gaps between the law on paper and law in practice.

The concepts of supremacy of law and the rule of law are still not fully accepted by all governmental officials. The general secretary of the party, Jiang

ZeMin, has called for "governing the country by law", which rekindled the desire of the legal scholars to push for formal recognition of the concept of the rule of law. The question really is whether the party and the government are subject to law or whether law is merely an instrument of the government in governing the country. There is no doubt that law has to a great extent been elevated to a central position of society, but during the process of implementing the law, interference come from various directions, such as party policies, governmental powers, the network of relations and local protectionism. Those external factors have often rendered law a secondary authority (Hu YuTeng 1997, 1).

Therefore, it is naive to rely purely and solely on legal rules to solve all issues encountered in the country. Chinese traditional law has ruled the country and the people's minds for 4,000 years; the traditional legal culture had rooted in the social structure, and it is not so easy to overcome this. Therefore, it is not difficult to explain why the weakness of traditional law still can be found in some aspects of the modern Chinese legal system. Furthermore, the long practices of planned economy and the old socialist system which concentrated on the supremacy of the party and the rule of man have had a tenacious influences on both officials and the people. In such a social context, the supremacy of law may to a certain extend continue to remain in legal rhetoric for a period of time (Wang ChengGuang 1999, 14).

People's Congresses at different levels, governmental branches with different functions and at different levels have the power to issue laws and regulations. The laws they make sometimes are inconsistent, and even contradictory among themselves. Furthermore, the constant changes promoted by reform and social transition make some of the existing legal rules out of touch with social reality; new amendments and supplementary provisions, especially the judicial opinions, render the legal rules rather complicated (Li BuYu 1999, 45). Lack of legal expertise is still a wide-spread phenomenon; as many administrative rules and regulations are not published systematically, there is no comprehensive and authoritative way for rule-finding, and there is no sufficient and effective way to challenge legal rules on the basis of the Constitution.

It would seem that a large number of laws and regulations produce a sound basis for a country's development, but in fact, the implementation of law remains a major challenge to the nascent legal system. The credibility of law is challenged by the incomplete implementation. The tenacious plague of "triangle debts", the difficulty in enforcing verdicts and awards, and the relative weakness of the Bankruptcy Law and the Copyright Law are examples of this problem.

These problems are destructive and pose an imminent threat to the future of Chinese law. The great task lying ahead is to solve these problems, thus assuring that Chinese legal reform can follow a right and effective way.

D. CONCISE SUMMARY OF THE CHINESE POLITICAL SYSTEM

Politics, economy and culture can be seen as the three fundamental components of a society. Their relationship can be seen as one of superstructure, economic base and ideology. They are an integrated body and interact with each other, so one should not concentrate on the economy of a country without considering the political environment it is involved in. Getting to know the political system of a country is a crucial step before doing business in the country. This chapter is designed to provide a general concept of the political system of the People's Republic of China.

1. THE STATE STRUCTURE OF CHINA

The People's Republic of China has set up the Presidency and Vice-Presidency, National People's Congress, the State Council, and the Central Military Commission. They are the state power organs operating at the same level.

a) National People's Congress

The National People's Congress sets out the way in which the political power and the fundamental system of the state operate. The Constitution provides a definition of the scope of the National People's Congress, it includes the following five parts (Li ShuChu 1997, 105):

1) all powers are in the hands of the people; this is the core and basic principle of the state system of the People's Republic of China;

2) the organs through which the people exercise their rights are National People's Congress and the Local People's Congresses;

3) National People's Congress and the Local People's Congresses are elected by the people, responsible for the people and supervised by the people;

4) state administrative organs, judicial organs and procuratorial organs are elected by the People's Congress, responsible for it and supervised by it;

5) the political system is called "*Democratic Centralism*".

The National People's Congress is considered the highest state power organ of the People's Republic of China. It is composed of deputies elected from the provinces, the autonomous regions, the municipalities directly under the control of central government and the armed forces. The permanent organ of the National People's Congress is the Standing Committee. It is elected for a term of five years and holds one session each year. A presidium is elected to preside over the meeting.

The functions and powers of National People's Congress (NPC) are as follows (Li ShouChu 1997, 113-115):

- Legislative power: the NPC can amend the Constitution, formulate and amend Criminal Law, Civil Law and other basic laws;
- Nominative power: the NPC elects and approves the choice of and the removal of the leaders and relevant members of the highest organs of the state when necessary, such as the Vice-Chairman, the Secretary General of National People's Congress, the President and Vice-President; the Chairman of the Military Commission and others;
- Decision-making power: the NPC enjoys the decision-making power of the important affairs of the state. It examines and approves the plans for national economic and social development, and it reports on the operation of the plans;
- Supervising power: the NPC supervises the implementation of the Constitution and the work of the highest state organs;
- Other powers: the NPC performs other functions and powers that should be exercised by the highest organs of the state.

The Standing Committee of the NPC is composed of the Chairman, Vice-Chairman, Secretary-General and other members. The members of the Standing Committee can not hold posts in government, judicial or procuratorial organs. The procuratorial organs perform a supervisory task on the judicial system. The Chairman, Vice-Chairman and Secretary-General form the chairman's meeting, which handles the important day-to-day work of the Standing Committee. Under normal circumstances the Standing Committee meets every two weeks.

The NPC has nine special committees, covering: ethnic affairs; law; finance and economy; education; science, culture and health; overseas Chinese affairs; internal and judicial affairs; environment and natural resources protection; agriculture and rural affairs.

The special committees which are the components and work organs of the NPC carry out special work and activities according to the powers of the Standing Committee of the National People's Congress, so that the NPC can exercise its power and develop its matters exactly, efficiently and timely. There are a number of special committees attached to different state power organs with varying duties (Pu XingZu 1999, 36-39).

According to the Constitution, the duties of the special committees are studying, deliberating and drawing up motions. The special committees study the problems concerning the NPC and its Standing Committee and put forward proposals. The study work of the special committees includes listening to the people's opinions, listening to the reports of the state administrative departments, judicial department and procuratorial organs and others, trying to understand the situation and discussing with the department concerned. The special committees deliberate the motions put forward by the presidium of the NPC and its Standing Committee. They deliberate the inquiring cases raised by the presidium of NPC, listen to the reply of the organs which are under inquiry, and if necessary, put forward a report to the presidium and the Standing Committee.

Another duty of the special committees is to deliberate the administrative rules, decisions and orders of the State Council; the orders and regulations of the ministries of the State Council; the decisions, orders and regulations of the government of provinces and of municipalities directly under the central government which are considered going against the Constitution or laws. The special committees are also are in charge of deliberating the drafts of laws put forward to NPC and the Standing Committee. The committee of ethnic affairs also deliberates regulations on the exercising of autonomous and specific regulations raised by the autonomous regions to the Standing Committee, and it reports on this. Drawing up motions and putting them forward to NPC and its Standing Committee also belongs to the duty of the Special Committees (Gao GuoBin 1998, 267-280).

b) The President of the People's Republic of China

The President of the People's Republic of China enjoys powers similar to the presidents of many other countries of the world. But there is one difference, that is, he does not make decisions alone but exercises his power according to the decisions of the National People's Congress and its Standing Committee. The Constitution stipulates that the President of the People's Republic of China acts as the representative of the state, only exercising duties of representation; he does not exercise administrative duties (Li ShouChu 1997, 136).

The President and the vice-president of the state are elected by the National People's Congress, for a term of five years. The powers of the President are the following:

- to promulgate law: the President promulgates the laws after the NPC and its Standing Committee have passed them; then the laws go into effect. The chairman does not have the power of veto;
- to promulgate orders: the President of the state can promulgate orders of absolution, order of martial law, declare war and promulgate mobilization orders;
- to appoint and remove the members of the State Council: the President appoints and removes the Premier, Vice-Premier, the member of the commissions of the State Council, ministries, heads of the commissions of the State Council, the State Auditor and the General Secretary of the State Council;
- to award state honorary medals and titles.

The above are the powers related to internal affairs. The president also has power concerning foreign affairs including:

- to ratify or abolish the treaties and agreements signed with other countries in accordance with the decisions of NPC;
- to accept diplomatic envoys of various countries, to dispatch plenipotentiaries who will be sent abroad and to recall them.

c) The State Council

(1) Function

The central government is the State Council of the People's Republic of China; it is the executive arm of the highest organ of the state power and state administration. Law defines the functions of the State Council. It is composed of Premier, a number of Vice-Premiers, a number of State Councilors, ministers, the Chairmen of all state administrations, the State Auditor and the Secretary-General. The functions and powers of the State Council involve all aspects of politics, economy, culture and social life. Its functions can be illustrated as follows (Li ShouChu 1997, 142-143):

- to stipulate administrative measures, formulate administrative regulations, promulgate decisions and orders;

- to put forward the motions to the NPC or its Standing Committee;
- to stipulate the missions and functions of all ministries and commissions, guide their work and guide the administrative work that are not under the governance of the ministries and commissions;
- to lead administrative work of the local state organizations, stipulate the divisions of the central and provincial governments, autonomous regions and the municipalities directly under the central government;
- to draw up and conduct the plans of the state economy and social development as well as the state budget;
- to lead and administer education, science, culture, public health, sports and family planning work;
- to lead and administer civil administration, public security, judicial administration and procuratorial affairs;
- to administer foreign affairs, sign treaties and agreements;
- to lead and administer nationality affairs, protect the equal rights of minor nationalities and the rights of autonomous regions;
- to protect the rights and benefits of overseas Chinese, the returned overseas Chinese and their family members;
- to lead and administer national defense affairs;
- to change and remove any improper orders, instructions and rules issued by ministries and commissions;
- to change and remove any improper decisions and orders issued by local administrative organs;
- to ratify the division of provinces, autonomous regions and municipalities directly under central government, as well as to ratify the organizational system and divisions of autonomous prefectures, counties and cities;
- to take decisions and to issue orders of martial law enforced on provinces, autonomous regions and municipalities directly under central government;

- to examine and approve the authorized size of administrative organs; to appoint, remove, train, examine, award and punish administrative staff in accordance with the law;
- to perform other functions and powers authorized by the NPC and its Standing Committee.

(2) Structure

The State Council of the People's Republic of China has set up a General Office and ministries, commissions and offices.

The ministries of the People's Republic of China, 23 in all, cover Foreign Affairs, National Defense, Education, Science and Technology, Public Security, State Security, Supervision, Civil affairs, Judiciary, Finance, Personnel, Labor and Social Security, Land Natural Resources, Construction, Railway, Communication, Information Industry, Water Resources, Agriculture, Foreign Trade and Economic Cooperation, Culture and Health. The *Bank of the People's Republic of China* is not a ministry, but is put at the same level as a ministry.

Commissions, 5 in total, include the State Development Planning Commission, the Economic and Trade Commission, the Science, Technology And Industry Commission, the Ethnic Affairs Commission and the Family Planning Commission.

Finally, there is one office in place at the moment, the National Auditing Office.

d) The functions of the selected ministries

Here, the direct and indirect relationships of the ministries with the foreign participant in Chinese market will be taken as a criterion to distinguish which ministries should be highly paid attention to. A brief introduction will be given to illustrate the functions of those directly related ministries.

(1) The State Development Planning Commission

The State Development Planning Commission is a macro control department attached to the State Council, which is responsible for the strategy, planning, overall balance and restructuring of national economic progress and social development. Its major responsibilities include to study and propose the strategy of national economic and social development, middle and long-term planing and annual development planing (Shi Zhu 1998, 2). The functions connected with foreign market participants are to study and propose the development strategy for utilization of foreign investment and the goals, policies for overall volume balance and structure optimization, being in charge of foreign debt volume control, structure optimization and supervision and balance of international payment (Guo ChaoRen 1999, 105).

(2) The State Economic and Trade Commission

The State Economic and Trade Commission is responsible for monitoring and analyzing the economic operation, regulating the daily operation of the national economy; organizing and enforcing national industrial policies, and supervising industrial structure adjustment, as well as organizing the drawing up of comprehensive economic regulations and policies for various sectors and business.

The most important responsibilities concerning foreign market participants are defined as: to study and regulate the *investment layout* of competitive industries, promulgate *project investment guiding catalogues* regularly; *guide the direction of investment* and commercial bank credits for those industrial and commercial enterprises that do not enjoy state allocation; conducting *project registration*, filing and supervision, making projects a portion of the total volume balance of the State Development and Planning Commission; studying and formulating policies concerning *utilization of foreign capital*; *supervising* the industrial and commercial enterprises using foreign capital (including foreign direct investment projects), making foreign investment industries guiding catalogues in industrial and commercial enterprises if they use foreign loans; studying and formulating the policy concerning *property transfer of State Owned Enterprises*, sharing and putting into practice of *rights to foreign business people* and enforcing supervision; supervising enterprises conducting international operations, and enforcing the plans of *overseas enterprises* (Guo ChaoRen1999, 106).

(3) The Ministry of Foreign Trade and Economic Cooperation

The responsibilities of the Ministry of Foreign Trade and Economic Cooperation (MOFTEC) are rather self-explanatory: formulating drafts of laws and regulations concerning foreign trade and foreign investment; quota, licenses and related import and export tasks are also performed by MOFTEC. MOFTEC is in charge of the formulation and enforcement of the policies and managerial regulations of technological trade and the policies concerning encouraging export of technology and complete sets of equipment, analyzing and studying the state of foreign investment and reporting the situation to the State Council; rectifying contracts and regulations, and amending large-scale foreign investment projects. MOFTEC also performs foreign trade meetings and exhibition. In general, MOFTEC is a powerful ministry dealing with foreign market participants on a large scale, and related areas (Guo ChaoRen 1999, 114).

(4) Organs of the State Council

The State Council of the People's Republic of China has set up 17 organs directly under its control, namely:

- General Administration of Customs
- State Administration of Taxation
- State Environmental Protection Administration
- General Administration of Civil Aviation
- State Administration of Radio, Film and Television
- State General Administration of Sports
- National Bureau of Statistics
- State Administration for Industry and Commerce
- State Press and Publication Administration
- State Forests Administration
- State Bureau of Quality and Technology
- State Intellectual Property Office
- State Drug Administration
- National Tourism Administration
- State Administration of Religious Affairs
- Counselor's Office of the State Council
- Government Office Administration of the State Council

The administration organs of the State Council are the following:

- Overseas Chinese Affairs Office
- HongKong and Macao Affairs Office
- Legislative Affairs Office
- Economic System Reform Office
- Research Office

The institutions under the direct control of the State Council are:

- XinHua News Agency
- China Academy of Sciences
- China Academy of Social Sciences
- China Academy of Engineering
- Development Research Center of the Sate Council
- National School of Administration
- China Seismological Bureau
- China Meteorological Administration
- China Securities Regulating Commission
- China Insurance Regulation Commission

There is a total of 21 national bureaus of the People's Republic of China, administered by ministries and organs of similar level, including:

The ...	... is administering the ...
State Development Planning Commission	State Grain Reserve Administration
Ministry of Natural Resources	State Oceanic Administration State Bureau of Surveying and Mapping
Ministry of Information Industry	State Post Bureau
State Economic and Trade Commission	State Administration of ... ... Internal Trade ... Coal Industry ... Machinery Industry ... Metallurgical Industry ... Petroleum and Chemical Industry ... Light Industry ... Textile Industry ... Building Material Industry ... Tobacco Monopoly ... Nonferrous Metals Industry
Ministry of Personnel	... Foreign Experts Affairs
Ministry of Culture	... Culture Heritage
Ministry of Health	... Traditional Chinese Medicine
General Administration of Customs	... Entry, Exit and Quarantine
Bank of China	... Foreign Exchange

The State Archives Administration and the National Administration for Protection of State Secrets are the subordinate organs of the Central Committee of the Communist Party of China.

e) The Chinese people's political consultative system

The political consultative system is a basic political system of China; various parties, people's groups, minority nationalities and the representatives of all social circles organize a political consultative conference to consult on the country's policies and principles. The political consultative system has the following characteristics:

- the Communist Party leads the political consultative conference;
- it consists of various parties, people's organs and organized circles, and represents the interests of these groups;
- the contents of consultation includes the Communist Party's lines and decisions; the policies and principles of the state, important problems concerning the national and the people's future as well as the economic problems of the state and regions;
- the organization form of the system is the Political Consultative Conference;
- the result of the consultation does not have legislative effects and does not form the state's will. However, it can be used as suggestion, reference and consultation opinion when the Communist Party and the state perform their work. Furthermore, it influences the decisions of the Communist Party and of the state to some extent.

2. REFORMING THE POLITICAL SYSTEM

The reform of the political system of the People's Republic of China began in 1979, after the third session of the thirteenth plenary session of the Communist Party. The reform covers the leading system, administrative style, definition of organs, the cadre system and the legal system. The purpose of the reform is to make the formation of the government organs, the implementation and the operation of the legal system meeting the needs of modernization construction, as well as making the state machine administer public affairs and serve the socialist construction more efficiently. The political reform is a vital part of the overall reform of China. It is the perquisite of the economic reform and cultural progress.

The reform of China began in the economic domain. With the economic transition from planned economy to socialist market economy, the old political system was perceived as a barrier to the economical development. Especially after 1984, the reform penetrated into all areas of the society. The contradictions between the advanced production power and the backward production relations intensified more than ever before. Therefore, the political reform became an irrevocable trend. The combination of the political reform and economic reform paved the way for social progress.

Critics often focus on perceived malpractice's in the current political system of China, such as power centralization, over-lapping organization, incompleteness of the cadre personnel system, incompleteness of democracy and of legal construction. Such malpractice's may lead to instability of the society. The Chinese government is contributing great efforts to eliminate these factors, though it may encounter numerous difficulties in the process of reform (Zhu XinMin 1999, 214-219).

E. BRIEF OUTLINE OF THE EDUCATION SYSTEM

1. GENERAL INTRODUCTION TO THE DEVELOPMENT STATE OF EDUCATION

Since the founding of the People's Republic of China in 1949, the educational system went through a winding development process. It is widely acknowledged that the People's Republic of China was founded on the basis of a backward society. The successive wars damaged multiple aspect of life; education was one example. During the 17 years from 1949 to 1966, the educational reconstruction achieved certain progress. According to the statistics of 1965, there were 434 universities and colleges, 10% more than 1947; 670,000 colleges students, which is three times the number of 1947; 14,320,000 secondary students, which is seven times that of 1946; 85% of school age children started school; there were 116,210,000 primary students, which was four times higher than that of 1946. In addition, universities and colleges educated 16,000 postgraduates students, 1,550,000 college students and 2,950,000 middle vocational school graduate students in those 17 years. These graduates became the major force in the construction of the country.

The steady education work of this period was interrupted by the Cultural Revolution. Education was damaged in an unprecedented manner during Cultural Revolution period, and the consequences were disastrous: teachers suffered from prosecution, the relationship between teachers and students worsened, schools were in turmoil, the quality of the teachers and the educational level went down sharply. Numerous universities and colleges were closed down; intellectuals was condemned as the lowest class in the society. From this point of view, calling the Cultural Revolution "ten years of disaster" may not be seen as an exaggeration. The Cultural Revolution denied the importance of education and tried to cancel education; its direct consequence was that it delayed the growth of a whole generation of young talent and lead to the serious shortage of educated people who were needed for the construction of the country. From 1976 to 1978, education began to return to a more normal track.

In April 1978, Deng XiaoPing held an important speech at the National Education Conference. He pointed out that the quality of education had to be further improved; science and education level had to be raised; schools should strengthen order and discipline and try to bring up a new generation of intelligent people; education had to conform with the requirements of the development of the national economy; teachers had to be respected. From then on, the discriminating policies in the education field began to change, and education, knowledge and intellectuals were respected again by the Communist Party and the people.

In 1977, the National Institutions of Higher Learning unitary entrance exam recovered after being canceled for ten years. After the third plenary session of the 17th session of the Central Committee of the Communist Party in December of 1979, the focus of the national work was put on the economic construction. Therefore the role and position of education was highly paid attention to. The Communist Party promulgated "the decision on the reform of the education system" in 1985. The education policy was defined as "education must serve the socialist construction, socialism must rely on education" (Shao BingRen 1999, 25). From then on, educational reform was carried out nation-wide. The basic task was to change the educational system, the education structure, educational ideas, education contents and the education methods that could not meet the needs of social development. Facing the intensified competition of the world economy as well as science and technology, Deng XiaoPing put forward the famous judgment "science and technology are the first production power" (Xi GuangQing 1998, 34).

These celebrated thesis demonstrated the relationship between science, technology and production power forcefully. On the one hand, it confirmed that science and technology are production powers, meaning that science and technology can create value. On the other hand, it highlighted the importance of science and technology and put science and technology in the first and foremost position among the various essential factors of productive powers. From Deng's idea it was deducted that without the educational reform, there would be no development of science and technology, therefore no development of the production power, and as a consequence of such a chain reaction, there would be no social progress.

In March 1995, the Education Law of the People's Republic of China was put into effect. The strategy of "using science and education to advance the country" (Shao BingRen 1999, 25) was illustrated in the law. Since 1980, more than 200 pieces of laws and administrative regulations have been passed, such as the "Compulsory Education Law of the People's Republic of China", which was passed in April 1986. The aim of the law was to promote nine years of compulsory education and thus to give every child the right of going to school. China is a country that still has many illiterate people. In order to change this phenomenon, the State Council promulgated the "working rule on eliminating illiteracy" in April 1988. The effective enforcement of the law helped to reduce the illiterate people greatly, 4,000,000 per year on average since the 1990ies. The "Teacher Law" was passed in 1993, and in 1995, the "Rule on Teacher's Qualification" was promulgated. In accordance with this law, a set of systems to check the teachers' qualifications was set up soon after. The qualification rate of the teachers' education background raised enormously. By the end of 1997, the qualification ratio of the Chinese primary and secondary school teacher had risen from 47.1% and 9.8% in 1978 to 93% and 84% respectively. The promulgation of these laws and regulations was designed to adopt some compulsory measures to standardize and speed up the process of educational reform.

From the results of the implementation, it can be observed that these reform measures have been effective. By the end of 1998, the cover rate of the nine years compulsory schooling is 73% of the total population; 2,242 cities and regions passed the checking test of nine years compulsory education. There were 609,000 primary schools in 1998, the entrance rate of school age children was 88.93%. There were 65,400 secondary schools, 50.7% students continued to study after graduating from secondary school. High school level students reached 9,306,000. There was a total of 1,022 national common institutions of higher learning, with 590 universities and colleges as well as 432 training schools and vocational technical institutes. Among them, there are 736 institutions which are qualified in educating graduate students, with 408 higher learning institutes and 328 research organs. There were 962 adult higher learning institutes; among them there were 45 broadcast and television universities, 567 staff and workers higher learning schools and 3 higher learning schools for farmers, 153 cadre management institutes, 190 educational institutes as well as 4 independent correspondence schools. In addition, as part of external education, China has established education exchange and cooperative relationships with 150 countries. From 1978 to the end of 1997, China had dispatched 300,000 students to more than 100 countries; 100,000 have returned to China.

2. EDUCATION CLASSIFICATION

Education is divided into four categories in China: elementary education, vocational and technical education, higher education and adult education.

Elementary education is composed of pre-school education, nine years compulsory education, and general high school education. Nine years compulsory education refers to the education that school age children and teenager must attend. The law stipulates that country, society and family must guarantee the education. According to the current lengths of schooling, elementary school can be five years primary school plus three years secondary school, or six years primary school plus three years secondary school, or five years primary school plus four years secondary school or nine years in all without differentiating between primary and secondary school. It should be noted that in China both eight years of school and nine years of school are referred to as "nine year compulsory education". Different regions can select any form based on their specific situations. Because it is safeguarded by law, all of them are called "nine years compulsory education". Pre-school education refers to kindergarten; high school education is three years education after finishing secondary school. The law does not have mandatory regulation about the attendance to these two types of education (Jin YiMing 1999, 29).

Vocational and technical education can be classified into three levels: elementary level, middle level and higher level. *Elementary* level recruits primary students, which is equal to secondary school in educational levels, but the contents of education focuses on vocational techniques. *Middle* level recruits middle school graduates. The schools providing this kind of education include vocational high schools, ordinary middle vocational schools, technical schools and adult middle lever vocational schools. Middle level vocational and technical education is the focal point of the three level education. *High* level education recruits high school graduates students (JinYiMing 1999, 30).

Higher education can be classified into training school education, undergraduate education and post-graduate education. *Training school education* recruits high school graduate students; the length of schooling is two to three years. There are training schools, colleges and universities providing such education. Training school education focuses on training middle level technical personnel; undergraduate course education is the major component of higher education. Its task is to train advanced professional people. *University course education* awards graduate students with bachelor degrees and corresponding certificates to prove their educational background. After finishing this period of education, the undergraduate could become a scholar, high school teacher, manager, engineer, a chartered accountant or lawyer, to name but a few. University subjects include philosophy, economics, law, education, literature, history, science, engineering, agriculture, medicine and management; they are called first level branches. There are sub-branches below them, 71 in all. There is a total of 249 subjects available. *Postgraduate* education is composed of two levels: master and doctorate. The length of study to obtain master's degrees is two to three years; doctor's degree education is three to four years (Shao Bing-Ren 1999, 31).

Adult education refers to further education to those who have already worked. The focus of adult education lies in professional education to raise professional knowledge and to further education. The major forms of the adult education include attending distant learning, self-studying and going to adult colleges to study. With the increase of social demands, adult education has developed rapidly. For example, all kinds of training schools, such as English training schools, computer training schools, self-study training schools and many other kinds of schools were set up in many big and middle cities. The concept of further education is commonly accepted, especially among young people.

In China, the term "charging" is often used when attending training schools. This term compares men to a battery – after a period of use, the electricity of the battery is not enough to generate something; therefore it needs to be recharged. People face a similar problem: after having worked for some time, the knowledge is not enough to catch up with the rapid development of society, so recharging is needed too. Recently, people have started to realize the value of life-long study. They have actively extended studying from school study to further study and then to life-long study. The development of the concept indicates that people are aware of the need to develop their potential actively.

This concept conforms with the educational policy of China, which emphasizes to train students in three aspects. One aspects lies in the training of a sense of *responsibility*. Once one has the awareness to take up social responsibility, one will have the motivation to develop oneself, thereby contributing to the development of the state. The second aspect emphasizes the training of *curiosity*. It goes without saying that curiosity is the source of creative ability and the basis to study new things. The third aspects is the training of *self-study ability*: the ability to study knowledge in books and to learn practical techniques. This ability is regarded as the fundamental ability of human beings if they want to make progress constantly in the information age, because the volume and quality of information one masters is used to judge a person's value. This kind of self-study ability includes screening and setting of targets by oneself, looking for the subjects oneself and determining study methods and the way of study oneself. At the same time, people should manage the study process themselves. It should be noted that the congruence of people's ideas and of government policy is not a coincidence (Shao BingRen 1999, 179). It is an indication of the fact that the needs of the individuals and the needs of China as a whole are identical, that is: development.

F. ECONOMIC REGIONS

Since the founding of the People's Republic of China, China has not divided its comprehensive economic regions formally, but several division methods are used in practice. The first method is to organize economic production based on administrative regions. In this method, administrative regions are equal to economic regions (Li JingWen 1999, 136). The disadvantage of this method lies in the fact that the separation of administrative regions might cut off the economic relationships between economic regions, due to protectionism of local governments.

Inner and coastal economic regions had been used in 1950ies as the second way of economic region division, but it is not used very often today, since it is too rough to describe the economic characteristics of such large areas.

During the 1960ies, *six* economic regions were used to organize national economy. They are DongBei, HuaBei, HuaDong, ZhongNan, XiNan and XiBei (Huang ZuoPing, 1999, 26). But this kind of method failed to function very well; nevertheless, people often use it to describe China's economic regions.

The method that has been commonly used in the economic field in the 1980ies is to define *three* economic regions, which are East, Middle and West. The purpose of this method is to adjust the unequal economic development among these three regions. Due to the policy advantages given towards the Eastern Region, and due to the disparities in economic conditions existing between these regions, the economic development state of the Eastern Region is more advanced than middle and Western Regions. Observing the gap, the Chinese government has drawn up numerous policies trying to promote the development of the Western Region. For example, 60% of the loans from international financial organizations and foreign countries and governments should be used in the Western Region (Zhou DianKun 1998, 5).

The definition of three economic regions conform to the needs of national economic development. But if it was used as the geographical basis of the market research, it would be too rough, since the areas are too large, and the disparities in economic development within each of the regions are too big to be neglected. Therefore, the specific market features of each region would not be covered as thorough as it would be necessary. Based on the above analysis, it is assumed that the regional division should not be too rough if it has to serve as a basis for market studies, and it should be convenient to abstract the common characteristics of the components of the markets. Thus, a new method was needed which had to be pragmatic for theoretical study as well as for practical economic development.

With the intensifying of economic regional studies since the opening-up of China, many new comprehensive economic regional division programs were developed. One of them is the *ten* economic regions vision, which intents to divide China into the following ten economic regions: DongBei (LiaoNing, JiLin, HeiLongJiang provinces); HuaBei (BeiJing, TianJin, HeBei, ShanXi and ShanDong provinces); HuaDong (ShangHai, JiangSu, ZheJiang, AnHui, JiangXi and FuJian provinces as well as TaiWan); HuaZhong (HeNan, HuBei and HuNan provinces); HuaNan (GuangDong, GuangXi, HaiNan, HongKong and Macao); XiNan (SiChuang, YunNan, GuiZhou provinces); XiBei (ShanXi, GanSu and QiHai provinces); Inner Mongolia, XinJiang and Tibet. This division is attributed to professor Yan ShuZhen of Beijing's People's University (Li JingWen 1999, 439).

The definition of *six* comprehensive economic regions belongs to the study achievements of professor Liu ZiaXing. These six regions comprise DongBei, the middle and lower reaches of the Yellow River, the middle and lower reaches of Yangtse River, DongNan coastal region as well as XiNan and XiBei regions. Under each main region, sub-regions are defined.

Zou JiaHua, the Vice-President of the State Council, formulated the "*seven* economic regions vision". Under his theory, China is divided into the Yangtse Delta and coastal region, BoHai region, DongNan region, XiNan, HuaNan and DongBei regions, the five middle provinces and XiBei region. The program was designed to meet the needs of the national economic situation and development. After being put forward, it became an important basis for the government to study regional problems. However, the program put too much consideration on the influences of reform and opening-up of the economic regions, and less comparison and judgment were given to the nation-wide regional structure (Li JingWen 1999, 439). For example, seven regions overlap in space, and provincial administrative boundaries were not respected, thus making the implementation of economic policy a difficult task.

On the basis of the previous study achievements, professor Li JingWen put forward a new vision which divides China into *nine* economic regions. Professor Li took the similar contradictions in the components of each region and differences between various regions as the basis of defining economic regions. It is pointed out that China's traditional economic structure has changed greatly, and the new regional structure is determined by the degree of reform and opening-up as well as by the state of the development of the industrial structure. The state of the two factors determine the development level and contradictions of each region. Based on the specific level and contradictions, the government can adopt different policies to each region (Li JingWen 1999, 440).

The nine economic regions program can be summed up as follows:

1) BoHai economic rim region, which is composed of BeiJing, TianJin, LiaoNing, HeiBei and ShanDong provinces;

2) Yangtse River delta region, including ShangHai, JiangSu and ZheJiang provinces;

3) Southeast coastal region, composed of FuJian, GuangDong, GuangXi and HaiNan provinces;

4) Northeast inner region, composed of JiLin and HeiLongJiang;

5) North Inner region, comprising Inner Mongolia, ShanXi, ShánXi, GanSu, QingHai and NingXia provinces;

6) Central region, composed of HeNan, AnHui, JiangXi, HuBei and HuNan provinces;

7) Southeast region, composed of Sichuan, YuNan, and GuiZhou provinces;

8) XinJiang region, XinJiang autonomous region;

9) XiZang region, XiZang autonomous region.

One of the greatest advantages of Li's nine regions method can be found in its compliance with the other division principles. That means, this method can serve the purpose that the other methods intended to serve, or, in simple words, this methodology solves the problems that the other methodology only intended to solve.

G. MARKET ECONOMY AND THE CHINESE PEOPLE

Market economy is a completely new term in the economic history of Mainland China. It reveals a free market vision before Chinese people. Facing the new market regulations, Chinese people are puzzled and wonder: "Who am I? What is the next step I should take? What is the way to live a comfortable life". This kind of thoughts embodies the contradiction between the old value concept and modern civilization.(Qi XiaoYing 1997, 21).

Chinese people have to ask themselves many questions. They have to think hard to solve these questions. During the process of asking and answering, Chinese people are changing their mind and behavior to adapt to the changes of the society. Chinese people are evaluating themselves and others, judging the market movement, choosing their way of living. In one word, the Chinese people who were used to be planned by others now have to plan by themselves. The market economy gives the Chinese people the right to form themselves and to act as a individuals, and to be relatively more free in thought.

a) The concept of Chinese to market economy

Then, what is market economy? How is it perceived by Chinese people? A mini-case may be very interesting in addressing this question:

> *One day, a passenger in a bus did not have small change, and he gave 100 Yuan to the conductor. The conductor did not to have enough money to give him change. The conductor said: "Please get off and get some small change." The passenger replied: "You have got no right to ask me to get off the bus and get small change myself". He argued that preparing small change before getting on the bus was typical during the times of planned economy, but that now it was the age of the market economy; therefore the old rule should be abandoned. He wanted to pay the fare, then he should enjoy the service without any additional conditions.*
>
> *It is a small thing in itself; however the significance lies in the awareness of the passenger. He could connect his situation easily with the concept of the market economy. It indicates that the concept of "market economy" has penetrated his thoughts deeply. He resisted to accept the plan of others even though it was only a small one. This indicates that he got the awareness that in the market economy, he now is a free subject that has the right to act according to his own choice. In the meantime, the conductor, as the other subject in the market, should take up her responsibility of providing adequate service; her behavior should be guided by self-discipline.*
>
> *This small case reflects that Chinese people perceive market economy as a kind of thing that gives freedom to choose what one desires, but in the meantime, asks one to take up the responsibilities that belong to oneself. Therefore, market economy has a double connotation: one is rights, the other is duty. One could conclude: a free person who is responsible for him/herself is the embodiment of the market economy in China.*

b) *The alteration of identity*

Because of the adoption of the market economy, Chinese people possess a new identity: "salesperson", is now a fashionable concept among Chinese. Products, ideas and value concepts are the things they sell. By selling these things, they harvest economic or spiritual benefits either directly or indirectly. The level of sales decides the benefits they harvest. Furthermore, people's identity is uncertain: today, one may be an employee, tomorrow, self-employed. But they would continuously of the identity of being a salesperson.

The Chinese sales concept can be analyzed as having two layers of connotations: one is the work of selling, the other one is to establish good public relations. Chinese sales sometimes are named "public relations department". From this point of view, the complexity of Chinese marketing art can be seen. Chinese promotion work does not evade personal relations and emotional factors, but tries to establish such relations and to use them efficiently. This kind of marketing concept still preserves the features of planned economy. It also indicates that the Chinese market is still immature, for a certain lack of commonly acknowledged commercial principles and laws to regulate the business operations leads to the importance of depending on personal relations. But as a phenomenon of transition period, it has nothing to be condemned.

As an important part of sales work, people promote themselves. In the planned economic system, people did not need to "sell" themselves. Even if one wanted to sell, the others would not accept it. Nowadays, marketing oneself has already become an essential part of social life. The purpose is quite clear: let others understand one's value, thus realize one's value. The most commonly used form of promotion is recruitment promotion. It is not so easy for Chinese people to gather the idea of promotion after so many years of constraining of spirits. Humility has always been respected as a virtue by Chinese, while promotion asks them to reveal their advantages to others. The old and new standards for behavior exist simultaneously. But needless to say, this change of outlook on the world has epoch-making significance in Chinese economic history.

c) *The effects of market economy*

Reform and open-up policy bring imbalance to people's psychology. But this time, the imbalance is embodied in the economy form, that is, a gap between rich and poor appears. The Chinese people who had been ruled by the idea "Do not worry about being poor if everyone is as poor as you are" feel the imbalance strongly. In the rural areas, peasants contract land and make money out of their different productive technique; any gap between them is relatively narrow. In the cities, "the iron rice bowl", which meant that people lived in

State-Owned Enterprises and had little difference in income, was broken completely, while a new balancing system has not yet been set up (Duo ChunSheng 1997, 42). In this situation, many Chinese feel they are surrounded by crisis.

Furthermore, many enterprises are in a state of depression, numerous people's real income has fallen, and the unemployment rate has risen. It is estimated that one-third of the staff in State Owned Enterprises will lose their jobs. Corruption is a growing threat to economic development. Facing this situation, people are desperate for a job in order to make a good living. Striving hard to make a living is a common focus for many Chinese people. Those who have managed to cover the basics are considering the next steps: how to make a high quality life? The knowledge structure of many Chinese people does not fully meet the needs of the market economy. The traditional education system often did not provide people with enough information that necessary for people's self- development.

The knowledge structure is another issue that has to be addressed. Nowadays, people call those who can not communicate in English and do not have computer skills "illiterate". It should be noted a large part of the Chinese people are "illiterate" by these standards. Recently, there is a new term appearing in academic circles: "*Zhi Bei Jia*", meaning people who possess a lot of knowledge and make money out of their knowledge. Another yet related term is "intelligence capital" (*Zhi Li Zi Bei*), expressing that intelligence has the same value as financial capital. The appearance of such new terms reflects the changes in people's concepts.

d) Chinese belief

"Spiritual shackles" has often been used to describe how the feudal ideas constrained people's mind. Now, the market economy has started to take the "shackles" away, and the question may be asked: where is the way forward for Chinese people's minds? Family relationships have been a stable factor throughout Chinese society. But now, with the changes of the social-economic structure, the family concept is not as strong as before. The sense of responsibility towards the family, originally binding people together, are becoming less strong too. Many young people put themselves is first, the family ranks only second. If a husband does not provide a comfortable life to his wife, then the wife would probably ask for divorce, since Chinese men to some extent are still assumed to take up the duty of earning money.

If Confucius' ideas looses dominance, then how about emotion? For many, emotion does not possess an important position in a family anymore. If you happen to hear people ask "How much for one kilogram emotion?" please do not be surprised. The concept of "three cardinal guides and five constant virtues" has already been thrown away into the dustbin of history. Economic independence gives Chinese women unprecedented equal rights in society. Nevertheless, the equality status of men and women varies between cities and rural areas.

In cities, women are on average better-educated than those in rural areas; therefore, they possess a relatively high self-esteem. Furthermore, the city labor markets provide more opportunities for women to participate in social life and thereby make economic independence possible. Nowadays, in accordance with such change, an issue has been brought up: What is the normal relationships of couples? What responsibilities should both husband and wife take towards the family? What kind of concept should couples embrace towards the family? If personal needs and family needs contradict, which aspect should take priority? Certainly, many other problems exist. The stability of the family, as the core of the society, has great significance. The introduction of the market economy, at the origin of such social problem, contributes a lot to the economic development; the problems it brings at the same time can not be neglected. However, from the point of view of liberation of thoughts, it can be judged positive that women's self-awareness increases.

There is not one consistent belief in Chinese history. The believes of Chinese people are greatly influenced by ideology. People's believes are restricted by the authorities' believes. With the habit of believing in state power, Chinese people struggle how to deal with the freedom of belief given by the market economy. Suddenly, Chinese people seem to loose their spiritual basis: Buddha, Jesus or Gods, who could bless and protect Chinese people best? To some extent, Chinese people experience a loss of ideology, which may lead to confusion in world outlook, because believes give moral instructions to people. More seriously, it can lead to confusion in action (Duo ChunSheng 1997, 82). Most Chinese people at this time do not have a belief, or at least they do not believe in anything but themselves: if it is right to believe in oneself, the market could test this and provide an answer.

One of the greatest advantages that Chinese people harvest from the market economy is the individual awareness. Before the economic reform, Chinese people have been parts of collectives, so that their individual identity was rather neglected (Li QiShan 1996, 49). Thus their creative ability was oppressed, because they did not have the right to think freely. Their value concept had to conform to the collective value tendency. Now, the market economy provides a lot of opportunities for people to develop their creative ability. People like using the image of a "sleeping dragon" to describe ancient China, but now, the Great dragon is awaken. The dragoon's full potential is probably beyond imagination; its unfolding remains to be seen.

H. THE PSYCHOLOGY OF THE CHINESE CONSUMER

Consuming psychology refers to the complicated process of selecting and comparing before a consumer takes the decision to buy something. It is a kind of model of thinking dealing with consuming behavior. Hence understanding the consuming psychology of Chinese is a necessary approach when thinking of entering into the Chinese market.

There are many factors that influence and restrict a person's purchasing decisions, such as purchasing power, value concepts, aesthetic standards and so on. People's consuming psychology varies according to these factors. Therefore it is not sufficient to just giving a simple definition of what Chinese consuming psychology is, considering the variety of Chinese consumer groups. What will be stated below are only trends commonly existing in Chinese consumers; if it used in a specific situation, a thorough investigation of the specific consumer group is essential.

1. SAVING PRIOR TO CONSUMING

Saving prior to consuming is the first striking feature of Chinese. See if this joke rings a bell (Qi XiaoLi 1999, 18):

> *An old Chinese lady meets with an old American lady in heaven. "Hi", the Chinese lady is greeting the American proudly, "I finally bought a beautiful house with all my lifetime savings, and I lived in it for a day." – "How good", says the elderly American, "just before I came here, I finally paid back the mortgage for the beautiful house I lived in my entire life".*

This joke is currently doing the rounds among mainland bankers and their clients, as the Chinese government is encouraging the people to open their wallet. Although it is only a joke, it reflects Chinese people consuming psychology to some extent. It is no exaggeration to say that Chinese save a life for buying or building a house, especially in rural areas. Chinese people always say there are two things of very significant meaning, one is building a house, the other is marriage, and both of them are costly. As the farmers incomes are relatively low in China, they have to save even if they do not have enough to eat. Though the situation has changed quite a bit recently with the improvement of farmers income, the fundamental reason that restricted the speed of such change – the backwardness of the agriculture economy – still has a long way to go.

Being industrious and economical in managing a household has always been a virtue of Chinese people. The concept has penetrated Chinese people's mind deeply; therefore even if a person has a certain amount of money to spend, he would rather not spend it casually. Otherwise, he would be condemned as wasting. Another reason contributing to the conservative consuming habits is the rapid social development. Chinese are used to stable lives for years, however, with the introduction of reform in both political and economic spheres, the steady pace of a peaceful life is put into question. The rapidly changing social environment makes people adjust themselves constantly to fit into the society. Such constant adjustments make people feel unstable all the time. In order to reduce the negative influences of such instability, people choose saving in case of unexpected spending.

In urban areas for example, people were less conservative due to the economic situation being better than in the countryside. Before the enforcement of the housing reform policy, city residents did not need to buy a house; they lived in a house built by the government for free. They had a pension to live on after retirement, they enjoyed medical treatment for free. Certainly, they had nothing to worry about with the state taking care of everything; hence they could spend their money freely. – But now, with the overall reform of China, many workers are laid off and anyone could lose his job at any time. Furthermore, people have to buy their house, to take care of a part of medical fees and some day, their pensions may be canceled. All these factors lead to the city residents consuming attitudes becoming conservative little by little.

The government lowered the deposit interest rates five times from 1st May, 1996 to 1st July, 1998, but deposits still increase continuously. From this point it can be seen, that people do not want to spend money due to lack of confidence in further income increase. A statistic shows that the saving to consumption ratio has increased rapidly in the last few years: the ratio was 1.48 in 1996, 1.98 in 1997 and 2.51 in 1998 (Lu Zheng 1999, 3). By the end of 1998, individual savings grew to 5,340.7 billion Yuan, up 17.1% from 1997. It is not deniable that such highly increasing rates are based on the Chinese moral concept. For many Chinese, it is morally wrong to spend tomorrow's money for today's pleasure. To spend within one's means has for a long time been the principle of Chinese consumers. If one can not balance one's budget and has to borrow money from the others, it is considered a shame and others would look down upon that person.

The Chinese government has launched an individual credit policy for purchasing a house, a car and some durable goods step by step. The China Construction Bank is so far the most successful bank in terms of providing housing loans. Up to the end of February 1999, the bank's ShangHai branch issued a total of 18.8 billion Yuan in individual house loans, accounting for 90% of the city's market (Qin XiaoLi 1999, 19). This achievement is remarkable in changing Chinese people's consuming concept, but further work has to be done in promoting the policy in medium and small cities, and also rural areas. It should be observed that consuming credit service is new in China; banks do not have much experience with it, and some areas do not have the prerequisite conditions for providing such financial services. People need time to accept the idea.

2. PURCHASING COMPETITIONS

Competing in purchasing is a second feature of Chinese consumers. People of the same income group tend to compete with each other when comes to purchases. They tend to do so for protecting their "face", because face represents a person's dignity and position, which are regarded as very important by Chinese. For example, many city residents have bought large-screen television sets in recent years. This indicates people's living standard has gone up. But some people bought 36 inch television sets and put it in a small sitting room, just because their friends or colleagues also had bought one. In order not to lose face before the others, Chinese would rather buy it, even if it may not match their small apartment.

Another interesting phenomenon happened when it comes to wedding ceremonies. Now, it is widespread to hold a banquet on wedding day. On that day, friends, colleagues and relatives of the new couples and their parents' are invited. Sometimes, even people they are not familiar with or lost contact for a long time will be invited. It is a common practice to invite some powerful people to attend banquet and treat them as guests of honor. The reason to do so is to show to the other guests: "look, we are respected by such important officials". The underlying meaning is to let others think highly of themselves, as well as building excellent relationships.

As a consequence, the grade and scale became higher and larger due to the competitive mindset of people. The cash gifts for the new couples become higher and higher as well, just to demonstrate the good relationship with them. In fact, sometimes the new couples are not willing to do so because some day they have to pay back such gifts. Chinese people like calling such gifts "emotional debt", and it must be paid back some day. On wedding day, new couples will rent cars to pick up friends and relatives. Sometimes, the car parade is composed of more than twenties cars (Zhang PeiZhi 1998, 299). The normal price to rent a Mercedes for a day is 3,000 RMB in Beijing, a price that most normal Chinese families can not afford. Of course, a portion of the expenditures are covered by the gifts. This consuming mentality fits very well with a Chinese expression: "to slap one's face until it is swollen in an effort to look imposing." Certainly, this psychology is not very healthy. It causes enormous wastes. Eventually, the government may want to make policies to regulate such behavior, such as: the number of wedding cars may one day be limited, and government officials may not be allowed to take part in weddings.

This competitive mindset also has a connection with the Chinese idea equality. Chinese people do not mind to be poor if the others are as poor as they are themselves, as long as they are equally poor. Furthermore, they tend to like competing with each other in almost everything to find some psychological balance. For example, they like comparing whose child can go to a famous university, whose wife is the most beautiful and so on. And inevitably, they will compete in consuming to keep their psychological balance. Nevertheless, with pragmatic ideas being promoted, Chinese may eventually pay attention to personal life quality rather than to consuming more and more.

3. BRAND LOYALITY

Chinese tend to be brand-loyal: once they choose a brand, they would use it for years. Therefore, it is not easy to promote a new brand. Chinese do not like to try new things if there is no reputation guarantee. Many sellers give free sample when trying to promote a new brand; in this way, they encourage and attract the consumer to try. When it comes to items of high value, Chinese tend to choose a famous brand. The results of a research project on the popularity of famous brands among Chinese consumers in ten big cities including BeiJing, ShangHai, ShenZhen, WuHan, QingDao, NanJing, ChongQing, JiNan, ShenYan and ShiJiaZhuang were released in 1999: eighty per cent of those surveyed owned famous brand products. In families where the combined income was more than 3,000 Yuan per month, there was the highest consumption of well-known brand names. For example, Haier is the first refrigerator brand and RongSheng, XinFei, ShangLing, MeiLing were after it, with XiaoYa, Narcissus and RongShiDa following (Shi Zhu 1999, 40). The above research was undertaken by a Beijing based magazine called China Quality and Panorama Social Economic Research. There are many such organs in China to make this kind of public appraisal of the quality of different products. The result of such studies are often leading people's consuming choice because of the brand effect.

Chinese would consult their friends prior to making a purchasing decision because they sometimes trust the other's judgment more than their own. They believe the judgment of several people are cleverer and more correct. There is a Chinese saying that "three shoe-makers' wisdom is higher than the wisdom of

Zhu GeLiang". Zhu GeLiang was a strategist during the Spring and Autumn and the Warring State Period, famous for his wisdom. It is very common for a Chinese to take a long time before making a final decision; comparing the same goods in three stores is part of the philosophy of most Chinese. In this way, they could find out where to get good quality at a low price. Hence, one has to be patient and to help Chinese to form a decision quickly, if one wants to develop the Chinese market.

4. SPECIAL CONSUMING PSYCHOLOGY

The current family planning policy allows each Chinese family to have only one child. As a consequence, most Chinese families have only one child, at least in the cities. Chinese have the tradition of bringing up child with loving care. Now with six adults to look after one child, naturally, a child becomes the center of the family. Children are called "little emperors" in China: it indicates they enjoy a form of absolute superiority in the family. In the family consumption patterns, child expenditure is prior to others needs. That is the reason why child's goods are more expensive than others. Many manufactures take advantage of this situation and make huge profits. One of the important expenses related to bringing up children are educational fees. Children are sent to various schools to learn piano, gymnastics, dancing, English and some other courses, and the training fees are rather expensive. For the purpose of educating the child to become a knowledgeable person, Chinese parents in many cases think it is worthwhile.

With the implementation of Deng's policy "let some people become rich first", a lot of millionaires appeared in China in the 1980ies. It is commonly acknowledged that those people were not well-educated. They took advantage of the preferential policy of the government and became rich first (Zhai Ye 1998, 2). Compared with the hard-earned money of the ordinary people, their money came in easier. Hence, those people usually hold a different point of view on consuming. They would spend thousands of RMB in one dinner, or they would purchase something without thinking about the price. Another kind of consumption of this group is on gifts: in order to build good relationships with government officials, they would buy expensive goods, such as imported video cameras, golden watches or branded wine, and send it to the related officials who help them earn more money. Of course, such valuable gifts must be sent at the right time, to the right place and with the right excuse to the right people. It is commonly recognized those suddenly rich people like showing off through the way they spend money, because of it can raise those people to a higher class.

There are other kinds of rich people who are different from the newly rich. They are well-educated, and some of them returned from abroad. They earn money through their intellectual capital. Those people are gathering in the big cities, and their consuming focus is on the high quality. Grand hotels and elegant shopping centers are the place they tend to go. They are willing to pay for high-quality services and luxury enjoyment.

Conclusion: In recent years, many private and foreign enterprises were set up. And as a consequence, a white collar class appeared. They can earn higher salaries than staff in State Owned Enterprises. Most of them believe in the principle "work hard and play happily". Various bars and clubs are the places they would tend to go to; famous brands are what they seek after (Yu KunQi 1999, 93). It can be seen their consuming concept is influenced by Westerners to some extent.

At the end of this analysis, it should be noted that different consumer groups have a rather different consumption psychology, although generally speaking, Chinese are conservative in consuming. Therefore, to distinguish the specific consumer group and to promote products and services according to the specific psychology is of great value when wanting to do business in China successfully.

I. BUSINESS ACTIVITIES AND GOVERNMENT OFFICIALS

1. THE RELATIONS OF BUSINESS AND GOVERNMENT IN CHINA

In China, the business world and the government are closely connected. One of the vital aspects of doing business in China is to deal with government officials due to their special role in commercial life (Yuan Wang 1997, 94). The Chinese government systems permeate business at every level, from policy-making to specific operations. Therefore, to deal with government officials is a course that one should learn if wanting to do business successfully in China.

The close association between authority and economy characterizes the Chinese business culture. The reason is that state-owned economic elements have dominated the economy of China for a long time. Public ownership puts the officials in a position of governor of the country and manager of the enterprises simultaneously. This kind of situation results in some ambiguity of political power and enterprise ownership. There was a rule in China's State Owned Enterprises: the director of the enterprise must be a party member; every enterprise must have a party organization, which holds more power than the director. Therefore, it can be seen that economy is largely controlled by government officials.

In recent years, as part of China's reform program, the government has began to reduce bureaucratic control over commerce wherever possible. For example, in the management process of SOE's, the policy regulates that the director of the enterprise is responsible for the overall operation, while the party organization is only responsible for ideological work of the staff. The SOE is responsible for the management itself, and the government would not interfere with it. However, policy is policy, and it may take some time before the policy can be really be enacted. Although the current policy is trying to build up a "socialist market economy", its context focuses on the combination of the state sector and the private sector (Fan Gang 1999, 74). That is to say that there are two kinds of ownership in the market: public ownership and private ownership. The government still draws up policies to coordinate their relationship and to guide their operation, thus making sure that the national economy is still under the control of the macro-economic policy of the state. As a result, compared with developed countries in the West, the role of government in China's economy is powerful and pervasive.

Besides functions common to most governments, China's various governmental organizations play an important role in many economic areas. For example, the State Development Planning Commission is in charge of arranging the major foreign capital projects and the overseas investment projects and would sent officials to supervise them. It will formulate price policies and supervise their enforcement. It will control and adjust the general level of prices. It will regulate and decide the prices of some important commodities that are governed by state.

The State Economic and Trade Commission conducts macro-management and guides all kinds of enterprises with various economic elements, studies the policy and the measures for the development of large enterprises, directs the strategic reform of SOE's, directs the management of SOE's, and compensates deficits and eases the burden of these enterprises (Guo ChaoRen 1999, 106).

The Ministry of Personnel is in charge of the appointment and the removal work of the large SOE's and SOE groups; in charge of the choice, examination and training of the director of SOE's and SOE groups; it also studies and guides the personnel reform of enterprises (Guo ChaoRen 1999, 110).

The Ministry of Labor and Social Protection is in charge of the formulation of certified management methods of the foreign organizations that work in the fields of labor recruitment, consulting and training. The Ministry of Foreign Trade and Economic Cooperation examines and approves the contracts, regulates and modifies large foreign investment projects; it supervises and examines the performance of laws and regulations, contracts and rules on foreign invested enterprises; it guides and manages the import and export activities of foreign enterprises (Guo ChaoRen 1999, 114).

From the above examples, it can be observed that the Chinese government is involved in almost every aspect of economic life. Naturally, the government officials who are in charge of the detailed operations are powerful people. The above judgment is not only based on practical economic and political power, but also on a number of other factors in social, cultural and administrative spheres. These factors includes:

The Chinese tradition advocates hierarchical values rather than values of law, which still exerts impact on modern Chinese; they would be inclined to respect officials automatically.

Business success is typified by a striving for a "seamless relationship between business and officialdom". Certainly, a seamless relationship is set up easily on the basis of mutual benefit. That indicates most Chinese business people still believe that official power is a kind of passport for success in business (Cheng QiHua 1999, 153).

China's resources are often in a state of shortage. The central government is not always able to satisfy all the demands made upon its financial, material or administrative resources. It is very hard to guarantee that these resources which are controlled by the officials are channeled equally. Some officials may take advantages of their rights to further their own interests, which makes a co-operative relationship with officials even more necessary (Yuan Wang 1997, 100). Having recognized the importance of Chinese government officials, the next step would be to identify and to appropriate the skills of contacting with officialdom; this can be seen as one of the keys to exploring new business opportunities in China.

2. COMMUNICATING WITH GOVERNMENT OFFICIALS

Because of pervasive bureaucracy in almost all governments in the world, companies outside China tend to employ or engage professional lobbyists to deal with governments and government officials. In China, however, lobbying is not a profession. Although there is an increasing number of public relations companies that claim to have special connections with government officials at different levels of the Chinese government, few of these organizations can really offer a service of dealing with government officials on behalf of the client on a regular basis (Li Yong 1995, 254). Furthermore, on most occasions it is impossible to have anyone substitute one's own representation of one's company. Therefore, it is necessary to understand some skills in communicating with officials.

A Chinese proverb maintains that “strangers should follow local customs” (*ru xiang sui su*), a concept know in the West as “in Rome do as the Romans do”. It is advisable for a foreigner in China to learn about local life, if one wants to be accepted. Since China has its own unique administrative and political system, and one can not easily change it, it is more prudent to learn how to play the game by Chinese rules. The following are some rules summarized by Chinese business people.

a) Focus solely on business world (zai shang yan shang)

This is the principle that Chinese business people uphold. The principle emphasizes that a business person must follow the rules of commerce and concentrate on business itself, and should not involve in politics. One thing should be noted: not to involve in politics does not mean, not to pay attention to politics. On the contrary, understanding government policies towards the business would be quite crucial for any business operation (Chen QiHua 1999, 152). Politics here means those issues that the Chinese see as belonging to China’s internal affairs, such as China’s political system, or the policy towards the unification of the country, to name but a few. Chinese believe that those things are internal affairs, and that they do not need any others to interfere with and comment on.

If in the initial stage of contact, sensitive political comments are issued by foreigners, they will be suspected to have some evil motivation or aims. In the later period of discussion, the officials in charge of the business would be very cautious about dealing with them. The worst result can be, that officials may decide to discontinue negotiations on the ground that the motivations of their foreign partners are doubtful (Yuan Wang 1997, 102). Therefore, the first advice would be: do not publicly or indiscreetly raise political topics with Chinese officials, even if it is only out of your personal curiosity and not intended to cause offense. This is the first and most important commercial principle in China, so one should follow and respect if.

b) Respecting official’s authority

Because China is a society that has a strong historical and contemporary sense of hierarchy, Chinese officials often mix the authority of a position with personal authority. They often see the respect to the authority of the position as something that is owed to themselves, and they are sensitive about such respect (Yuan Wang 1997, 102). To deal with officials, one should learn to like them. For the purpose of expressing respect, one can invite the appropriate officials to visit the project office or plant on a regular basis. This creates good-will, particularly while awaiting a project approval or licensing. It is a good way to consult the officials on some problems that he knows more about than oneself, such as "the reason for China's rapid economic growth" or "the future of China's economy." Various questions are possible, but one should avoid too simple and too sensitive questions. In this way, one leaves an impression of being interested in China and eager to learn something. The official would appreciate the modest attitude and study spirit. Modesty has always been a good morality in China. Certainly, such exchange of view will help narrowing the gap between one another. The method should not be used without sincerity; otherwise it will be perceived as impolite.

Chinese have a special way to address officials. Quite different from some Western countries, Chinese people are not accustomed to calling each other by their first names, except to show that an intimate relationship already exists. On most occasions, especially where any kind of hierarchical relationship is involved, Chinese people call each other by their surname followed by their position title. This custom is strongly reflected in the social interaction of Chinese officials and others. Chinese officials definitely expect others to call them by their position title, such as "Mayor Li“ or "Secretary Zhang“. It is not wrong to call them "Mister Li" or "Misses Zhang", but it has a very positive effect if one refers to them in the correct way: they immediately feel that they are respected.

c) Friendship contact through a personal channel

It has often been said that it is more important who one knows than what one knows – this is certainly also true in China (Yuan Wang 1997, 103). Through personal relationships, some business activities can be extraordinary successful. For example, if one is competing for a bank loan against ten other business people. And one has known the director of the bank before. In this case, even if one's own debt repaying ability is not stronger than the one of the other applicants, one might get the loan by paying a personal visit to the director and asking him to do a favor. The reason is that Chinese pay attention to interrelationship more than to principles of the organization, on condition the favor does not too much go against the principles. They do not want to offend someone who might be of help in later business cooperation. Personal relationship based on feelings and trust are essential psychological components to take care of for a successful business outcome.

In this world full of human touch, friendship can be a resource that can reveal wonders for the person who uses it properly. Of course, officials are human beings, so they have human emotions, too. Therefore, to built a sound relationship with Chinese government officials and to make good use of it has always been the focus of Chinese business people. Chinese business people believe that personal relationships can surpass official principles, and that flexibility of the officials is only shown to people of whom they have a good impression. Therefore, one should not be surprised that if a business deal is discussed at home or at an informal occasion, it is sometimes treated with more seriousness than business raised in an official forum. The reason is that Chinese officials are more considerate in dealing with individuals privately.

For this reason, it is preferable to spend a substantial amount of time becoming familiar with Chinese officials. One needs to discover an individual's likes and dislikes, ambitions and special talents, by combining business and recreation . It should be noted, however, that not every Chinese officials likes such personal relationships, especially the high-ranking ones who tend to be rather busy. The above statement does not intent say that good relationships are the only crucial point to run a successful business in China. After all, honesty and credit are the business principles that should be followed all the time.

In accordance with the complexity of the Chinese government structure, the responsibility and the rights of each official are not clearly divided. So perhaps one will find that one official says "yes" while the other says "no". The question than is, who has the decision-making power? It is an intelligent and economic way to find out who is the ultimate decision maker before dealing with a group of officials, and to focus on communicating with that person. Relationships of Chinese officials are very complex; therefore the best way is to treat them as a network and not to offend anyone. If necessary, one should reconsider ones principles and position oneself right in the network; one will find that there are many points of access, but that it still takes energy to get in. It has to be pointed out that "reconsidering ones principles" does not recommend to commit bribery. One should find a way between bribery and building good relationships. This is what many Chinese seek after, quite in the tradition of Confucianism: "the doctrine of the middle way".

J. GIFT-GIVING IN CHINA

1. GIFT-GIVING AND COURTESY

Chinese highlight that courtesy demands reciprocity (*li shang wang lai*). If someone gives a gift to somebody else, then that person is expected to give something in return, maybe in some other form. Through such exchange of gifts, people's relationship are strengthened. Whenever there is a need to ask for help, one can count on the people with whom one has exchanged gifts regularly. As part of Chinese culture, gift-giving has been a common practice that serves two purposes:

- One purpose is to express *good wishes* between the gift-giver and receiver. For example, when a couple has given birth to a new baby, their friends would send gifts to congratulate on the occasion; the couple would be very happy to receive the gifts because they know there are others sharing their happiness. Birthday gifts and wedding gifts also belong to this kind.

- The another purpose is to ask for a favor. The favors being asked may be of various kinds. Perhaps it is special treatment or some convenience, or opening a "back-door". Generally speaking, this kind of gifts do not require gifts to repay, and they are usually given by lower towards higher ranking people. This kind of gifts are different from the first kind because it is not purely an exchange of emotion, but more an exchange of benefits. Gift-giving in a commercial context belongs to this kind.

It is not an exaggeration to say that gift-giving has penetrated every aspect of life in China. Sending gifts to officials is likewise a Chinese phenomenon. A common Chinese expression maintains that "an official never blames a gift-giver". Officials, like anyone else, like to receive gifts, including appropriate gifts from business people. Because Chinese pay great attention to the human touch, keeping emotional communication open remains an effective way of maintaining harmony between people; thus people resort to gifts to express their desire to build such harmony. Of course, keeping in harmony with Chinese officials is important due to the special role of Chinese officials in commercial activities.

In Chinese business culture, sending gifts to officials has a number of specific functions, such as catching an official's attention, building up goodwill, exploring the possibility of establishing a personal relationship for the purpose of long-term cooperation, obtaining the official's support and hoping for reciprocation in the form of say issuing an operating license or approving a business in a legal and timely fashion (Yuan Wang 1997, 109).

Considering the importance of gift-giving, business people are encouraged to familiarize themselves with the wisdom of this custom. However, various questions have to be considered first: Whom should the gifts be sent to? If they were to be sent, will they reach the expected effects? When should it be sent and in what manner? In China, gift-giving is a kind of social science that may be worth studying. If one does not have the knowledge, perhaps one can consult a Chinese business person with a modest attitude, for modesty is always appreciated in China. Only once the answers are found one can use the method effectively, otherwise it may exert a negative effect. For example, when in comes to choosing a gift, the gift should match the identity of the official; it should not be too cheap nor too expensive. If it is too cheap, then it can not express respect as is the purpose; if it is too expensive, then it might be suspected as bribery.

The meaning of the gifts is also what one should take into account of. Works of arts, home made articles full of unique flavor, or some high quality goods that one can not find in China might be proper gifts. The way of sending the gifts should also be considered very carefully. The principle would be: if someone intends to display respect that "gives face" to the official, or tries to strengthen the relationship of two organizations, the gift should be sent in public; if one intends to obtain individual support, then send it privately may be the better option. In dealing with such issues, attention has to be paid to the law and the relevant regulations, in order not to commit bribery. One should rather stay within the limits of law and conform to the general behavior standards.

According to Chinese customs, when receiving the gifts, one should be modest and polite (*ke qi*). Normally, one would say: "You are too polite to bring so many gifts, next time, please do not do that again." One does not have to take those words literally. It is just a way of expressing politeness. In fact, the receiver of the gift may be very happy with the situation. Under such circumstance, an appropriate answer could be: "A small gift cannot express my great esteem for you".

2. GIFT-GIVING AND CORRUPTION

Before launching a discussion on corruption, it is worth defining what is considered a gift and what a bribe. There are several criteria to distinguish gift and bribe, but the difference is very subtle and involve both cultural and economic issues. A lot depends on the way the receiver obtains the item and the way in which the gift is conveyed. The ambiguity has led to difficulties in judicial practice; it is difficult to judge what is a legal gift and what is a bribe. Therefore, in dealing with such cases, judicial staff is required to analyze carefully according to the specific situation of each case. The following are factors they usually take into account in an investigation (Cheng ZhengYun 2000, 335):

- First, whether the gift-giver and receiver have a close interaction on a regular basis, whether they frequently send gifts to each other. Everything has its reason, so does gift-giving: the prerequisite of gift-giving is that both sides care about the counterpart's matters and seek for mutual benefit. However, if the two sides did not have any relationship before and suddenly gift-giving takes place, this may be an indication of bribe.

- Second, whether the amount of money or goods is out of proportion. Since gift-giving is a kind of pay without asking for compensation, the amount will not be too much. If normally accepted amounts are exceeded too much, this may be an indication of bribe. For example, if an official's son gets married, and someone would send 1,000 Yuan while the normal level for a gift is 100-200 Yuan, then the action would likely be bribery. Furthermore, if a gift-giver is in a poor economic situation but sends large amounts, then again this would be an indication of a bribe.

- Third, whether the gift-receiver sought benefits for the giver. Gift-giving has no illegal purpose, while bribe is an action that seeks for private benefit using an official's power.

- Fourth, the way of accepting and giving gifts is also another factor to judge the case. Gift-giving usually happens publicly, while bribes happen secretly, and the two sides do not let others know about it. But it is not an absolute criterion to distinguish between gift and bribe.

- The identity and the social status also stands as a criterion to judge the case: if there is an enormous gap between the two sides in social status and identity, and they do not contact each other regularly and do not have a family relationship, then the gifts may be illegal bribe (Cheng ZhengYun 2000, 292-293).

From the above statement, it can be seen that there are no absolute rules to distinguish between bribes and gifts. Because of the corresponding vagueness in judicial practice, officials may be tempted to take advantage of the situation and to get involved in corruption. At present, corruption in China is becoming a serious problem. The centralized control of commercial activities, the underdeveloped Chinese legal system and the influence of a seamless relationship between business and officialdom all have encouraged corruption at various levels (Yuan Wang 1997, 111).

According to statistics, from January 1993 to October 1997, procurotorial organs have filed 290,513 cases dealing with bribery and related crimes. Among them, 100,655 cases of graft, 69,415 cases of bribery, 60,537 cases of misappropriate use of public funds. – 4,845 cases involved large sums of money, i.e. over one million Yuan (Cheng ZhengYun 2000, 35).

These cases have exerted negative influence on society; among them the case of the former deputy mayor of the Beijing municipality, Wang BaoSen, was notorious. Wang grafted 250,000 RMB, 20,000 US dollar, and misappropriate used 350 million Yuan of public money (Yan ShuWen 1997, 45).

Although the Chinese government has been contributing great efforts to fight against corruption, the total amount of crimes increases, and the types of crimes have expanded. There may be various reasons: people's moral concept is changing constantly, there may be a lack of morality to regulate behavior; the old social systems were reformed but the new policies are not completed yet, thus providing opportunity for corruption.

As a foreign business person, one might encounter and suffer from corruption since business activities always have something to do with government officials. Perhaps, someday one would be asked to provide free overseas study or sightseeing or economic support to someone. In such cases, how should one deal with the request? Clearly, one has to handle the issue strategically, so as to gain official help in business without having to resort to corrupt practices. Direct refusal is not recommended; one would better find a reasonable excuse to refuse the request without letting the other lose face. One may want to say that the company has strict rules regulating such offers, or that one does not have the power to authorize such requests and has to report this to senior management. If such requests come in often, perhaps one can discuss the matter over with higher ranking officials in private. Because of the subtle relationship between business activities and Chinese government officials, having a careful consideration of the issue and drawing conclusions that save ones interests is probably a good move.

3. CONCLUSION

In light of the close connection of business activities and government officials, keep a normal and constructive relationship seems the only way out for the foreign business person. As to the standard of normal and constructive, according to the common understanding of Chinese can be: have contact often, not only in the time that problem needs to be solved but in normal time, actively contact with them; not to be too intimate and try to keep certain distance, just like the distance between friends and colleague, have both working ties and friendships. When dealing with Chinese officials, just think no matter how high their position is, they are human being, so human being have human touch. Therefore, expressing the most emotional aspect to the officials might change empathy in return.

K. NEGOTIATION IN CHINA

1. INTRODUCORY REMARKS ON NEGOTIATION

People coming from different countries have different negotiation styles due to their various cultural backgrounds, value concepts, standpoints and experience. Chinese tend to think that the typical American is enthusiastic and active and likes to make a "one package" trade; the typical German pays attention to efficiency and seeks for perfection, while he can not give concession easily; the stereotype English is seen as kind, gentle, flexible and actively reacting to constructive suggestions. The typical French is seen as having three distinctive characteristics: he has a firm standpoint, uses French as only means of communication, and maintains dignity at all times (Yuan QiGang 1995, 377). A judgment cannot be given as to which style falls best with the Chinese. A good negotiator should understand both his own style and his the style of his counterpart. It should be acknowledged that every culture can train excellent negotiation specialists with unique styles.

Chinese are good at negotiation; many ancient Chinese show wisdom in negotiation. Zhu GeLiang, a strategist in SanGuo times, and the first emperor of the Han Dynasty, Liu Bang, were examples of distinguished negotiators. The modern Chinese learn a lot of knowledge from the cases provided by their ancestors. But China is rather late in taking negotiation as a subject of study. With China's position raising to one of the important economic powers of the world, many foreign experts began to study the Chinese negotiation style. They have concluded that Chinese negotiators can be characterized as having strong self-respect and taking a skeptical attitude.

This character can be seen in many Chinese. It is a reflection of the influence of Chinese traditional culture. There is a saying in China: "a gentleman may be killed but may not be insulted". Many historical figures were respected as heroes in Chinese history because they valued their honor higher than their life. A story passed down in China for thousands of years gives a vivid illustration of Chinese self-respect. It goes like this:

> *A person who was about to starve was given some food to eat, but together with an obscene word. He refused to eat the food and eventually starved to death, in order to maintain his dignity and face.*

Sometimes, Chinese would rather sacrifice economic benefit to protect face in a negotiation, which is sometimes difficult to understand for a foreigner. In recent years, Chinese begin realizing the importance of economic benefit, but the deep-rooted concept of face-protection can not be removed easily. Therefore, it is a skill of a foreign negotiator to let Chinese give concessions but not to let them feel losing face.

The skeptical character of many Chinese is closely related to the history of China. Almost all powerful countries invaded China in the past 160 years as described in the part on history. Chinese can not forget the humiliation and the disasters that history brought to China. Therefore, when a Chinese sits at the negotiation table with British nationals, perhaps what he is thinking of is not the negotiation but the Opium War and the NanJing treaty (Yuan QiGang 1995, 381). Furthermore, since the founding of the People's Republic of China, in many cases, Chinese business people were cheated by foreigners. For example, outdated technology was introduced as state of the art, together with high charges for technical investment. This has made the conservative Chinese even more careful when dealing with foreigners. Chinese can be described as conservative and unwilling to take risks; they may distrust Westerners they do not know. But once friendship has developed, Chinese will treasure it for long time. For Western business people, once they understand the cause of Chinese characteristics, ways can be found to communicate with Chinese effectively, that is, in an open and sincere manner.

2. CHINESE NEGOTIATION STYLE

China is referred to as "etiquette country". Chinese treat the guest generously and considerately (Ding JianZhong 1996, 57). Chinese are used to treat a the foreign business person with etiquette. When doing business with foreigners, a Chinese business person will always ask to negotiate in China, so that the agenda can be controlled by the Chinese side. Chinese like observing the guests and building up their trust that the Chinese side is sincere in doing business and establishing friendship with them. For the Chinese who think highly of face, etiquette is related to prestige and dignity. Chinese give the opponents face by not refusing their suggestions directly. In the meantime, they need the counterpart to give them face in public. Therefore, no matter what one negotiates, no matter if one is young or old, holding a high position or a low one, one should pay attention to his courtesy. This is the first step to achieve a successful negotiation with Chinese.

Chinese business people are accustomed to "etiquette first, military force second"(Ding JianZhong 1996, 57). This is a military term of China. Chinese often compare business to battle and quote military terms in business operation. Nowadays, these strategies are deemed to be a source of advice to both Chinese and foreign business people. Whilst treating the opponents with etiquette,

Chinese also consider if the tough hand could be used, especially when they are forced. Therefore, when arguing with Chinese, do not let them feel that one is forcing them to submit or that one is taking advantage his superiority excessively. If excessive words harm the Chinese sense of self-respect, they will teach one a lesson by providing an even more difficult condition. So, if there is really a divergence, one would better inform the opponent in advance and give them room to prepare psychologically. For example: "this question may not be proper, but I raise it in advance, and please help me analyze it." Under such circumstances, Chinese would give the question careful consideration.

As has become clear by now, Chinese think highly of interpersonal relationships. Rather than launching immediately into direct business discussions, Chinese negotiators will most probably first wish to talk with their counterpart on a whole range of non-business related subjects. These may include broad discussions about culture, art, history or food customs, and will usually also involve friendly questions about one's social or personal life (Yi SongZhi 1998, 271). The purpose of this is to judge whether an interpersonal relationship can be established between the counterparts before the negotiation begins. Chinese business people have a great desire to demonstrate their respect for their counterpart as a means of establishing mutual credibility. This is a genuine attempt at establishing a friendship relationship, but it is also a strategy to maximize opportunities and to ensure the success of the negotiations. Notwithstanding, all business people are capable of breaking promises or changing contracts. However, the Chinese believe that a strong personal relationships can not easily be ruined or broken. Many Westerners are particularly task and efficiency-orientated, and often see little need to attend to non-task-related topics in conversation with their Chinese counterparts. They usually want to come straight to the point. However, if negotiations are to be successful then task-orientated individuals will have to look at the benefits of adopting their strategy to complement, not to clash with the Chinese negotiating style (Yuan Wang 1997, 50).

Chinese are diligent, but the general work rhythm may appear slow. Chinese often designate more negotiator than their counterpart (Liu Yuan 1999, 287). The negotiation within the Chinese group will prolong the negotiation process. Also, the hierarchical social values and the special characteristics of the Chinese managerial system makes that negotiators do not dare to say "yes" without consulting the authority and listening to the other's opinions. Obviously, this contributes to the prolonging of negotiation process. Etiquette and tactical concerns contribute to the length of negotiations. A foreign counterpart may wish to reduce time-consuming activities wherever possible. However, one should be careful. One's Chinese counterpart may take advantage of any impatience, especially if he has exhibited anxiety about signing the contract because of time restraints or expenses incurred. One must be prepared to negotiate longer than one would otherwise like to. Meanwhile, one can be looking for a reasonable excuse to justifying the negotiation to be limited in certain time.(Alston 1997, 113). The other negative effect of trying to reduce time-consuming activities may be that one could be regarded as having a lack of sincerity in cooperating and establishing a long-term business relationship. Therefore, one should not take the risk of violating the Chinese rules.

Chinese business people tend to be implicit, and they dislike indicating their attitude directly. In the primary stage of negotiations, Chinese rarely put forward their requirements and suggestions. They always ask their counterpart to introduce the characteristics of the product; listen attentively to their counterpart's ideas and suggestions on transaction. In the negotiation process, Chinese technical experts often ask for detailed information about the product and make a comparison with the products of their counterpart's competitors. If the questions and the products of their counterpart surpass the authority limitation of the negotiators or the questions are hard to answer, they will ask for instruction from their leader or discuss together until a common understanding can be reached. Chinese believe a limited power is real power, and it is also a good excuse to say "no" to their counterpart. Therefore, if one does not have a clear picture of Chinese thoughts, one should keep calm and not express ones own thoughts too early. Furthermore, one should not change one's stand point easily without knowing the counterpart's intention (Liu Yuan 1999, 287).

Chinese are good at sticking to principles, and they demonstrate flexibility. Chinese tend to think that the two negotiating sides are equal; there should not be one that is particularly strong or weak (Yi SongZhi 1998, 103). The negotiation should be mutually beneficial. When the negotiation goes into crucial stage, Chinese business people often ask to reach a letter of intent first, and to discuss the details later. Chinese would not give away in questions of principle; they can be rather stubborn in this aspect. When Chinese find the principle is challenged or the content of the negotiation is not conform with the long-term target, they can show a serious and unyielding attitude. – Meanwhile, they show great flexibility in specific affairs. Because Chinese seek for equality and balance, they would balance gain and loss in the process of negotiation. As the counterpart of Chinese, one should have a careful consideration on all the conditions. In this way, one can evaluate the standard of equality and reduce any imbalance.

Chinese people show distinguished talent in bargain. They will try every way to ask the counterpart for a lower price. Chinese use two tactics in lowering the price: firstly, only if the counterpart's prices are lowered, they will commit to buy a large quantity, otherwise, the order can be very small, or there is no order at all. The foreign business person can choose between a lower price and giving up trade. The other way is to let the suppliers compete with each other; if Chinese want to buy an important commodity, they will ask an offer from several suppliers and then give a comprehensive consideration on quality and price. Sometimes, they will ask the suppliers to compete to lower prices face to face, until the ideal result is achieved (Yuan QiGang 1995, 384).

The following checklist provides an illustration of some typical characteristics of Chinese negotiators:

- strong self respect, face protection, strong historical sense;
- strong guidance by policy and principle;
- prudent and suspect, harsh terms, always on guard against someone;
- thinking highly of friendship, loyal to friends, enthusiastic;
- good at bargaining;
- lack of business knowledge, low proficiency.

Successful foreign business people use certain strategies to cope with Chinese characteristics. They include (Yuan QiGang 1995, 384):

- modesty, protection of face, not harming Chinese self-respect;
- patience to wait;
- attention to establishing long-term friendships, achieving Chinese trust;
- giving a higher price at every step, and not lowering prices easily.

Chinese hold views on agreement or contracts that are quite different from Western customs. For Westerners, signing a contract means that both sides have agreed to cooperate on fixed conditions that only have to be implemented. However, for Chinese people, a signed agreement merely marks the end of the initial stage of cooperation, subsequent cooperation is contingent on the condition that supplementary negotiation may be required before, during or after implementation. Chinese business people argue that there is no agreement without loopholes, and that there will be problems that cannot be anticipated at the time of initial negotiations, especially for complicated or large-scale projects (Yuan Wang 1997, 56).

Another factor is that some Chinese business people do not have a strong sense of the strict legal effectiveness of a contract or agreement. Since business relationships in China are based on personal feelings, these are considered more important than legal documentation. Many Chinese believe that although the main features of an agreement or contract must be observed, many points can be subject to change, depending on the depth of trust and the development of the relationship. This ambiguity is sometimes quite frustrating for foreign negotiators. To reduce the potential for dispute, one should work with, and not against Chinese counterparts. Carefully identifying the items within the contract that are for all intents and purposes beyond reasonable dispute, it is also necessary to explain and reaffirm with the Chinese negotiating side what is the exact nature of an agreement or contract before signing it. This takes patience and time, and is most effective if based on a friendly relationship.

3. THE ROLE OF BANQUETS IN THE NEGOTIATING PROCESS

When talking about banquets, a few sentences have to be added here which intend to explain why doing business in China is closely related to eating. Eating is a kind of culture in China. As part of a splendid cultural tradition, the current dietary habits reflect the psychology of the Chinese nationality and the Chinese way of life. Furthermore, it embodies to some extend the national ethnic and moral concepts as well as religious ideas. Chinese dietary culture includes food culture, tea culture and spirit culture, which have been handed down by generations and finally formed a kind of cultural tradition full of national characters (Lian YongJie 1999, 291). Chinese people like eating; it is an important aspect of life. Most Chinese think that eating is a kind of enjoyment rather than pure necessity. It reflects the Chinese attitude towards life. In feudal society, the Chinese family was of large size, with several generations living under one roof and all family members eating at one table. Under such circumstances, harmony was created, and eating provided the family members with an opportunity to exchange views and feelings, and to share happiness and sorrows together. Therefore, eating is a legacy of Chinese, and it is still treasured by many Chinese who naturally uphold the philosophy that "eating is the heaven for common people".

In China business is always related to eating; practically every foreign business person who has been visiting or working in China has received an invitation to a formal banquet. For many Westerners, one of their most lasting impressions of China is the variety of food. There are many forms of banquets and farewell banquets (Yuan Wang 1997, 58). Foreigners are often shocked by the grand feast with only a couple of people to enjoy. To them, it is not understandable to cause such a waste. They may interpret such banquets as a Chinese business tactic to soften their foreign counterparts by making them feel important.

Actually, the meaning or function of banquets in Chinese culture can not be explained in such a simple way. Whether banquets would cause positive or negative effects in business depends on how one perceives, understands and then makes use of this important social activity. If one thinks "these Chinese business people eat and drink with me, then lie and cheat me with a smile on their face", then one will stop to make good use of the attitude of hospitality during banquets. If on contrary, one can show how willing one is to establish long-term business relationship with China, Chinese in return will show their sincerity; banquets will be a symbol of business achievements. The example below can give some indication about the function of banquets:

> *Michael Pointer is the managing director of his sheepskin trading company in Australia. He says that nothing upsets him more than hearing Western business people complaining about having to go to a banquet. "I do more business over banquets than I ever do in negotiating rooms," he says, "all we ever do in negotiating rooms is having a long argument to arrive at the point that we reached the evening before over dinner." Over the meals, which many Westerners find stiff and strange situations, Pointer makes sure he develops nice, friendly, personal relationships with the Chinese. He asks individuals about themselves, their role, their family and where they come from (Carol Yun 1997, 128).*

Chinese not only treat foreign business people with feasts, but also any other people who have a business relationship with them, whether the person is an official, business counterpart, potential partner, top manager, expert authority or department head, a customer or a supplier: all could be guests at the same banquet table. In every large and medium city in China, and especially in those in GuangDong province, business people are eating and doing business, the cost incurred by the host is taken for granted as a necessary and essential business expense. For this reason the administration budgets of most Chinese enterprises and organizations cover the expenses of banquets. It may sound strange to foreigners, but eating is the heart and soul of Chinese business culture. There is little doubt that one must understand the role of banquets in Chinese business, if one wants to succeed in China. Banquets have four main functions:

- The first is establishing an initial business relationship. For Chinese business people, the easiest way for strangers to get to know each other is to talk in a relaxed atmosphere. At a banquet, both the host and guest can easily engage each other in topics of conversation as diverse as personal life, culture and, of course, business.

- Demonstrating a capacity to conduct business. Most successful negotiations in China are based on mutual trust, respect and confidence. Chinese business people believe the size, turnover, performance and assets of a particular enterprise or company – they are important elements of a successful business equation. They also believe that the banquet table is a reflection of this, but more importantly, of their financial power and political support. In order to help the business partner build up a picture of their firm's credibility and connections impressively, a Chinese business person will choose the best restaurant, and invite Chinese officials or other relevant important figures to join them even if they have no business relationships with each other.

- Exploring the possibilities of further cooperation. Clearly, most Chinese business people prefer to discus deals in an informal setting rather than in a formal meeting. In a sense they feel that the potential embarrassment of a public rejection represents an intolerable loss of face and therefore take steps to make the whole process less formal and therefore less risky. For them, it is much safer to raise demands at an informal or private occasion. Under these circumstances, a Chinese counterpart may not feel a loss of face even if their demands are rejected.

- Taking a break from negotiation. Conflict and argument in the negotiation process often lead to an impasse when neither side is wanting to compromise. Once this occurs, the Chinese side may attempt to break the deadlock by holding a banquet to relax the tension of negotiations and give both sides an opportunity to evaluate their commitment to a deal.

4. THE STRATEGIES USED IN NEGOTIATION

Do Chinese really possess strategy in negotiations? The answer is positive. But where are the sources of these strategies, and why are Chinese so intelligent and at ease in using them? To find answers to these questions, a review of the story of the famous strategist is indispensable.

In China, virtually all educated people know Zhu GeLiang, whose story is well-known from the historical novel "Three kingdoms". This book ranks as the number one among the four Chinese classics; the remaining three being "A Dream of Red Mansions", "Journey to the West" and finally "Outlaws of the Marsh". Of all celebrated strategists, none is more celebrated, respected or honored than Zhu GeLiang. Zhu was born in 180 AD, during the warring days of the Han Dynasty. He was invited as advisor by Liu Bei who was a warrior-general. By using strategy, he helped Liu Bei win many wars. One example of Zhu's brilliance was demonstrated when fighting with Cao Cao's troops. Cao Cao was a powerful warrior-general, too. Zhu's own forces ran out of arrows; in order to remedy the situation, he had his troops tie straw bundles to the sides of war boats and then go back and forth along the river under the enemy's fortress walls during a foggy night. The enemy, suspecting an attack but unable to see the boats clearly at night, fired many arrows at the river below, wave after wave of arrows descended upon the boats all night long. In the morning, Zhu's men had a full supply of fresh arrows, and the enemy sitting behind the fortress walls had depleted his supplies.

Sun Zi was another outstanding strategist in Chinese history. Little is known about Sun Zi's life story. He lived during the Spring and Autumn Period, around 500 BC. The real name of Sun Zi was Sun Wu; his grandson was Sun Bin another great strategist. Many latter strategist have studied Sun Zi's "Art of War", which was his military masterpiece, such as Qin ShiHuang (the emperor of the Qin Dynasty), Cao Cao (the above mentioned powerful warrior-general in the Spring and Autumn Period), Napoleon (the French General and later Emperor) and Mao ZeDong (the first chairman of the People's Republic of China). It is assumed that the "Art of War" has been completed between 496 BC-453 BC; it includes thirteen articles, a total of 6,000 words (Fan QiAn 1999, 3-5).

Perhaps one would ask: why talk so much about strategists here? Latter on, one will know how these strategies are forcefully used by Chinese business people. Chinese people often see the market like a war field; therefore they tend to apply the essence of martial strategies in business management. Negotiation is one of the crucial parts of business management and involves the direct encounter between two sides. The side that can gain more advantages in negotiation is the side that will make more profits. Therefore, it is to proper to compare the negotiation table to the battle field. Some strategy will be discussed below; it might be of help to negotiate successfully:

"Know yourself and know your counterpart and you will win every battle" (*zhi ji zhi bi, bai zhan bai sheng*). It has always been respected as the first wisdom in Chinese warfare history. It means: to have a thorough analysis about advantages and disadvantages of both sides will ensure success (Liu SiQi 1994, 116). By understanding these preparations, one can always be in a favorable status. One can use his advantages to take initiative, one can reduce the risks of failure to maximum level by knowing his advantages. If one knows the advantages of the counterpart, one can strengthen one's defense work in advance. Knowing the weaknesses of one's counterpart will help one find the right point to attack. According to Sun, if one just knows oneself without understanding the counterpart or one knows one's counterpart without understanding one's own character, one can only win half the battles.

"Attack where he is unprepared; go forth where he does not expect you". In negotiations, this is precisely what Chinese tend to do. The optimum lies in adjusting the strategy according to the different situations of both sides, and in using this strategy flexibly. Therefore, one can not have a stiff rule to copy. For example: one is powerful and has the ability to win the war, but one pretends to be weak and not being able to stand a blow. Or: one wants to start operations soon, but pretends to move in the distant future. Towards a powerful enemy, one should strengthen the defensive work and avoid to meet him; towards a fierce and irritable enemy, one can force him to surrender according to his character; towards an enemy that wants to rest and reorganize, one should try to make him run around and to get tired. At the negotiating table, these strategies can be used to put one's counterpart under control. For example, if the foreigner does not have the patience to hold a long talk, the Chinese side may prolong the conversation on purpose and wear down their will. One is well advised to understand these strategies in advance and to be on guard against them.

What is valued in war is a quick victory, not prolonged operations. It is better to get one's deal done quickly, with the least waste of resources and expenditure of time (Brahm 1997, 45). Long talks will make the negotiating teams tired and put their motivation to a test. In addition, expensive hotels, conference rooms, air tickets and other luxurious expenditures will be a burden for the companies. Considering from these two aspects, long negotiation are discouraged. Before leaving for negotiation in China, one should think of the disadvantages of a long war.

"Use stratagem to attack the enemy." Sun Zi said, the best policy in war is to attack the enemy's strategy, the second best way is to disrupt his alliances through diplomatic means, the next best method is to attack his army in the field. The worst policy is to attack walled cities. Attacking cities is the last resort if there is no alternative. If these methods were to be used in negotiation, one would better develop a plan before proceeding to perform a negotiation. On the basis of understanding the enemy's policy, one can posse a favorable status to attack the weakness of one's counterpart. In China, direct argumentation at the table will result in disaster; emotionalism has to be dismissed from the negotiation stratagem (Brahm 1997, 50). If one want to predict the success rate of one's negotiation, the following four criteria can function as a reference.

- he who can form a judgment at the right time, and balance gain and loss, knowing exactly when to negotiate and when not to, will win;
- he who knows how to use different stratagem according to different conditions of each side;
- he whose negotiation team is united in purpose will win;
- he whose leader of the negotiation team is able and not interfered with by outside forces will win.

Sun Zi said: "invincibility lies in the defense, the possibility of victory in the attack". One should defend oneself when one's strength is inadequate, and attack the enemy when it is abundant. Thus, by adopting defensive and attack policies alternatively, one is capable of protecting oneself, and of gaining a complete victory. When it comes to settle disputes in negotiation, one must protect oneself from the outset. One way of doing so is to adopt careful arbitration language in one's Chinese contract. Since Chinese do not like direct confrontation with their partner, they prefer friendly negotiation. In case the negotiation is not as friendly as one would like it to be, arbitration might be resorted to as a tool to defend oneself. If one knows that the counterpart is in a unfavorable condition – for example, badly in need of the equipment or the materials that are the object of the negotiation – then one may offer a high price; most likely, the other side will not take the risk of breaking the negotiation by refusing the offer.

Sun Zi said: "he who occupies the field of battle first and awaits his enemy is at ease; he who arrives later and joins battle in haste is weary". Therefore, one skilled in war brings the enemy to the field of battle and is not brought there by him. Since most negotiations are conducted in China, on the one hand, the foreign party has to came to China with a time schedule. Hotels and air tickets are booked in advance. Meetings are arranged in advance to the last minutes. On the other hand, the Chinese Partner makes preparation easily at home and waits the foreign party to come in. They can afford to plunge in or withdraw from the negotiation without causing too much waste. On this aspect, the Chinese side possess the initiative; when the Chinese party senses that its foreign counterpart is fixed to a deadline, half the battle is won. By simply bidding time, the Chinese party will often force the foreign side into a position where it is bargaining against itself (Brahm 1997, 68).

A tactics might be used in accordance with Sun Zi's art of war can be illustrated as follows. Show sincerity to the counterpart and tempt them to express intention, at this time, one can keep calm and avoid destination being known by counterpart (An Ping 1997,142). By this way, one can estimate the situation by comparing the identical and different part of one's counterpart's position. On contrary with it, the counterpart do not know the one's real intention, therefore they dare not to ask for big concession in case of the great possibility of being turned down.

Knowing the terrain is of great assistance in military operations. It is necessary for a wise general to make assessments of the enemy's situation correctly, in order to create conditions leading to victory, and to calculate distances and the degree of difficulty of the terrain. If the doctrine is applied to negotiation, that means knowing the local situation is critical to negotiating in China successfully. One should really take care to inquire into the nature of one's Chinese partner, given the complexity of Chinese business environment. A number of questions would be looked at, such as: is the enterprise well-managed, is it profitable, is it trustworthy, what is their real aim in seeking the cooperation? Does the enterprise have the capacity to work towards a defined goal?

Use of spies. Sun Zi said that war is a money-consuming activity; it will be the cause of backwardness of a national economy and miserable living conditions for the people. Under such circumstances, spending money but remaining ignorant of the enemy's situation is against humanity. – Corporate espionage is a critical element behind many negotiations. One should not assume, when one sits in the back seat of the car discussing the day's events, that the driver assigned by the other side to shuttle the guests around does not understand English. One should not assume that – during the negotiation – the other side who appears to rely so much upon translators does not either (Brahm 1997, 112). Chinese have the tradition to use spy in warfare in order to gather information about the enemy. In the commercial field, industrial espionage may be employed to steal information from revivals. At the negotiation table, espionage may be used to detect the real situation of one's counterpart. Therefore, as a foreign partner, one can do two things: to be on guard against espionage, and to send a spy into the Chinese side.

Conclusion: in this part on negotiation, the discussion has focused on four aspects, which are: the characteristics of Chinese, the style of Chinese negotiators, the role of banquets in negotiations, and the strategies in negotiation. These theories are deducted from the experience of the early negotiators. However, judgment and advice is often based on subjective opinions. Therefore, in practical situations of negotiation, different phenomenon may exist, making it necessary to consider the specific situation and to form a suitable strategy.

V. RESULTS

Using the example of China, the data and information presented in the last chapter result in a guide to doing business in a foreign culture that has the improvement of showing how culture, ethics and the current state of the society have to be taken into account in the business process. The process of building business is outlined step by step: after preparing for market entry, understanding government policy and relevant laws and investigating the environment, the operation can be started. I am also providing some insights in areas that are especially important in China: Human Resource Management and relationship building, including personal and public relations.

A. PREPARING FOR MARKET ENTRY

1. THE DIFFERENCE OF SOCIAL ENVIRONMENTS

Before entering the Chinese market, one should be fully aware that China is a place that can be quite different from one's own country in terms of political environment, business environment and cultural tradition. China is a socialist country; communism is the highest ideal that Chinese struggle for. The Communist Party is the leading party of China, and every party member is required to be loyal to the leadership of the party. China is a state in which state policy and law enjoy almost the same status; therefore China is a country with a strong political atmosphere.

Both policy and law can be used to adjust social relationships. They are closely connected with each other and work as complementary factors to govern the country. Law reflects the will of the state, possesses a strong mandatory power, and the whole society must abide by it. Some policies may not reflect the will of the state. For example, party policy. Some policies have the characteristics of law, but the policy maker and the procedure of drawing up were not so authoritative as the legislative organs. Therefore, they may possess weaker mandatory power than law. – In China, the competition between policy and law for commanding a governing position underwent a winding process. In the primary period of the founding of the People's Republic of China, China highlighted the rule of law, policies as supplementary element. Then, the coming Culture Revolution used only policies to govern the country. From1978 till now, China is developing from rule of law and policy towards rule of law. However, the phenomenon of policy overriding law still exists in some areas (Li BuYu 1998, 86).

Politics penetrates a wide range of aspects of life, from business operations to the world of literature. Therefore, making sure that one would not be shocked by the important role of politics in China is the first psychological preparation one must make. In correspondence with the strong political atmosphere, the role of government in business in China is particularly strong, and one has to deal with government officials at different levels in order to run a smooth business, for these officials possess rights in determining the success or failure of a business. Therefore, whether one can fully accept this phenomenon of China is also a question one should consider.

China's legal system is far from being completed; the administrative system of official regulations is still developing; Chinese commercial laws have not been completely implemented. As a consequence, one may find oneself in a situation where a law does not give a clear definition of a problem, or it will take time and energy to get one. Under such circumstances the question could arise: does one still have the patience to continue? It has often been said that China has an enormous market, but what is sometimes neglected is that it does not have a mature rule for the participants to obey. Chinese business people have developed their ways of earning money; some may take advantage of their relationship with government officials to get a scarce resources at a low price, perhaps giving a high commission to the person who is in charge of purchasing goods.

In China, because of the ambiguity of property ownership, sometimes there may be a conflict of interest between the company and the individual. Some people would use their rights to make money for themselves illegally while disregarding the company's benefit. This type of activities has intensified with the complexity of the Chinese business environment. It is commonly recognized that connections (*guanxi*) are a vital factor for a successful business in China (Chen QiHua 1999, 69). Among the various relationships, personal relationship with your business partner will be very important, because China is still a country in which human touch is highly appreciated. That means, showing your sympathy and understanding to the others will probably result in the others giving their understanding and sympathy in return. Specifically speaking, the other may give priority rights and preferential policies and other convenience in business.

Therefore, taking fully advantage of public and personal relationships and making them conform to one's business need is a qualification one needs to have. The advice here is: if one is not familiar with the Chinese business practice, one should be careful and try to spend some time in understanding it. Those who do not get ready to accept it and are reluctant to adopt it risk failure.

2. ECONOMIC ENVIRONMENT DIFFERENCES

China is a developing country. Development lies in many aspects, including the development of production capacity and purchasing power. Development comes with uncertainty; purchasing power is no exception. On account of the continuous reform of the social productive structure, the employment state can change rapidly. People do not know when they will out of work; when their salary will be raised or cut. Consequently, such uncertainty in income must lead to uncertainty in consuming and purchasing power. Market demand changes accordingly; it is one indication of the uncertainty of the Chinese market. On the other hand, the Chinese economy is undergoing a transformation from planned economy to market economy. During the process, numerous challenges appear.

> *For example, the prices of the products that were regulated by the State Price Bureau previously become subject to market supply and demand after the implementation of the market economy. But because of market competition, market participants may compete to lower prices in an attempt to gain market share. Such price strategies can lead to deflation, and in fact, deflation happened in China in a number of years. – This has fueled debate as to whether the government should set minimum price levels or leave the market subjects behaving as they wish to. In a more general sense, the question is what effects government policy could produce, and whether the market subjects have the ability to do self-regulation.*

The above example just wants to indicate that the Chinese market is still in an infant stage; the market participants, market rules, self-balance ability and competition are still developing. Therefore, having a psychological preparation on these specific issues will reduce the risk of failure.

China's economic development is not quite balanced. The Eastern area is the most developed region, central China and the west are relatively more backward. For example, in the Eastern Region, the population is 40% of the total population, but it possess 70% of the total investment and 60% of the total consumption (Lu Zheng 1999, 115). The imbalance embodies in the standard of living of people: in the Eastern Region, people's consumption focuses on buying an apartment and a car, while in the Western Region, people are struggling to have enough to eat. The differences between cities and the countryside are enormous. Some city residents are millionaires and enjoy a luxury living, while many farmers are still living in low dwelling and depend on good whether to make a living. Taking color TV as an example: the popularization rate is 94% in cities, against 27% in rural areas (Lu Zheng 1999, 39). So do not be surprised if you see great gaps in living standard between Chinese people.

Another difference between China and many other countries lies in the way of getting information. In China, some market data and some kinds of business information are very difficult to get, because they are thought to be secrets. Foreigners may find this strange, but in China it is rather normal to have secrets in various levels, such as state confidential, marital confidential, personnel confidential, business confidential and so on.

3. TRUST ISSUE

It goes without saying that trust between partners is of great value; but how should a foreigner be trusted by a Chinese partner? *Firstly*, respect Chinese culture even if some aspects are very different from what you are used to. If you really can not understand something, it is better to keep silent and not to comment or criticize it, for Chinese people have a strong sense of national honor. No Chinese would like to cooperate with people who look down upon Chinese culture.

Secondly, put your Chinese Partner in the same status as yourself. Remember you are equal as a person, no matter whether your social position is high or low. Try to keep away from a mindset that one can take advantage of Chinese. The cooperation should be mutually beneficial. Without mutual benefit, the Chinese would think they are taken advantage of by someone, and they would probably not stay in such an unpleasant working environment.

Thirdly, communicate with your Chinese Partner regularly. A foreigner should be open to his Chinese Partner and should exchange views frequently with him, because there may be quite different viewpoint on some question. Things that a foreigner would take for granted could make the Chinese feel uncomfortable. For example: to "go-Dutch", meaning everyone pays his own bill, is unacceptable to many Chinese; they would rather treat each other in turns than paying the bill in a restaurant, for they tend to think they could lose face before the others if they do otherwise. The reason is that "treating" in China has a two-fold meaning: one is to show the economic ability of the host, the other is to demonstrate the good relationship between the host and the guest. Certainly, "going-Dutch" does not serve these two purposes, and Chinese could be unhappy with it. Because of the differences between the Chinese and the Western way of thinking, effective communication possesses a very important position in establishing trust. Make your Chinese partners understand your working progress and target if necessary, and give them the feeling that you are working together towards the same goal – this can encourage your partner to a great extend.

Other than business-related communication, Chinese pay close attention to personal feelings to someone. Therefore, to spend some time to chat with your Chinese Partner on some topics that he might be interested in, and to show your understanding to their thought will be a good way of establishing trust. The topic can concentrate on family matters, study, interests and so on. Your Chinese Partner would think: "This guy has human interests!" and will treat you more considerately. There is a Chinese saying: "to win a heart by giving true consideration for the others heart". That means: if you want to get the other's trust, trust them in advance. Do not show your suspicion easily. From the above analysis, you can see that communicating with a Chinese Partner can be a rather complicated thing. Therefore, before entering the Chinese market, you may want to ask yourself: "Can I reach a relationship of mutual trust with my Chinese partner? – Have I ever thought of such trust issues?"

4. CULTURE SHOCK

When you come to China for the first time, get ready to experience a quite different culture. Because Western countries tend to be not very well-informed about China, China is a rather backward country in the Westerner's mind. The image may have many sources, such as old books written by travelers who came to China many years ago, or from Western media which may not provide an accurate picture. Some foreigners say they thought Chinese still live in one-story dwellings and wear dark and deep-blue Mao suits. When they got off the plane in Beijing, they were shocked by the scene of a modern big city. The high buildings, the never ending and rather modern cars, mixed with the impressions of the Forbidden City, the Imperial Palace and the Great Wall struck them at first sight. They immediately had the impression that China is a country composed of a charming ancient civilization, and high-level modern civilization.

But how long will the impression last, and what is China really like? The answer can only be obtained on condition that they live in China long enough and merged into Chinese ordinary people's life. Here are some references to what they thought to be unique about China; however it can only be taken as a general idea, since every person has their own understanding about culture:

- Most Chinese are atheist, and they often do not know how comparatively important religion is in Western countries; perhaps they would use religious terms very casually in some occasions, which might offend a foreigner. Knowing this point in advance will help you to reduce misunderstanding when such an incidence happens.

- China has many dialects; some dialects are very difficult to understand. Even Chinese find it sometimes difficult to communicate with each other, if they come from different regions. Thus knowing something about the language environment of China in advance will reduce the feeling of unfamiliarity.
- There are gaps between Chinese and foreigners, when it comes to eating, living and entertainment. For example, Chinese food is quite different from Western food, living space is relatively small etc. But with the increasing of cultural exchange, the gap is reducing gradually. One can now find Western restaurants everywhere. As to entertainment: bars, gymnasiums, bowling alleys, swimming pools and discos can be easily found in big cities. It is important to be psychologically ready to accept the differences in living environments.

B. UNDERSTANDING GOVERNMENT POLICY AND RELEVANT LAW

Since the opening of doors to foreign investment in the late 1970ies, the People's Republic of China has made significant progress in putting into place a comprehensive legal framework for conducting international business transactions. This has included not only the promulgation of literally thousands of new domestic laws, regulations, decrees and administrative rules, but also the ratification of numerous international treaties and bilateral agreements by China, dealing with trade and investment matters. For the purpose of promoting foreign trade and investment, China has worked out many preferential policies. One the one hand, these laws and policies regulate the operation of foreign business participants, and they attract and promote foreign trade and investment. On the other hand, they help safeguarding the benefits and rights of foreign business people. Therefore, to have a preliminary understanding of these policies and laws will help the would-be market participants to make good use of them, thus to gain maximum profits and reduce risks to the minimum.

1. RELEVANT LAWS AND REGULATIONS

The laws and regulations concerning foreign economic relations of China cover the subjects of business contracts with foreign elements, foreign trade, foreign direct investment, technology import, international transportation, taxation and finance, industrial property rights, environmental protection, customs, commodity inspection of import and export goods, arbitration and lawsuits. A list of laws is given for reference:

a) Commodity Inspection and Environmental Protection

- Regulations for the Implementation of the Law of the People's Republic of China on Import and Export Commodity Inspection
- Procedures for International Navigation Ships entering and exiting Ports of the People's Republic of China
- Regulations on Establishment of Foreign-funded Import and Export Commodities Inspection and Appraisal Enterprises
- Provisions for Imposing Administrative Penalties concerning the Import and Export Community Inspection of the People's Republic of China
- Provisions for the Exemption of Import and Export Commodities from Inspection
- Law of the People's Republic of China on Import and Export Commodities for Inspection
- Methods on Supervision and Administration of the Quality of Imported Commodities in the Circulation Sector

b) Customs and Taxation

- Announcement of MOFTEC, the State Planning Commission, the State Economic and Trade Commission and the Customs General Administration concerning the Removal of Import Control Measures over Commodities
- Procedures of the Customs of the People's Republic of China on Protection of Intellectual Property Rights
- Regulations of the Customs General Administration of the People's Republic of China on the Management of Agent Declaration Enterprises
- Regulations of the People's Republic of China on the Customs Protection of Intellectual Property Rights

- Law of the People's Republic of China on the Administration of Taxation Collection
- Customs Law of the People's Republic of China
- Customs Regulations of the People's Republic of China of the Control of Luggage and Articles Carried by Chinese Passengers Entering and Leaving the Border
- Circular by the State Administration of relevant Issues concerning the Strengthening of the Collection and Management of Taxes on permanent Representative Office of Foreign Enterprises

c) Finance and Foreign Exchange

- Measures for the Control of Provision of Security to Foreign Parties by Organizations within the People's Republic of China
- Provisional Measures on the Administration of Shadow Margin Account scheme applied on a pilot basis to Imported Materials and Parts Inward Processing
- State Council Regulations for domestically-listed Shares held overseas of Companies Limited by Shares
- Procedures on Foreign Exchange Control in Bonded Areas
- Law of the People's Republic of China on Commercial Banks
- Law of the People's Republic of China on the People's Bank of China
- Guarantee Law of the People's Republic of China
- Insurance Law of the People's Republic of China

d) Foreign Investment

- Regulations on the Examination and Approval of Foreign-funded Enterprises serving as Agents for International Cargo Transport
- Catalogue for the Guiding of Foreign Investment Industries
- Interim Provisions for the Duration of Chinese-Foreign Equity Joint Ventures

- Interim Provisions on Guiding for Foreign Investment
- Law of the People's Republic of China on the Protection of Investment of Taiwan Compatriots
- Provisions on the Establishment of Foreign-Funded Construction Enterprises
- Regulations Concerning the Examination and Approval of International Freight Forwarding Agencies with Foreign Investment
- Detailed Rules of MOFTEC on the Approval and Control of resident Representative Offices of Foreign Enterprises

e) Foreign Trade

- Regulations of the People's Republic of China on the Control of Nuclear Dual-Use Items and Related Technologies Export
- Regulations of the People's Republic of China on the Administration of Controlled Chemicals
- Patent Law of the People's Republic of China
- China Maritime Arbitration Commission Arbitration Rules
- Rules for the Implementation of the Income Tax Law of the People's Republic of China for Enterprises with Foreign Investment and Foreign Enterprises
- Company Law of the People's Republic of China
- Auction Law of the People's Republic of China
- Labor Law of the People's Republic of China

The above laws are only a small portion of laws dealing with foreign business operations. With the appearance of new problems in the practical processes of foreign business participants, new laws and regulations are promulgated to meet any new needs. It may not always be easy to understand these laws immediately; therefore, one may want to entrust a competent lawyer to write a report on possible legal issues that may affect one's business. Of course, once a business is established in China, a legal advisor needs to be consulted regularly.

2. BASIC POLICY ON CHINA'S UTILISATION OF FOREIGN INVESTMENT

a) Macro policy

Before going into the depth of specific foreign economic and trade policy, a bird view of China's macro economic policy might help to understand the general development tendency of foreign trade and economic cooperation. On the basis of such understanding, a sound positioning strategy can be formulated in an early stage of a market entrance decision. The macro economic and trade policy can be explained in six parts:

1) Emphasize overall opening-up, development of trade and economic cooperation along a bi-direction way. Specifically speaking: take fully advantage of internal and global markets, and optimize the resource structure; take part in global competition and strengthen global economic cooperation; implement the opening-up policy of Special Economic Zones, coastal areas and boundary, extend center cities and let these districts influence and promote the development of other districts; continue to enlarge international trade. China wishes to develop trade and economy with all countries of the world on the basis of equality and mutual benefit and to strengthen multi-lateral cooperation with international economic and trade organizations (Sun GuoBin 1997, 8).

2) Emphasize the reform of trade and of the economic system. China uses exchange rates, tariffs, tax and credit to regulate economic activities, and will lower the general level of tariffs and adjust the tariff structure reasonably. China intends to modify the operational mechanism of foreign economic and trade enterprises and let them become self-operational, self-developing, self-regulating and responsible for profits and losses themselves (Sun GuoBin 1997, 11).

3) Emphasize the principle of equality and mutual benefit, and take contracts seriously and abide by them; this is the usual principle of Chinese foreign economy and trade. Try to perfect regulations to ensuring the enforcement of this principle.

4) Emphasize maintaining good quality. Quality is the passport to the global market; therefore, all work should maintain good quality. Try to build up a good reputation in the global market.

5) Implement a comprehensive economic and trade strategy. "Comprehensive economic and trade strategy" refers to integrating

foreign trade, economy and foreign investment. Strengthen the integration of foreign trade and economy and industry, agriculture, technology and commerce; thus: promote foreign economy and trade fulfilling industrialization and globalization (Sun GuoBin 1997, 12).

6) Strengthen the unification and transparency of the policies. In order to ensure the unification of policies, systems and regulations dealing with foreign trade and economy are promulgated and organized to enforce by MOFTEC. This has been authorized by the State Council. Some of the policies should be promulgated by National People's Congress and its Standing Committee, and by the State Council. All laws and regulations, policies and rules are promulgated publicly. Internal policies known only to the government should be sorted out; those that are still valid should be promulgated, thus increasing transparency.

The above listed policies are macro policies serving as an instruction document in the field of foreign trade and economic cooperation. However, these policies do not provide any detailed contents concerning the operation of foreign trade and economic cooperation. Therefore, some of the detailed policies will be explained in the following.

b) Industrial policies

According to information released by the State Planning Commission, by the end of 1996, 50% of the actual amount of foreign investment was concentrated on common processing trade, 30% on tourism, hotels and real estate, 1.5% on agriculture and 1.8% on transportation; infrastructure such as electricity or petroleum held a share of just 10% (Shi YongHai 1996, 20). Such an industrial structure was not compatible with projections for economy and social development.

In June 1995, the Chinese government promulgated "Interim Regulations guiding Foreign Investment" and the "Industrial Catalogue guiding Foreign Investment", which aimed at directing foreign investment into compliance with national industrial planning. The regulations and the catalogue divide industrial projects into four categories: "encouraged, permitted, restricted and prohibited". Foreign investors are *encouraged* to invest in agricultural as well as in high-tech projects, export-oriented high-tech projects in agricultural comprehensive development, and in energy, transportation and crucial raw material industries, and in projects which make full use of the advantages of the Midwest regions. The *restricted* projects refer to those technologies that China has developed or used for a long time, and to production capacity that can meet the demands of the Chinese market. Projects that produce traditional Chinese products are also restricted. Projects that will bring harm to the natural environment will be *forbidden*, and those concerning state security, are unfavorable to the national economy or social development will be firmly forbidden.

The National Planning Committee, the National Economic and Trade Committee and MOFTEC have carried out a revision of the "Industrial Catalogue guiding Foreign Investment" to adopt it to the development of the economy, and have promulgated it on December 31st, 1997. The revision highlighted the industrial focus, complied with the principles of industrial restructuring and introducing advanced technologies, and also embodied the principle of encouraging foreign investment to the Midwest regions (Shi Zhu 1998, 21).

c) Regional policies

Due to factors of geography and policy guidance, the geographical distribution of foreign investment is seen as less than satisfactory. In order to accelerate the development of the central and Western Regions, the state will put more emphasis on the utilization of foreign investment in central and Western Regions, improve the investment environment, enhance its attractiveness to foreign investment, and encourage foreign business people to make investments in that region. Although the economic development of the Midwest regions lag behind that of coastal regions, the Midwest regions have their unique comparative advantages such as 85% of China's land resource, 60% of the total population, 60% of the mineral resources, 70% of coal and 83% of water energy (Shi YongHai 1996, 21).

Currently, the major policies that encourage foreign investment to invest in the Midwest regions are as follows (Shish 1998, 21):

- Selected industries and projects with advantageous effects to the Midwest regions, after being approved by the State Council, can enjoy the policies on encouraged projects in the catalogue. The conditions for market openness and establishment of projects belonging to the restricted category and limited foreign equity can be more flexible than those in eastern areas.

- The domestic loan facilities corresponding to foreign investment in Midwest regions will be increased by an appropriate percentage, while foreign government loans and preferential loans from international financial institutions will be mainly applied to key infrastructure and environmental protection projects in these regions.

- Provinces, autonomous regions and cities listed in the separated planning of the state will enjoy rights to examine and approve foreign investment, as coastal areas do.
- Foreign investors which have made investments in eastern areas are encouraged to invest in Midwest regions. As for projects with foreign investment of over 25%, equal treatments as those for foreign-invested enterprises will be given.
- Pilot projects for opening-up should be carried out both in eastern and Midwest regions concurrently.
- China will enlarge as priority a batch of projects in agriculture, water conservancy, primary energies and environmental protection in Midwest regions, so as to attract more foreign investment and intensify its support in funding and other relevant measures.

According to the "China Economic Information" of 11th May, 2000, giving support to the development of the Midwest will be the focus of State Development Bank in the time to come. The State Developing Bank has established a branch in LanZhou, and the service areas of the branches cover GanSu, QingHai, NingXia in January 2000. On 17th February, 2000, the ChengDu branch of the State Development Bank and the Sichuan Provincial Government reached a package agreement. The agreement stipulated to provide 53 billion Yuan credit to the government, to be put into transportation, telecommunication and water resource projects, in the hi-tech field and in city construction. At the same time, investment projects were formulated, such as the building of eight expressways in the coming 20 years, or 18,000 kilometers of railway construction; generally speaking, projects focus on infrastructure, ecological construction and development of advanced industries as well as on structural adjustment. The formulation of these policy demonstrate the unyielding will of the Chinese government to accelerate the economic development of the Western Regions. With the implementation of those policies, the investment environment will be improving.

In addition to earlier preferential tax policies, the State Council promulgated a notice dealing with reducing tax for foreign invested enterprises on 8th December, 1999. The notice said that the policy will be executed in the Midwest regions, which refers to ShánXi, Inner Mongolia, JiLin, HeiLingJiang, AnHui, JiangXi, HeNan, HuBei, Hunan, ChongQing, Sichuan, GuiZhou, YunNan, XiJiang, NingXia and XiZang. It encouraged industries and projects with foreign investment, listed in the Foreign Investment Guiding Catalogue, and it encouraged advanced industries and projects with foreign investment. The policy stipulates that those fulfilling the above requirements can enjoy an income tax break of 15% for three years after the termination of the current tax policy; the notice entered into effected on 1st January, 2000 (Fang Xiang 2000, 4).

d) Gradual opening of the service sector

According to the actual circumstances, China will gradually and on a trial basis open trade in services related to finance, telecommunication, insurance, foreign trade and airlines. China will reduce its restriction on ten aspects in services trade. These ten aspects are listed as follows:

1) China has canceled the regional restriction to foreign business people investing in the financial field. Foreign financial organs can apply to establish financial organs anywhere in China (Jin Wen 2000, 4). In the meantime, China will gradually extend trial regions and operational scale for overseas financial organs to deal in RenMinBi.

2) In 2000, the Chinese government has licensed four capital insurance companies to run business in China. In the meantime, the open regions will be extended beyond the current ShangHai, GuangZhou, ChongQi, DaLian and TianJin. Hereafter, China will gradually extend the trial regions for foreign capital accession. China will extend the insurance categories that foreign business people are allowed to run, and reduce the restrictions on the shareholding structure.

3) China has promulgated "Interim Measures on the Establishment of Pilot Foreign Commercial Enterprises". The pilot areas expanded to provincial capitals, municipalities directly under the control of the central government, planned cities and Special Economic Zones. In the meantime, BeiJing, TianJin, ShangHai and ChongQi are allowed to run pilot foreign invested wholesale companies (Shi Zhu 1998, 23).

4) Extending the operational scope of holding companies set up by international companies. Holding companies are allowed to sell products within or beyond the border of China on condition that the products are produced by its invested enterprises and allowed to provide after-sales service. The holding companies are allowed to purchase and export the needed products and put into the global network of its parent company directly in China. Holding companies are allowed to set up research and development centers and to provide technical support to the enterprise. The related regulation will be promulgated in due course.

5) The pilot areas and the number of foreign trade companies will be further expanded. At the same time, the investing functions of Joint Venture Trade Companies and the related regulation on establishing such companies will be reconsidered.

6) The pilot of intermediary service companies, such as foreign invested certified public accountants, evaluation organs, legal and consulting companies will be expanded. At present the concerning regulations are being worked out.

7) China will increase the number of foreign invested airline companies.

8) China encourages companies that are rich in capital and technology to cooperate with the powerful big domestic companies in the global market, and to set up project companies; they are encouraged to contract large-scale projects in China or overseas.

9) China will explore and research actively on the openness of the telecommunication market in a systematic way. The detailed steps are: breaking the state monopoly; value-added telecommunication services are chosen as pilot for absorbing foreign capital and extended to basic telecommunication industry gradually; finally permit the flow of foreign capital into the Chinese market.

10) In tourism, "Interim Measures on the Pilot Travel Service Joint Venture" will be enforced quickly; pilot areas and numbers of travel service Joint Ventures will be extended.

Except the above trade, China has decided to study specific measures to extend the openness in the fields of medical care, education, municipal construction and infrastructure (Jin Wen 1999, 5).

e) Preferential policies

The National People's Congress passed the "Income-Tax Law of the PRC for Enterprises with Foreign Investment and Foreign Enterprises" in 1991, and the State Council stipulated the "Rules for the Implementation of the Income Tax Law of the PRC for Enterprises with Foreign Investment and Foreign Enterprises". According to these regulations, various foreign enterprises can enjoy the following preferential tax policies:

- Income tax on foreign-invested enterprises is set at a rate of 30%, and a local income tax rate of 3%; the total is 33%.

- Foreign-invested enterprises established in Special Economic Zones and productive foreign-invested enterprises established in economic and technological development zones enjoy a 15% income tax rate. Enterprises whose income tax may be levied at a reduced rate of 24% include: export-oriented foreign-funded enterprises with production capabilities established in coastal economic open zones or in the urban cities where Special Economic Zones or economic and technological development zones are located (Shi Zhu 1998, 23).

- Enterprises with foreign investment established in coastal economic open zones or in the old urban districts of cities where special economic and technological development zones are located, or in the other places stipulated by the State Council, if the involved industries of these enterprises are energy, transportation, wharf, harbor or the other projects encouraged by state, can enjoy a reduced income tax rate of 15%.

- To these productive foreign invested enterprises scheduled to operate for not less than 10 years shall, from the year in which they start to make profits, be exempted from income tax for the first two years and allowed a 50% reduction for the following three years (Zhang ZhiYong 1997, 24).

- Export-orientated foreign-invested enterprises can, after the termination of exemption and reduction periods according to tax regulations, enjoy a income tax cut of 50% from the regulated tax rate, if the export value reached 70% of the total productive volume of that year.

- Any foreign investment that directly reinvests its share of profits obtained from the foreign-funded enterprises into that firm to increase its capital, or uses the profit as capital to set up other foreign-funded enterprises for not less than five years of operation shall, upon approval by tax authorities of an application filed by the investors, be refunded 40% of the income tax already paid on the reinvested amount.

Foreign invested enterprises, if they import materials with foreign capital or additional investment to fulfill ratified contracts, are exempted of tariffs and import stage value added tax and commercial tax on imports, if they meet the following requirements:

- They import advanced machinery, equipment and materials not available domestically for installing and affixing the machines and for building workshops.
- They import machinery, equipment and materials directly needed for the prospecting and exploration of oceanic petroleum co-operative development projects, as well as spare parts and materials needed for making machinery and equipment needed for oceanic petroleum exploration and production.

f) Application of national treatment to foreign invested enterprises

It is a fundamental policy of China's absorption of foreign investment to apply national treatment to foreign invested enterprises. At the early stage of reform and opening-up, China's domestic economic operation system, enterprise management, production management, material supply and salary systems were different from those abroad, due to the long-term planned economy. At that time, in order to facilitate the smooth establishment and development of foreign invested companies, the Chinese government adopted policies for foreign invested companies which were preferential and different from those for domestic enterprises. As a method of attracting foreign capital, these policies were quite necessary.

In recent years, however, with the improvement of the investment environment and the maturing of market regulations, which brought about improved self-control ability of the market participant, better self-balance ability of the market when supply and demand is not in balance, and relevant laws and regulations which control the behavior of market participants, some new issues appeared: "Should foreign enterprises be put in a different status from domestic enterprises, and should they enjoy preferential polices? What is the fundamental way to attract foreign investment, other than by using preferential policies?" After studying the questions comprehensively, many experts point out, that the policy of attracting foreign capital should change from preferential policy to improving investment environment and opening the potential enormous market (Huang KeAn 1998, 15).

For example, strengthening infrastructure construction, perfecting the legal system and providing legal insurance, perfecting the employment system and extending information channels were seen as appropriate means. Therefore, under the current circumstances, some tariffs were to be adjusted as well as income tax policies and fee charging standards, thus making the treatment for domestic and foreign investment enterprises more uniform. This is one aspect of national treatment of foreign enterprises. Another aspect was seen in improving treatment in areas were foreign enterprises were given lower standards than domestic enterprises: higher charges will be cut down, and preferential policies for domestic enterprises will be given to foreign enterprises, too. Therefore, it can be seen that the adjustments are oriented in both directions; the aim is to treat foreign enterprises like national ones. To apply national treatments for domestic and foreign investment companies was seen as means to enable fair competition between foreign invested enterprises and domestic ones.

3. CHINA'S FOREIGN TRADE POLICY

The foreign trade policy of China can be illustrated in the following aspects:

- To keep the *general balance between import and export* is the basic foreign trade policy of China. The purpose of expansion of export is to import a) advanced technologies and equipment which is necessary for the economic construction, b) material assets to make up for domestic shortages, and c) consumption goods which meet the needs of people's living. In order to keep import and export in balance, China adopts active measurements to expand export, rather than passive methods to reduce imports (Liu Xiang-Dong 1998,151).

- China encourages domestic enterprises to raise the processing depth, precision, quality and grade of export goods. To improve the structure of export goods, to promote the export of finely process finished goods rather than roughly process finished goods, and to increase the exports of high value-added products are the policies towards export goods. Enterprises are encouraged to adapt to trends of global trade, take fully advantage of labor resources, natural resources and technology, and to increase the variety of export goods, as well as to develop export of processed or improved material and assembled parts supplied by clients (Liu XiangDong 1998, 66).

- China adopts policies to encourage export and promote growth of export trade. For example: perfecting the export rebate system, setting up export goods development funds and risks fund, subsidizing goods whose global price fluctuate greatly, setting up a State Import and Export Bank, thus providing credit support and risk guaranties for capital and goods export.

- On condition that export creates foreign exchange, a certain amount of foreign exchange reserve is kept. China actively expands import based on the principle of import and export balance. The focus of China's import lies in: advanced technology, equipment, crucial parts and raw materials that are in shortage in the domestic market (Hou GuiSheng 2000, 177). Furthermore, the objective is enforce necessary quotas and control a limited number of important import commodities with licenses, as well as, according to the international practice, to adopt trade protection measurements to infant industries. China does not advocate protectionism; the market of China is open to countries all over the world. If the foreign products conform to the industrial policy guidance and possess competitive force, then they are to have access to the Chinese market.

- China conducts macro-regulation and the principle of free operation to import and export trade. China encourages to establish integrated companies to manage goods concerning state plans and people's living, strategic resources, monopolized goods in the global market and goods possessing leading position in the global market.

- China emphasizes adopting various ways to do trade: expanding spot trade, barter trade, carrying trade, leasing trade, multinational trade and frontier trade are encouraged.

- Perfecting foreign trade operations coordinating service systems, as well as giving full play to coordinating, guiding and consulting functions is the work that the Import and Export Commercial Association deals with. The Import and Export Commercial Association is a trade self-regulating organ; its major responsibilities are: to safeguard foreign trade operational order, to organize response to anti-dumping filings, to provide information and consulting services to member enterprises, to reflect the demands and opinions of enterprises to the government, and to put forward proposals to the government to help formulating policies; to supervise and guide enterprises to function according to law; to organize the operation of import and export goods quota bidding according to the authorization of the government in charge; to conduct economic punishment to the enterprises which violate the coordinating decisions of the commercial association or to put forward other punishment proposals to the department in charge.

Conclusion: the above laws and policies are at the macro-level of the foreign trade and economic cooperation policies system. One might think it is not detailed enough to serve as a guide in practice. One should not worry too much about this: when one decides to choose a particular field, one will find dozens of special policies, and one will be guided by these policies within the larger field of economic cooperation and trade. It is therefore advisable to position oneself in the market with a clear focus.

C. INVESTIGATING THE INVESTMENT AND TRADE ENVIRONMENT

Investigating the investment environment is a stage that every investor has to experience, for its decisive role in investment success. The aim of investigating the investment environment is to assess the advantages and disadvantages, and thus to form a judgment about how soon and how much return on investment can be expected, and about the associated risks. Then the question is: what is "investment environment"? Investment environment is a broad concept; every factor that influences the operation of an investment can be regarded as part of the investment environment. The whole social system, economic state and cultural characteristics are a portion of the investment environment. All the issues that have been discussed in earlier chapters belongs to the scope of investment environment. To be specifically, they are the soft side of the environment. On the other side, infrastructure, communication, transportation, natural resources, energy and so on can be defined as hard factors of the environment. Hard factors of the environment relate directly with investment activities and are imperative for the operation of an investment.

In the study of the investment environment, the soft environment is considered more and more important since the representatives of new productive capacity are less sensitive towards the material environment but more sensitive towards soft environment, such as knowledge, culture and so forth. In spite of the extreme importance of soft environment, people often still do not recognize it. Therefore, raising the recognition level of soft environment has become an issue of study. A new concept has been developed which is called "system environment" (Zhang ChuenFu 1998, 9). Here, system refers to a series of customs and regulations. Investment activities and decisions are restricted within the framework of this series of customs and regulations; it is referred to as "system environment".

As many aspects of the soft environment have been discussed in earlier chapters, this chapter will look at regional investment environments to illustrate this issue of investment environment. Regional investment environments will answer the question of which region and area the investment should be put into, thus ensuring maximum profits. China is in an unbalanced development state; therefore for the purpose of adjusting the imbalance of the economic state, economists usually divide China into three regions. In implementing economic policies, different policies are adopted to ensure balanced development. Therefore, three parts, namely the Eastern Region, the Middle Region and the Western Region will be used here as space basis to the investigate the investment environment. Furthermore, special economic districts such as Special Economic Zones, Bonded Areas and Hi-Tech Development Zones will be addressed separately in the following discussion.

1. EASTERN REGION

The Eastern coastal area is the most developed region in China in terms of economy and culture. The investment environment is quite different from the middle and Western Regions. An illustration will be given to explain the advantages and disadvantages of the investment environment of the Eastern Region.

The Eastern Region includes 12 provinces: LiaoNing, HeBei, TianJin, BeiJing, ShanDong, JiangSu, ShangHai, ZheJiang, FuJian, GuangXi, GuangDong, HaiNan. These provinces have several advantages compared with Midwest regions.

1) Natural geographical environment: the cultivated land of Eastern Regions accounts for 31% of the overall cultivated land of China. This region has broad plain, damp and fertilized soil, abundant rainfall and many rivers flaw in the regions. Such natural conditions create opportunities for developing agriculture (Xiu FengaXian 1999, 26).

2) Resources: there are rich oil and iron mines in the Eastern Region. Human resources account for 40% of the total number of China. Furthermore, the quality of labor is high, the average education length is 10.8 years, among them 18% are technical talent (Xiu FengXian 1999, 34).

3) Social economy and technology: The Eastern Region is near the sea and also close to the lower reaches of rivers; it has a long history of commercial ports. Judging from the evolution of society, China's commodity economy has developed from east to west and from coastal regions to the inland. Therefore, the eastern area has a long history and awareness of developing a commodity economy. The technical forces concentrate on the Eastern Region. Many culture, education and technology centers are located here. According to statistics, research and development staff working for governmental natural science and technology research and development organs are 557,001, which makes up 54.1% of the national total number (Zhou DianKun 1998, 171). In 1993, nationwide urbanization was 33%, while the Eastern Region was as high as 41%.

4) Infrastructure and completed set: Post and communication, transportation and education of the Eastern Region is at a relatively higher level compared with the other two regions. The total length of railways in Chinese was 54,360 kilometers in 1995, or 0.45 kilometers per person. The Eastern area provided 1.8 kilometers per capita, much more than at the national level. The density of the national highway network is 120.5 kilometers per 10,000 square kilometers, while the Eastern area's is 5,820 kilometers. These two sets of data are examples to show that the Eastern area has advantages in transportation, in railway, highway, cargo and sea transportation. Furthermore, the Eastern area is much more advanced in post and communication (Zhou DianKun 1998, 105). In terms of education level, most parts of the Eastern Region have commonly enforced nine year compulsory education, while in some poverty-stricken Western areas, children can not afford to go to school.

5) Policy and law: since the Eastern coastal area opened earlier to the outside world, they enjoyed earlier the preferential policies which have been discussed in earlier chapters. Over time, the Eastern area has established and perfected a series of laws administrating the operation of foreign investment. Relatively speaking, the Eastern area is very experienced in introducing, attracting and regulating foreign investment.

6) Social service environment: on account of the high urbanization level of the Eastern Region, better information services and public services are available for foreign investment. Furthermore, because of high-level labor force, work efficiency is higher than in the Midwest region.

7) Capital: the income of Eastern and Midwest regions vary greatly. The province with the highest income is GuangDong, 8,562 Yuan per capita per year on average. The lowest is GanSu, which is 3,597 Yuan per capita. The gap is 2.38 times. High income of the Eastern Region and high investment are interrelated. The investment ratio of the Eastern Region is 2.98 times that of the more backward Western Region; the Eastern area has attracted 86% of all foreign investment in China (Xiu FengXian 1999, 111).

Apart from these advantages, the Eastern Region has disadvantages in investment environment, such as: high population density which causes high employment pressure, especially in rural areas. Since large cities concentrate on eastern areas, people rush to these cities to seek opportunities, leading to high land price, house shortage, traffic jams and deterioration of public order. Some other disadvantages such as water shortages or the mixture of old and new industries will not be studied here explicitly.

Having perceived the strengths and weakness of the investment environment, the Chinese government is determined to improve the current situation through adjusting industrial structure and developing medium and small cities. The developing direction of the Eastern Region is to push technical-centralized and capital-intensive industries to be the leading industries of the region. On the other hand, a policy of restricting the development of energy and raw-material consuming and low-tech industries is adopted.

The above discussion of the investment environment has its scope within China. Its aim was to provide a basis of comparison between regions of China. To put this into a broader perspective, some information will be provided about differences between China and other parts of Asia. The most commonly used standard internationally to describe investment environments includes the following aspects (Zhang ChunFu 1998, 54):

- degree of currency stability
- current yearly inflation ratio
- degree of political stability
- ownership ratio allowed to foreign investment
- local capital supply ability
- difference in treatment and control between foreign and local enterprises
- attitude towards tariff protection

If the above standards were used to evaluate the investment environment of China's Eastern Region, then there is a big gap between developed countries in Asia and China. A qualified analysis is too complex to be done here, thus the result of the gap will be used to explain the issue: China attracts less foreign investment than Singapore, Indonesia and Korea. Several reasons might contribute to such gap:

Firstly, economic environment: China has just been freed from a completely centralized planned economy, and the level of market development is relatively lower than these countries. For example, SOE's still do not participate in the competition of the market completely. The interference and control of government over enterprises' operations is relatively mighty. *Secondly*, foreign investment and service: China's management and services provided to foreign enterprises is seen by many as inadequate and low in efficiency. Complicated procedures in approval and examination as well as bureaucratic behavior commonly exist. *Thirdly*, the legal construction is incomplete. There are some part of law in China that do not conform to international business practice, and this tends to handicap the interests of investors.

Through such analysis, the conclusion is: there is still room to improve the investment environment of the Eastern area, even if it is comparatively good in China.

2. MIDDLE REGION

The term "Middle Region" refers to eight provinces and one autonomous region. They are HeiLingJiang, JiLin, ShanXi, HeNan, HuBei, AnHui HuNan, JiangXi provinces and the Inner Mongolian autonomous region. The Middle Region is located the between Eastern coastal region and the Western inland region. The economic development level, population and land resources also lie in the middle level: higher than the Western, lower than the Eastern Region. In light of the geographic position and the important function of the Middle Region in communication between the eastern and the Western Region, the analysis of the Middle Region's investment environment will focus on the economic growth potential and social environment of this region.

Although the economic development of the Middle Region is less favorable than that of the Eastern Region, the market potential, development potential and resources reserves are promising, which might ensure a long-term benefit to investors. The Middle Region takes up 35% of the total population and has kept a 11% growth rate, which is much higher than Eastern Region. The huge population might exert great influence on the market potential. The income of the inhabitants of the Middle Region is lower than that of those in the eastern and Western Regions. The income per capita in urban areas in the eastern, middle and Western Region is 6267, 4484 and 4318 Yuan respectively (Xiu FengXian 1999, 111). Although the income level is low, the consuming tendency is stronger than in the two other regions. Therefore, with the development of economy, the market potential of the Middle Region will probably attract the more investors in the future.

China has put effort in large scale development construction in the Middle Region, put large amounts of capital in energy and mineral exploration, as well as in automobile, chemical and textile industries. Because of system and policy constraints, these investments did not produce the expected profits. But now, with market mechanisms being set up, loose policy control by the central government, and appropriate capital input, the large amounts of invested capital are expected to show positive effects. In terms of human resources as well as research and development capacity, the Middle Region demonstrates a medium development level, but in the mean time, it has demonstrated a good potential.

The Middle Region has thirteen kinds of mineral resources; its resources account for 40% of the national total. The cultivated land is 40% of the total area of China. The agricultural production capacity is low, therefore the potential for developing it is high (Zhang DunHou 1998, 68). The formation category and the development value of the Middle Region bring advantages to the agricultural and industrial development of the region.

In general, the Middle Region demonstrates high economic development potential, if appropriate policies are adopted, economic growth can be obtained, and if the region will create a favorable investment environment for investors where long-term profits can be expected.

Since the opening of China, the economic policy has given advantages to the development of Western coastal regions. Many preferential policies have guaranteed capital, resources and labor flowing into the region. The Middle Region has suffered from a comparatively slow developing speed. Furthermore, as a result of a chain reaction, in the part of management, market structure, wage system, personnel system and policy opening, there is much room for improvement to reach advanced and flexible standards. In addition, the degree of openness of the Middle Region is low, accounting for only 10% of the total foreign capital invested in China in 1995 (Xiu FengXian 1999, 65).

The people of the Western Region have deep-rooted concepts; they tend to lack commercial awareness. Critics say that old management ideas and methods as well as old attitudes towards labor and allocation are still in people's mind. Therefore, when new ideas and system are introduced, people tend to express strong resistance. In summary, the social environment is less favorable, and improvement is imperative. The general assessment of the investment environment of the Middle Region is: currently it appears to be less attractive; at the same time, development prospects are promising.

3. WESTERN REGION

The term "Western Region" refers to eight provinces, one municipality and one autonomous region, which are ShanXi, NingXia, GanSu, QingHai, XinJiang and GuiZhou provinces; ChongQing municipality directly under the control of central government, and XiZang autonomous region. The Western Region is an under-developed region in China. But now, the development of the Western Region is becoming a hot issue of the national economy. The

Chinese government has noticed the disadvantage of imbalanced regional economic development and formulated policies to attract investment to the Western Region. The Western Region also has some advantages in its investment environment.

- Firstly, the Western Region has rich mineral resources. Rare earth metal, mercury, titanium, platinum, magnesium potassium and asbestos accounts for 90% of the total reserves of China. Zinc, tin, vanadium, barite and natural gas take 60% to 80% of the total (Duping 2000, 145).
- Secondly, the energy industry has a great potential to develop in the Western Region. Coal reserves in the Western Region accounts for 57% of China's total. Rich water resources and petroleum resources are other advantage of the Western Region.
- Thirdly, the Western Region has extensive areas that were not polluted, which provide a good environment for the development of some special industries. For example, electronics and the astronaut industry. XiChang satellite launch center is being commercialized and has contracted the launch of business satellites of other countries. The development of this special industry functioned very well in promoting the development of the regional economy. The development of the electronics industry of ShangXi, SiShuan and GuiZhou provinces is also attributed to the local natural environment. In general, the special environment of the Western Region contributes to the formation of corresponding industries; these industries have helped to improve the regional investment environment.
- Fourthly, the Western Region is rich of tourism resources. The highest mountain of the world, the Himalayan, is located in Tibet. The beautiful mountains and lakes make Tibet a dream tourism site. Buddhism prevails in Tibet, and the 2,700 temples form a splendid unique cultural atmosphere in Tibet. The unique culture, customs and art have for a long time been a tourist attraction. Guangxi and YuNan are famous for their beautiful natural scene; GanSu and ShanXi are the hometowns of historical sites. The prairie of QingHai and Inner Mongolia attract those who appreciate the wonders of nature (Duping 2000, 114). In summary, the Western Region is a good place for developing tourism industry. It is definitely a positive aspect in the overall investment environment of the Western Region.

These above stated four advantages can be regarded as the hardware of investment in China's West. Certainly, the boundary trade of the Western Region with neighboring countries provide enormous markets for the Western Region. For example, Korea, Mongolia, Pakistan and India are direct trade partners. The market amounts to 0.1 billion Yuan. The twelve border countries which have a total of 1.4 billion inhabitants are the target of China's border trade.

From the above analysis it can be seen that the Western Region has an enormous development potential and market room. With the support of the state policy and the renewal of people's commercial awareness, the Western Region might be an ideal place to invest if one is prepared to do a long-term investment.

Apart from the advantages, as the most backward region in China, the negative parts of the investment environment can not be neglected. Currently, the economic basis of the region is rather poor, with industry output representing only 8% of the China's total, and low income and consuming levels. As a consequence, transportation, post and telecommunication is at a low development stage and development has a long way to go considering the 22% urban population in the region (Zhou DianKun 1998, 106). The low knowledge and educational level of the people is also one of the disadvantages of the Western Region. In addition, most of the Western Region is inhabited by minority nationalities; this can cause language problems. Furthermore, the interests of the minority nationalities should be taken into consideration when economic policy is enforced. This makes the investment environment more complicated than in other regions.

According to China's policy concerning the development of the Western Region, the focus will be on three aspects. The first is infrastructure construction which includes highway, railway, airport, telecommunication networks and so on. The second is ecological construction. The third is developing advanced industries and adjusting the industrial structure (DuPing 2000, 110-111). It can be concluded that, with the launching of infrastructure construction, the investment environment will improve.

4. SPECIAL ECONOMIC ZONES AND BONDED AREAS

Special Economic Zones are the earliest export-oriented economic areas that have opened to the outside world. They are designated by the state and given special policies to develop global economic and technical exchange and export-oriented economy. China's Special Economic Zones also serve the purpose of "opening the window", as base for opening-up of the country and trial basis of reform (Zhou WenZhang 1997, 17).

The SEZ of China have four features: Firstly, the major capital comes from foreign countries. The economic activities are regulated by market mechanism. Secondly, foreign enterprises are the major force in SEZ, and some in SOE, collective and private enterprises are included. The commodities produced in SEZ are export-oriented. Thirdly, preferential policies are granted on income tax. The procedures of import and export have been simplified, so that it is convenient for foreign business people to come. Fourthly, SEZ enjoy larger decision-making power and project examination and approval rights in foreign-related economic activity (Zhang DunHou 1998, 84).

There are five SEZ in China, namely ShenZhen, ZhuHai, ShanTou, XiaMen and HaiNan (Zhou WenZhang 1997, 7). From 1980 to 2000, after 20 years of construction, SEZ have formed an investment environment that ensures low risk, many development opportunities and good operational conditions. They have become an attractive investment choice in Eastern Asia. Twenty years of large-scale capital input in infrastructure construction have helped SEZ to improve municipality administration facilities, transportation and telecommunication networks, electricity and water supply facilities, commercial buildings and residential buildings construction and the corresponding facilities. These are the hardware of SEZ investment environment.

SEZ, like other areas in China, enjoy stable, long-term opening-up policies. In the area of legal environment, other than benefiting from the nation-wide legal environment which try to safeguard the benefits of foreign investors, local legislative power has been granted to SEZ. GuangDong and FuJian were authorized special legislative power to draw up their own economic laws and regulations to govern themselves. In addition, every SEZ was empowered to formulate rules and regulations dealing with foreign investment (Luo MuSheng 1999, 29-31). This increased the adaptability and flexibility of the related rules and regulations. In the aspect of international conventions, China has made great progress. China has signed double taxation agreements with countries including the United States, Japan, the UK and France. In the mean time, China has signed mutual promotion and investment protection agreements with Belgium, Finland, France, German, Japan , Norway, Romania, Sweden and the United States. In 1993, China joined the "Bern convention" which aims to protect intellectual property. Although good progress has been made in legal construction, there is still room left to improve the legal environment.

Foreign enterprises in SEZ enjoy self-governing power; the foreign enterprises can operate the enterprises in accordance with international conventions without being bound by China's current business management systems. Foreign enterprises can decide the organs that need to be established, the personnel arrangement, the recruiting, firing and rewarding and so forth.

Foreign enterprises also can formulate their salary standard and form. Foreign enterprises can draw up production, purchase and sales plan themselves within the limitation of contracts. Foreign enterprises have also been authorized to formulated price policies themselves (Luo MuSheng 1999, 32-35).

In general, the investment environment of SEZ is relatively good in both the hard and soft environment. Nevertheless, in order to meet the needs of unceasing development, the improvement of the investment environment must be conducted continuously according to the needs of the economic development.

A "Bonded Area" is a kind of new opening-up district in China. It is a closed comprehensive opening-up area supervised by customs. It is normally set up in a harbor or an inland port that is convenient for communication and trade. China's bonded areas resemble the free harbor and free trade zones of foreign countries (Lin QiHui 1993, 170). China has set up bonded area in the 1990ies; there are now fifteen Bonded areas: TianJin port, ShenZhen FuTian and ShaTouJiao.

China's bonded areas are located in coastal harbor cities, inland ports and inland river harbors which are near to the sea. On the one hand, they have convenient transportation conditions, good regional positions and social economic environments. These conditions will give them advantages in attracting foreign capital and developing foreign trade. On the other hand, bonded areas are small; the smallest one is ShenZhen – ShaTouJiao bonded area, which is only 0.2 square kilometers (Luo MuSheng 1999, 18). The largest one is ShangHai – WaiGaoQiao, which is 10 square kilometers (Gu YuMin 1994, 177). Small areas can easily being separated from surrounding areas, and it is easy to create a fully-separated investment environment.

China's bonded area started rather late, but large amounts of capital have been invested in the small areas to conduct land exploration and infrastructure construction. In a short time, customs, storage and transportation conditions were set up. The construction level of the infrastructure is higher than in SEZ and some economic development zones. Each bonded area has its own character. For example, TianJin port focuses on foreign trade, ShenZhen ShaTouJiao focuses on processing export (Gu YuMin 1994, 76). The program of these bonded areas follow strict principles. For example, ShangHai WaiGaoQiao is divided in five small districts: berth district, bonded storage district, management center and trade district, export processing district and life service district. Generally speaking, the "hard" environment of the bonded area is favorable for investment.

As to "soft" environment, China's central government departments and local governments pay great attention to legal construction. More than ten managerial regulations have been formulated, such as “ShangHai WaiGaoQiao bonded area management method”, “provisional management regulations on ShenZhen FuTian bonded area” and so on. These regulations guide the operation of bonded areas legally.

A series of preferential policies has been promulgated in order to attract foreign capital and run the bonded areas smoothly. These policies are the following (Lin QiHui 1993, 175-178):

- Goods can be imported and exported freely in bonded areas, import and export licenses are not required. Import and export tariffs do not apply.
- The sale of goods of bonded area to a non-bonded area is treated as export. The sale of goods of non-bonded area into a bonded area is treated as import.
- Trade between enterprises of bonded areas conduct protective duty. If the products are sold within the bonded area, production industrial and commercial unified tax does not apply.
- The production in productive enterprises of bonded areas is exclusively for export.
- Productive enterprises enjoy a preferential tax policy.
- A storage warehouse can be built after being ratified by customs.
- Trade companies can be set up. They can act on behalf of enterprises in the bonded areas; they can import raw material and spare parts
- Joint Venture financial enterprises can be set up in bonded area, foreign exchange current accounts can be opened and operate in foreign exchange; an excess of earnings after tax will be given to the enterprises within five years since after it occurred.
- Insurance and other service organs are allowed to be established.
- Business people can entry and exit bonded area freely.

The above policy guide the management of bonded areas and lead the work of attracting foreign capital has a rule to follow. Furthermore, many preferential policies are unique and it increased the attraction of bonded area, raise operational efficiency and the competitive force of the enterprises in the global market. The general comment on the investment environment of bonded area is positive by comparison with the general level of China.

5. HI-TECH DEVELOPMENT ZONES

China has established the first hi-tech development zone in 5th August, 1998: the Beijing hi-tech development pilot zone. Until the end of 1992, 52 national level development zone were established, 120 district hi-tech zones were established (Yu ZhiSong 1995, 39). Although the construction of development zones started rather late, it developed rapidly. Now it has advanced into developing stage. In terms of area, population, output, income, profit tax and export amount, some of the development zones have developed well and become the research, development and production basis of hi-tech products.

Hi-tech development zones are equipped with the following characteristics, forming the investment environment of hi-tech development zones:

- The "hard" investment environment is rather developed, similar to SEZ and bonded areas. The infrastructure which includes communication, electricity, gas and central heating supply, factory buildings and facilities have reached a certain standard. Most of the development zones started with the formation of the "hard" environment, e.g. ShangHai and NanJing development zones. Their infrastructure is developed according to a unified plan and unified construction, thus ensuring a relatively high standard and comparatively good quality. In fact, compared to traditional industry, hi-tech does not emphasize on hard environment. What plays a crucial function in development zones is the soft environment.

- The "soft" environment is in initial stage. China has a certain scientific and technological power and many technical staff who are well-educated and some talent people are concentrated in development zones. For example, BeiJing development zones has 138 scientific and research organs, which are part of the China Academy of Sciences, the State Council and Beijing municipality, as well as 269 organs which are a part of 50 colleges and universities. Scientific and technological staff approximately reached 80,000. Enterprises and advanced managerial talent have been trained in the development zones. This human capital formed the original driving force for attracting internal and external capital.

Other than these favorable aspects, there are unfavorable conditions in development zones, such as: low capital investment, low transfer rate of research achievements to products, low globalization. In general, China's hi-tech development zones are undergoing a maturing process.

6. OPENING STRUCTURE

Since much has been discussed about the investment environment of different regions of China, it might be helpful to introduce a new concept to help understand the reasons of the disparity between the investment environments. That is: the opening structure. Opening structure itself is complicated system. It is formed by six sub-systems, and each sub-system is composed of various factors.

The opening country structure determines which country China will open to. The opening regional structure refers to which district China will open to the outside. As to opening industry structure, it refers to what industry should be opened. Opening orientation structure deals with the import and export of the opening contents: if the total import is more than the export, then it is import absorption structure. In the reverse situation, it is external extension opening (Li HaiJian 1999, 4).

From the structure graphic it can be seen that what has been discussed earlier belongs to the regional structure of opening. Data shows that China has an imbalanced regional structure of opening, with the Eastern Region in the top and the Western Region in the bottom. In order to adjust this situation, China has adopted a strategy which is called "point, line and area opening policy".

- *Point policy* refers to opening the central cities of the Western Region. For example, XiAn and WuLuMuQi function as the central cities of the Northwest region, whereas ChongQing and ChengDu are the central cities of the Southwest region. These four cities can establish boundary SEZ on a pilot basis. The opening regions of the Northwest focus on the "Muslim economic circle" and extend to the "European economic circle". In later stage, the opening objectives of the Southwest will be the "Indochina economic circle" and extend to African countries later on.

- *Line opening policy* means setting up new opening points along the main line of communication, or open up the original central cities that are located along the main communication-line. There are the JingGuang railway across south and north, as well as the Yangtze River and LongHai and LanXin railways across north and east in the Middle Region. Therefore, open the cities along these communication-lines is the first step, and then opening the cities along the Yangtze River will follow. In April 1990, ShangHai Pu-

Dong new district opened, which is at the lower reaches of Yangtze River. The strategy is to drive the economy engine of the cities at the middle and upper reaches through the opening of the lower reaches, such as WuHan, which is a Middle Region city, and ChongQing, which is a Western Region city. The general comment is that the line opening policy functions better than the point opening policy in terms of promoting the economic growth (Li HaiJian 1999, 101).

- Towards the Eastern Region, the *area opening policy* is adopted. The Eastern Region can be divided into three strategically associated areas. One takes BoHai rim as center, including LiaoNing, HeBei, TianJin and ShanDong provinces, which is called northern associate area. The opening cities of this area mainly are the "Northeast economic circle" and extend to "North-American economic circle". The other area take Yangtze delta as center, including ShangHai, JiangSu, ZheJiang provinces which are referred to middle associate area. The trading and cooperation partners mainly come from the "Asia-Pacific economic circle" and extend to the "North-American economic circle". The third one is called south associate area, which takes ZhuJiang delta and Min-Nan delta as center, covering GuangDong, HaiNan and FuJian provinces. The business partner focus on the "Chinese economic circle" and export to expand to South-American countries.

The above stated opening strategy is being implemented. As a sub-system of the overall opening structure, it is closely related to other structures, thus when studying the opening structure, the relationships of each sub-system and how they interact with each other should be analyzed. But as a complicated new concept, the opening structure theory will not been studied in depth. It should only serve as supplementary material to understanding the investment environment.

SEZ, bonded areas, open cities and hi-tech development zones can fit in very well in the opening level structure. Bonded areas stand at the highest level, followed by SEZ. On third to tenth place are economic and technological development zones; coastal open cities, coastal economic open zones at city or county level, open cities along the rivers; boundary open cities (at city, county and township level), provincial capital opening cities; hi-tech industry development zones; national tourism and holiday areas (Li HaiJian 1999, 166).

A list of open areas will be given in the appendix to illustrate the opening level structure.

7. CONCLUSION

In this chapter, the investment environment of different regions and special economic development zones has been discussed. Actually, it is not a comprehensive study in depth and width, but it serves the function of introducing basic knowledge of China's investment environment. One more thing that is worth mentioning here is: the study of China's investment environment is in its infant stage, since investment is a relatively new concept, compared to other countries. But it can be assumed that, with the deepening of China's reform, more practical experience will be accumulated to promote the development of this field of study.

D. CHOOSING THE FORM AND AREA OF INVOLVEMENT

Considering the diversity of areas and the forms of being involved into the Chinese market, the foreign business person might be eager to know which form and which area can ensure the best future. This chapter is aimed at analyzing the forms and areas in terms of their developing state and their respective advantages and disadvantages so as to guide the foreign business person in the decision-making process.

1. A DISSCUSSION OF CLOSELY RELATED ISSUES

There are two main categories of doing business in China, one is *trade* and the other is *investment*. Within the scope of trade, there are various subcategories; various trade patterns exist (Jiang ZhuYan 1999, 161). Foreign investment includes Equity Joint Ventures, Sino-foreign cooperation, Wholly-Foreign Owned Ventures, Holding Companies and Cooperative Exploration (Wang LuoLin 1998, 5). During twenty years development period from 1979 to 1999, the Chinese authorities have embarked upon a series of ambitious reforms, covering not only foreign direct investment policy and the foreign trade system, but also the foreign exchange system and the taxation system. These reforms inevitably will have effects upon future flows of trade and direct investment. Therefore, an introduction of such reforms is imperative before further explanations of various trade and investment forms are given.

a) Reform of the foreign trade system

The traditional objective of foreign trade planning in China was to establish which essential materials and commodities were in short supply domestically and thus needed to be imported, and then to arrange for suitable quantities of selected exports to be produced in order to generate the necessary foreign exchange to fund these imports. Furthermore, at the beginning of the open-door policy in 1979, foreign trade was monopolized by twelve national foreign trade corporations (FTC) and their branches (Foster 1998, 97). Then, China experienced the first stage of the foreign trade system reform in 1984. The foreign trade system was considerably decentralized, when each province, autonomous region and Special Economic Zones established trade ports, and the branches of each FTC were permitted to operate as independent bodies. By the end of 1987, 300 enterprise were given foreign trade operation rights. All foreign invested enterprises enjoy self-operation trade rights (Liu XiangDong 1998, 223).

From 1988 to 1990, China enforced a contract system between MOFTEC and the FTC's, under which targets were given to each FTC for foreign exchange earnings. The amounts of foreign exchange earnings were to be remitted to the Central Government, and the export earnings or loss indicator could not be changed for three years. Because of the shortcomings in the system, it caused numerous disorders in the operation process of foreign trade. Since then, China went into the next stage of reforming its foreign trade system, that is, adopting the system of individual responsibility for profits and losses. During this period, the state canceled fiscal subsidies to export goods, the exchange rate was adjusted, the foreign exchange remittance ratio increased. In 1992, China has set a target of establishing a "socialist market economy", and the reform of China's foreign trade system also saw a significant movement: import duty rates were lowered on more than 3,600 tax items on two occasions (Wu YanGuang 1999, 29).

The new Foreign Trade Law of the People's Republic of China, which was promulgated on 12th May, 1994 which came into effect on 1st July, 1994, was a very significant piece of legislation: it ended mandatory planning for all trade enterprises. The new foreign trade system advocated a single exchange rate for the RMB. Furthermore, the measures included abolishing retained foreign exchange, the obligation on foreign trade enterprises to hand over foreign exchange, the system of settling and selling of foreign exchange and mobilizing enterprises' enthusiasm to export goods (Liu XiangDong 1998, 231). The law also abolished various foreign trade subsidies, and explicitly stipulated that managers should take responsibility for their own profits and losses. Each managers who is engaged in the import and export of goods or technology must be approved by the appropriate State Council department. Otherwise, trade must be undertaken through authorized foreign trade managers. Through the promulgation of the law, the contractual responsibility system was replaced by a tax system, and export refunds, risk funds and specialized financial institutions were introduced to help the exporters expand export in a legal and safe way (Foster 1998, 47).

One vital measurement in the series of reforms was the reduction of tariffs. China has lowered its import-duty rates four times since 1992. The average rate has been lowered from 43% to the currently 17%, and will be lowered to 15% in 2000 and 10% in 2005. At present, China practices a license management on 37 tax items. In 2005, China wants to abolish non-tariff measures (Wu Yan-Guang 1999, 29).

Through a series of reforms, China's foreign trade system has changed fundamentally and has begun conforming to the global standard. Nevertheless, there is still gap between the requirements of free trade and the China's foreign trade system. The system states: to enforce a foreign trade system unitarily, ensuring its transparency, granting imported goods national treatment, to guarantee free foreign trade operational rights, to lower tariffs and abolish non-tariff measures. Therefore, there is still substantial room for improvement of the current trade system in terms of the operational system and macro-management.

b) Development of the current foreign exchange regime

China's foreign exchange regime has gone through three stages. From 1951 to 1979, a rigid regime featuring centrally planned income and expenditure was practiced; from 1979 to 1994, the planning and market forces were integrated, and the system of foreign exchange retention and turning over to the State was still practiced. On 1st January, 1994, the regime has developed into a market regulated stage, with the system of buying and purchasing Forex (foreign exchange) through banks as the base (Xu HongDe, 1997, 26). The daily rate was set by the People's Bank of China on the basis of average prices at the major swap centers.

Under a new foreign exchange regime introduced in July 1996, China has attempted to introduce a kind of foreign exchange convertibility for current account items of foreign investment enterprises. Under the new legal framework, foreign invested enterprises will be able to obtain foreign exchange for current account items without the need to obtain government approval (Moser 1997, 165). Some foreign banks will be allowed to conduct business in RMB. Initially, this facility was limited to banks of the PuDong area of Greater ShangHai; in June 1997, it was announced that this scheme would be extend to foreign funded banks in ShenZhen (Foster 1998, 51).

c) Foreign direct investment tendency

Some issues around foreign direct investment and the taxation system have been discussed in the earlier text. In light of the great importance of foreign direct investment in the booming Chinese economy, the Chinese government is doing enormous efforts in simplifying the procedures of approval and creating preferential policies.

Foreign direct investment in China originates primarily from two sources, Chinese community investors – from HongKong, Macao, TaiWan and Singapore – and Western multinationals. Although more than 40 countries from all over the world have invested in China, almost three quarters (73.29%) of the total FDI in the country has come from the Chinese community (Kellet 1999, iii). The investment is focused on industry and real estate, which accounts for 73% and 10% of the total investment respectively. The investment areas are mainly open cities, coastal cities and Special Economic Zones, which account for 87% the total investment from 1979 to 1998 (Wang LuoLin 1998, 7-8). The Chinese government has already perceived the imbalance in development between different industries and areas. Therefore, the Chinese government is aiming to formulate policies to adjust the situation, e.g. the policy of encouraging development of the Western Region and the definition of the encouraged industries and areas. The fundamental target of those policies lies in guiding FDI development in a reasonable structure and eventually bringing China's economy onto a balanced developing road.

Apart from the above stated aspects, there are the financial system, infrastructure and some other issues that will influence the flow of foreign trade and investment. One should take these factors into consideration before choosing the form and area of involvement, and generate a feasibility research report based on reliable information to support one's choice.

2. THE MAJOR TRADE FORMS

a) Goods trade

According to the statistics of the World Trade Organization, China's export ranked ninth and import ranks eleventh. The total import value in 1998 was 1,401 billion US dollar, the export value was 1,837 billion US dollar. The export goods of China are mainly labor-intensive, low-technology industrial products. Machinery and transportation equipment accounts for 30% of total industrial export, which was 12% higher than in 1990. But compared with the global level of mechanical and electrical products exports, the Chinese level of exports is rather low. Primary products, which include food and live stock, beverage and cigarette, non-eatable raw material, mineral fuel lubrication oil and animals, as well as vegetable fat account for 11% of the total export value; industrial finished goods account for around 80% of China's imports since the 1990ies. Mechanical and transportation equipment cover 48% among all imported industrial products. Among primary products, non-eatable raw material and mineral fuel occupy a large proportion of the total amount, around 70% in recent years (Tang ChuanFeng 1999, 77-88).

Based on the above information, if one wants to do goods trade with China, then one has to make clear what the Chinese markets need, whether the market has already been occupied by other trade partners, and where the competitive edge of one's own products is. These internal and external factors should be taken into consideration.

China has focused on the following kinds of trade: general trade; processing and assembly operations; import material processing trade; frontier trade; batter trade; carrying trade; processing and assembly of imported equipment; foreign invested imported equipment, and compensation trade.

One of the special features of China's foreign trade is the substitution of processing trade for general trade. Processing trade is one of the major trade models of China. In 1998 processing trade import value reached 1,044 billion US dollar and accounted for 57% of total export. The import value of processing trade reached 695 billion US dollar, which accounts for 50%of the total import (Tang ChuanFeng 1999, 89).

Processing and assembly operations accounts for a significant part of China's exports and have been particularly popular with HongKong investors. Under this form of business arrangement, the Chinese party processes materials or assembles parts supplied from abroad by the foreign party and then ships the completed product back to the foreign party. The necessary production equipment is often shipped along with the parts and materials being processed. The foreign party usually pays the Chinese party a set fee for each unit produced; alternatively the Chinese party may retain a portion of the products. Processing and assembly arrangements are entered into not only for the traditional low-technology consumer goods that were typical for many processing and assembly arrangements in the early 1980ies, but also increasingly for electronic goods and other high-technology items (Moser 1997, 158).

Processing trade was non-existent prior to the reform of opening-up China in 1979, but its real expansion did not begin until the second half of the 1980ies. Under the combined impacts of Chinese measures and the evolution of the Asian economies, the Chinese government announced a development strategy in 1987 favoring export-oriented industries, and made the transformation and exportation of imported goods the key to industrialization in its coastal regions. Asian economic comparative advantages in HongKong, TaiWan, as well as Japan gradually diminished due to increasing wage costs, consequently, a vast relocation of industrial capacity has been observed due to the lower labor cost in China (Lemoine 1998, 66).

With respect to processing and assembly operations, the "Regulations Concerning the Control of Processing and Assembly Operations on behalf of Foreign Entities" were promulgated that entered into effect on 1st November, 1987.

b) Compensation trade

Compensation trade is a preferred alternative trading arrangement used by Chinese companies which often face difficulties accessing foreign exchange. A typical compensation trade arrangement involves the foreign party transferring materials, equipment or technology to the Chinese party in return for payment in full or in part in the form of products manufactured.

Compensation trade is an especially popular form of doing business between HongKong firms and Chinese enterprises in GuangDong and FuJian (Moser 1999, 16). In this form of trade, the Chinese party might pay cash to the foreign party, the foreign party will agree to the Chinese party a predetermined amount of products manufactured using the supplied materials, equipment or technology. Because of the risk to the foreign party that it does not obtain a product it can sell, the foreign party has a strong interest in the management and operations of the Chinese importers. Compensation trade is therefore somewhat of a hybrid between trade and investment.

One of the major attractions of compensation trade arrangements is that the payments in kind made to the foreign party are generally exempted from tax in China. Offshore sales to and purchases from China of goods are perhaps the most common forms of doing business with China. Most trade transaction are concluded through a standard form of contracts developed by China's state import and exports corporations. When the Chinese party is the purchaser, such contracts will usually provide for shipment on FOB (free on board) terms. And when the Chinese party is the seller, the contract will usually specify CIF (cost, insurance, and freight) terms.

China's international trading practices have in recent years tended to develop increasingly in conformity with international practice. For example, China is a signatory to the 1980 United Nations Convention on Contracts for the International Sale of Goods and to the 1958 United Nations Convention on the Recognition and Enforcement of Foreign Arbitrage Awards. Moreover, China generally adheres to the principles set forth in the Uniform Customs and Practices for Documentary Credits (UCPDC) complied by the International Chamber of Commerce (ICC).

The above provides some explanation of the major forms of goods trade in China. This information can function as reference when choosing one's trade from.

c) *Technology trade*

Technology trade refers to a special kind of trade between enterprises, economic organizations and individuals of different countries: the two sides agree to authorize, sell or buy the technological rights of use on general commercial conditions (HuoGuiSheng 2000, 183). It includes import and export trade. According to the Trade Law of the PRC and the related Technological Import and Export Management Regulations, technology trade includes the following forms: the license or transfer of proprietary technology; the license of transfer of trademarks; cooperative design, cooperative research; cooperative development ; cooperative production; the import and export of complete plant and production-lines; the import and export of crucial equipment (Jiang ZhuYan 1999, 161).

China has established technology trade relationship with more than 50 countries and regions, mainly concentrating on Japan, Germany, the United States, the United Kingdom, France, Sweden, Switzerland and Italy. In order to promote the development of hi-tech, China has formulated a series of policies encouraging the development of science and technology. Policies encouraging foreign business people to invest in hi-tech industries, technical research and transfer of advanced technology to China were formulated. Import contracts concerning hi-tech values 25% of the total of technology and equipment import. The technological import has been extended to special permitted operations, joint research and development and network transfer; all of them are new forms of technical import.

China's exports in computer and telecommunication, life science, electronics, computer integrated manufacturing technology, astronautic, photoelectric products, nuclear technology and biographical technology were in excess of 0.1 billion US dollar in 1997. But it only accounts for 4%-6% of the total export. It is much lower than in developed countries, e.g. technology export of Japan is above 56% of the total export, and in the United States it is 50% (Jiang ZhuYan 1999, 169).

As one of the major forms of technology trade, *technology licensing* is chosen to illustrate the characteristics of China's technology trade. Technology licensing typically includes the sale of equipment and the licensing of proprietary technology by a foreign company to a Chinese entity. Royalties may be paid in a lump sum, by installments, or as a certain percentage of product sales. Licensing arrangements will generally call for the foreign licensers to provide auxiliary services during the term of the contract, such as installation, training and consulting services (Hou GuiSheng 2000, 192).

Technology to be transferred must be advanced and appropriate, and capable of one or more of the following:

- developing new products
- improving quality and performance, increasing production efficiency
- maximizing use of local resources
- expanding exports and foreign exchange earnings
- promoting environmental protection
- promoting production safety
- improving management
- advancing scientific and technical levels

Most foreign companies face little trouble in meeting such requirements (Moser 1997, 155). Technology licensing is carried out within the framework of a legal regime which is growing in sophistication. National regulations governing technology transfer contracts were promulgated in 1985 and were supplemented in 1988 by a set of detailed implementation rules. Measures were also promulgated and put into effect in 1996 which significantly modified the system for governmental involvement in technology import contracts under the previous implementing rules. There are also local regulations governing technology transfer contracts in ShangHai, XiaMen Special Economic Zone, and the GuangZhou Economic and Technological Development Zone. In addition, China has a trademark law, a copyright law, a computer software law, and a patent law, all of which have substantial bearing on licensing transactions.

These laws seem complicated at first sight, but an explicit legal framework will certainly protect the benefits of the two sides. It also reflects that the Chinese government pays attention to technology trade for its function to fuel the nation's modernization drive.

The Chinese government has already realized the significance of developing technology trade, and is seeing the enormous advantages of developed countries in hi-tech industry. Furthermore, China is slowly losing the competitive advantages of low labor cost, which has enormous impact on the export of traditional products. Therefore, developing technology trade is regarded as key for the Chinese economy; it can promote the development of other trade and advance the external focus of the Chinese economy (Jiang ZhuYan 1999, 173). The Chinese government has formulated many policies in order to promote the development of this trade form. Therefore, it can be seen that there is a large room for doing technology trade with China, if performed on the basis of thorough understanding of policies, related laws, and a reliable market analysis.

d) Service trade

The service industry of China developed rather late, compared to the other industries. Currently, it only accounts for 30% of China's GDP. The employment provided by the service industry is 40%-50% below many developed countries. However, the volume of trade in services grew from 5,539 million US dollar in 1982 to 54,880 million in 1997 (Tang ChuanFeng 1999, 123).

China's service export was 24,583 million US dollar in 1997; the major export projects include tourism, commercial services and transportation services. These three items take up 49%, 31and 127% of the total service export respectively. At the same time, China's import valued 30 million US dollar, with transportation, tourism and commercial services ranking as top three of all the services imported, with 34%, 34% and 17% respectively (Tang ChuanFeng 1999, 124).

According to statistics, China's main trading partners in the export of services are HongKong, the UK, the U.S., and Japan (Shi Zhu 1998, 24). With the low development level, China has already seen the needs of developing its service industry. Certainly, the opening of the Chinese service industry market has been the focus of foreign business people. Here, a brief introduction will be given to illustrate the related regulations and degree of opening of different branches of the services industry.

(1) Financial Service Industry

The opening of the financial sector is covering Banking, Insurance and Security Exchange. Although the financial sector is more sensitive than telecommunication, the openness of the financial sector is higher than telecommunication sector. By the end of 1997, China had approved 544 Representative Office of foreign financial organs, and 170 foreign operational organs, among them 192 foreign bank branches, 5 Sino-foreign Joint Ventures, 7 foreign capital accounting companies, 8 foreign insurance companies, and one Sino-foreign Joint Venture insurance company (Yu YongDing 2000, 41). Considering the importance of financial security, the Chinese government adopts a prudent attitude towards the opening of the financial sector.

On 27th January, 1999, the People's Bank of China announced to cancel the regional restrictions on the setting-up of operational branches of foreign banks. That means, foreign banks can set up operational organs in any city; they are not any more limited to BeiJing, ShangHai, ShenZhen, HaiNan province and some other 20 cities. The areas opened for insurance industry are restricted to ShangHai and GuangZhou on a trial basis (Shi Zhu 1998,24).

Foreign invested banks and financing companies are only allowed to do foreign exchange business, and RMB business is allowed on a trial basis in PuDong, ShangHai (Yang ShengMing 1999, 167). The clients of this service are restricted to foreign invested enterprises and foreigners only. Foreign invested life insurance companies are only allowed to do life insurance business which is paid by individuals, and foreign invested property insurance companies are only allowed to insure properties of foreign invested enterprises. The security service industry is not open yet (Yang ShengMing 1999, 217).

With China's entry into WTO in December 2001, the financial sector will be a strategic plot that internal and external investors try to seize. However, the opening of financial sector has to be performed gradually, according to China's capacity to maintain the stability of the financial sector. Financial institutions with a long history, high credit rating and a high of strategic interest in China will gain access to the Chinese market. On the other hand, financial institutions that are considered as having potential to cause instability in the financial market will be confronted with resistance by China.

(2) Post and Telecommunication Service Industry

China holds a prudent attitude to the openness of the post and telecommunication market. Postal services, visual and video services are restricted, and not open for foreign business people. EMS service and value-added telecommunication service departments are allowed to set up Joint Ventures on a trial basis. The prerequisite for the establishment of such Joint Ventures is that the share of the foreign partners can not exceed 49%, there can not be less than 2/3 Chinese employees. The purpose of opening those areas is to promote the development of value-added services, which are almost vacant in China. These areas include electronic mail, voice mail, online information and database services, electronic data exchange, value added fax service, online data processing and so on (Huang KeAn 1998, 242).

China's post and telecommunication still face problems when talking about openness. It is undergoing a reform and reconstruction process itself. It has to survive without the support of government policy and financial support from the government, and balance the development of the Western and the Eastern Region, which are in a seriously imbalanced development state. The legislation work on post and telecommunication has not been finished, which is only factor among many that cause challenges and disadvantages in the development of telecommunication. However, looking at the global markets, the solution to these problems will not be refusal of reform and opening, as a growing number of experts is pointing out. Therefore, doing telecommunication service trade with China might be an interesting activity for foreign investors (Yang ShengMing 1999, 256).

(3) Transportation Services

Development and operation of transportation infrastructure by foreign investment is encouraged by Chinese government. But the Chinese Partner has to have a controlling share and to play a leading role in the development and operation of urban metros, public docks and civil airport projects. The development and operation of bridges and railway tunnels are forbidden for wholly foreign-owned enterprises. In international ocean transportation, overseas investors are allowed to set up Joint Venture shipping companies to offer international maritime transportation, including passenger and cargo services. But the Chinese Partner has to hold more than 50% of the registered capital of the Joint Venture (Shi Zhu 1998,25). In passenger transportation and aviation transportation, Joint Venture enterprises are the only form allowed; the foreign partner may only hold 25%. Railway, inner river and overland transportation is forbidden to foreign investors (Huang KeAn 1998, 247-248).

One could think that market access for trade in transportation services in China is quite open. The only restriction to market access is that wholly foreign-owned transportation operations are prohibited; there is no quantitative or geographical restriction on market access. When it comes to national treatment, there is no discriminatory provision in China's policies and regulations on the entry of foreign investors into China's transportation service market. The further opening of China's transportation service market will probably depend on the progress of bilateral and multilateral negotiations between China and other countries.

Looking beyond the financial, post and telecommunication as well as the transportation service trade illustrated above, the other areas of service trade are all in different degrees of openness. For example, the opening of domestic commerce of China is gradually proceeding from retail to wholesale, and from coastal regions to inland areas. The tourism industry is one of the earliest opened in China, and the tourism market is basically open. In the legal field, foreign law firms may establish offices in China; 15 cities have opened up to foreign investment on a trial basis. There are also some other service fields like accounting, engineering design, manufacturing and export commodities, consulting services that are gradually opening up. No matter what field one wants to step in, the development state, related laws and policies, the vision of the trade, and the benefits to the foreign and the Chinese Partner should be calculated carefully. The evaluation of one's competitive edge is also imperative.

3. FOREIGN DIRECT INVESTMENT

The forms of foreign direct investment include five kinds, which are Equity Joint Venture, Cooperative Joint Venture, wholly foreign-owned Joint Venture, holding companies and Joint Venture developments (Wang LuoLin 1998, 5).

Foreign investment is focused on industry and real estate. The industry sector accounts for 73% and real estate industry for 10% of the total investment, according to the statistics of MOFTEC. Foreign direct investment is mainly located in coastal areas. Two factors have contributed here:

1) China's open areas have developed gradually: at first, four Special Economic Zones were established in 1980ies, then fourteen coastal cities were opened, and economic and technological development zones were set up there in 1984. Then HaiNan, LiaoDong peninsula, ShangHai, ShanDong peninsula and BoHai region were added to the coastal open areas in 1988. ShangHai PuDong became a new development zone in 1990, and inland cities were opened since 1992.

2) HongKong, Macao and TaiWan occupy two-thirds of total FDI, since language and family relations of the investors are very close; the investment focuses on the coastal regions.

Foreign direct investment (FDI) contributes a lot to boom the economic development of China. Furthermore, the active role of foreign FDI in promoting the system transition, training talent and initiating new concepts are to the great interests of the Chinese economy. International FDI is referred to "one package creative investment" (Wang LuoLin 1998, 8), for concepts, techniques, management, marketing, and market networks are transferred to the Chinese Partner together with the transfer of capital.

Using foreign capital to promote the national economic development has always been the policy of the Chinese government. Therefore, the areas open for

FDI are wide, except those related to state security and media, which are considered to be close areas.

a) Equity Joint Ventures

An Equity Joint Venture takes the forms of a limited liability company. The liability of each party in a Joint Venture is limited to the capital subscribed by it. Parties to an equity venture are jointly responsible for investment and management, and they share risks, gains and losses. All assets are liable in the payment of debts (Brahm 1997, 25).

An Equity Joint Venture is formed by the injection of capital contributions by the foreign and Chinese partners. The contributions may be cash, capital equipment, know-how or industrial property rights. Generally, the foreign party will contribute cash and or equipment, as well as technology; the Chinese party will contribute cash or land, as well as buildings. There is no statutory limit on the foreign party's contribution to the Joint Venture, however, there is a required minimum foreign participation of 25 per cent.

Equity Joint Ventures are governed by a rather comprehensive regulatory framework. The most important legislation includes the Law of the PRC on Chinese-Foreign Equity Joint Ventures which was promulgated on 8th July, 1979, and the Regulations for the Implementation of the Law of the PRC on Chinese-Foreign Equity Joint Ventures which was promulgated on 20th July, 1983. In addition, a number of supplementary regulations have been put into effect, dealing with such matters as registration, labor management, land use, taxation and some other things.

In the Joint Venture law, 16 issues are addressed, including establishment and registration, form of organization and registered capital, ways of investment, board of directors and management structure, introduction of technology and tax. Apart from these central, high-level laws, the provinces, cities and autonomous regions have their detailed polices respectively to govern the operation of Equity Joint Ventures.

As investment vehicles, Joint Ventures are often preferred over wholly foreign-owned enterprises for a number of reasons. Joint Ventures may gain approval in certain sectors that are off-limits to wholly foreign-owned enterprises. Moreover, China's rather complicated government structure, production and marketing systems and regional differences often make a committed Chinese Partner a valuable assets (Moser 1997, 159). Equity Joint Ventures have become increasingly popular in recent years, and Chinese companies and officials have become very familiar with this form of investment. According to the statistics of MOFTEC, there are 183,051 Equity Joint Venture projects that were developed from 1979 to 1997, almost four times the number of Cooperative Joint Ventures.

b) Cooperative Joint Ventures

Cooperative Joint Venture are also referred to "Contractual Joint Ventures": that means, the foreign and Chinese Partner confirm the duties and rights of both sides through the signing of a contract.

The key characteristic of the Cooperative Joint Venture format is its flexibility. The flexibility covers two aspects:

- The investment of each side is not calculated in current volume, and does not take this as basis for shares and allocation of benefits and risks. The partners can negotiate the cooperative terms freely and confirm these terms in a contract (Zhang ZhuSheng 1997, 115). One of the parties could provide assets such as the buildings and the right of the use of land, while the other party could provide capital and equipment to jointly achieve a specific project.

- The organization of a Cooperative Joint Venture can alternate between legal entity and non-legal entity. A Cooperative Joint Venture and its shares have some of the characteristics of an Equity Joint Venture. But under this form, the Chinese Partner may provide natural resources or labor as parts of his contribution, which is forbidden in Equity Joint Ventures. A Cooperative Joint Venture without a legal entity is referred to as "pure" Cooperative Joint Venture. Under this form, each party bears its own costs, taxes, and liabilities relating to the Joint Venture according to clear specification in the Joint Venture Contract. The operation of the enterprise is administered by representatives from each sides. Sino-foreign Cooperative Joint Ventures are particularly popular for hotel and commercial complex projects and the joint development of offshore oil, and also for the production of simple manufactured goods for export.

Compared to Equity Joint Ventures, the following aspects of a Cooperative Joint Venture might be helpful to form a judgment how to chose between the two forms:

- less need to value capital contributions formally;

- greater freedom in choosing a management structure, including management by third parties;

- freedom to recover capital contributions prior to termination of the venture;
- fewer restriction on the form and sharing of profits.

c) Wholly foreign-owned enterprises

Wholly foreign-owned enterprises are the third type of foreign investment enterprises after the Sino-foreign Equity Joint Ventures and Cooperative Joint Ventures. Wholly foreign-owned enterprises are owned exclusively by one or more foreign investors and can therefore offer a mechanism for control over management, technology and other know-how.

As to the business scope, wholly foreign-owned enterprises are more limited than Joint Ventures. All sectors which are closed to Joint Ventures are also closed to wholly foreign-owned enterprises. However, some sectors in which Joint Ventures may operate are not open to wholly foreign-owned enterprises. For example, wholly foreign-owned enterprises may normally not engage in retailing and other service industries. Moreover, to gain approval, wholly foreign-owned enterprises are often required to use newer technology, be more export-oriented and make higher quality products then Joint Ventures in the same sector (Moser 1997, 166).

During recent years, the investment of wholly foreign-owned enterprises has increased rapidly, and the total investment values 155,5.1 million US dollar, second to Equity Joint Ventures. The reason might be that wholly foreign-owned investment enterprises have many advantages, in the sense that they are entirely controlled by the foreign partners and there is no need for interference from a local Chinese Partner in respect of management issues. Nevertheless, many foreign investors prefer to have a local partner to help them understand the market situation and deal with problems which the Chinese Partner is much better equipped to handle.

d) Holding companies

In recent times, some multinational corporations have been given approval by MOFTEC to establish foreign invested holding companies, which are also called "umbrella companies" or "investment companies". The purpose of establishing a holding company is to hold interest in subsidiary enterprises in China and to provide a range of centralized services to these subsidiaries. Although a holding company is prohibited from acting as a trade intermediary for any of its investors without special approval, a holding company is a useful vehicle for providing assistance to subsidiaries. The business scope includes (Brahm 1997, 59):

- to assist, or act as an agent, in purchasing machinery, equipment and office appliances for their own use;
- to assist, or act as an agent, in purchasing raw materials, components and parts used by the enterprises for their own production, for domestic or overseas markets, as well as to distribute the products in both domestic and international markets, and to provide after-sales service;
- to balance foreign exchange and expenditure among the enterprises with the consent and under the supervision of the foreign exchange administration authorities;
- to assist the enterprises in the recruitment and employment of personnel and to provide technical training, market promotion and consulting;
- to assist the enterprises in seeking loans to provide guarantees.

e) Joint developments

Chinese and foreign companies have employed joint development arrangements in connection with the development of offshore oil and gas reserves. Under this type of arrangement, foreign investors agree to conduct exploration programs at their financial risk. The petroleum produced is distributed to the parties in accordance with a fixed contractual formula that takes into account exploration costs, development expenses, and applicable profits. Now, the development arrangements have been expanded to onshore oil and gas fields and other mineral deposits (Moser 1999, 20).

Conclusion: In this part, different forms and areas of doing business with China have been introduced. It may not be complete in explaining the various characteristic of each form, since each form has its own complexity in practical operation. Furthermore, choosing a business model is a complicated task that can be performed successfully only with a thorough understanding of the possible related issues. Therefore, the advice here is: one should carry out an analysis according to the specific situation, and balance advantages and disadvantages carefully.

E. FINDING A GOOD PARTNER

If one chooses a Joint Venture as the form of involvement, then selecting a good partner becomes the crucial step to establish business in China. A lot of foreign business people choose Joint Ventures as their involvement form because they think their Chinese partners are familiar with the business environment and will lead them into a permanent operation without going too much of a winding road. Other than the advantages of Joint Ventures, there are risks, such as differences in managerial models, differences related to profits. These differences can cause many specific problems in the operational process, such as: how to allocate capital and manpower? What standard should be adopted in producing goods? Who is the final decision maker?. Most Joint Ventures have to cope with such problems; however, the solving of the problems depends on the closeness of cooperation of both parties. Therefore, the selecting and contacting before forming Joint Ventures became a crucial issue to determine success or failure of a business.

1. IDENTIFICATION OF PARTNERS

In the early days of joint venturing in China, the identification of partners was a somewhat random affair, and Western partners visiting China for the first time often said that they lost their way. English-language publications in China are full of lists of local manufacturers seeking foreign venture partners, but one might get little more information than the company's name and telephone numbers, a list of the products it makes, and how much money it wants the future partner to invest. As a result, one "often has to make a decision based on little more than intuition", some investors complain. Currently, this phenomenon has been improved to some extent, for China has found many ways to introduce cooperation projects and to guide potential Joint Ventures partners to form a reasonable decision.

For example, the construction of government websites has begun in January 1999. Almost all the government ministries have their website to propagate their administration function and the policies promulgated by the ministry. A name listed will provided in the appendix. The departments in charge of foreign relations and trade at different levels provide information on investment projects publicly. The government promulgates the foreign business people investment directory catalogue, in which the list of activities that are encouraged, forbidden or restricted is illustrated in more detail. Through these websites, foreign business people can have an initial choice, and then contact the partner they are most interested in.

Another easy way to meet a Chinese Partner is to participate as an exhibitor or simply to attend one or more of the many trade and industry fairs and exhibitions under the auspices of the principal Chinese ministries in Beijing, ShangHai or GuangZhou, or organized by the municipalities or provincial governments in their major cities. With the insatiable Chinese thirst for Western technology and Western products, these fairs and exhibitions are well-attended. This exposure is excellent for foreign manufactures seeking to form an impression of the market, for their products and processes, or to win customers, but much less useful for developing potential partners. Chinese companies offering themselves as partners were, by definition, a self-selected sample drawn from those attending the exhibitions, and often may not be best potential partners available (Jonathan 1995, 213).

Other Western companies were led into China by "old China hands", foreign business people with a personal experience of China, but inevitably with a limited range of contacts and local knowledge within a given Chinese industry. The experience of these "old China hands" may be valuable, however, a combination of their experience with one's own on-site investigation is encouraged before making a decision. – Also, there are expatriate Chinese who claim to be familiar with Chinese corporations or to be acquainted with high-ranking officials or their families. It might be interesting to listen to the advice of these people. However, the promise of these individuals can not always be taken as the only criterion to identify the suitable partner due to the limitation and the reliability of personal experience.

Another popular method of making contact with a Chinese Partner is participation in trade missions. The mission may be jointly organized by a foreign country specialist trade association or government with a Chinese ministry, provincial or city government, to visit China by invitation. The other form of missions is organized in a similar way for Chinese delegations of officials and selected companies to visit a foreign country.

On such occasions, the presses are running hot with reams and reams of lists, each containing hundreds of what is called projects right across the entire spectrum of commercial endeavors. For each such project, brief data is given about the partner, the product, anticipated sales volumes and required investment. One can meet a lot of people at those functions. They are one way of seeing what China has to offer in different areas, and what is in demand. The Western business person needs to be aware of what is going on, since many of the officials present will have little or no role to play in any business one may intend to do. One is faced with a constantly changing array of different kinds of organizations, factories, and enterprises (Rainer 2000, 91-92).

No matter what trade mission it is, efforts are made to satisfy visitor's requirements ahead of the trip by lining up the country's enterprises to meet. Such missions are beneficial for major corporations, where more intensive partner-matching has been carried out in advance, often at a higher, semi-official level. For small companies, the benefits of trade missions are more doubtful, although participating in a group of key corporations may seem prestigious and will certainly give some overview of the Chinese business scene. As the mission organizations will have selected the sample in advance, it may not match the needs of smaller companies (Jonathan 1997, 214).

Most foreign governments maintain commercial sections within their embassies and consulates in China. They are of varying capability, but generally the advisory services offered are of a non-specific nature in terms of partner identification. There are some professional consulting companies providing services including helping Chinese and foreign companies to establish business relationships. However, sometimes these profit-driven companies can not provide qualified service, or they do not live up to the responsibility they have. One major problem is that it is very hard to execute market research in China, because in China, market data are often considered to be top secret.

An Australian businessman commented: "Everything tends to be treated as a state property not to be divulged unless there are very good reasons. It is very frustrating when you are trying to obtain what would be considered basic public data in most other countries, and find it veiled in secrecy. Only as you go up the ladder of command can one find openness – if it suits the other side to do so." (Geoffrey 1994, 156).

Therefore, one should not expect that one can do a complete research in the name of a foreign enterprise. Furthermore, the government has made policies to regulate the investigation activities of foreign organizations. Thus the best and reliable way is to entrust a legal market research company to help doing the job. These companies often claim that they have close relationship with government, meaning they could get reliable market data from the government, and government was the only authorized organ that could provide such data. If that claim is true still will depend on the specific situation. In fact, the reputation of these companies might be a good reference to judge their credibility.

In establishing a short-list of potential Chinese Joint Venture partners, it is important to apply a filter of selection criteria in terms of the partner's ability to:

- assimilate and exploit the technology and know-how to be transferred to the Joint Venture;
- operate effectively at the level of production envisaged for the Joint Venture;

- absorb global quality standards and maintain them in the Joint Venture;
- provide competent management, and maintain an entrepreneurial role in directing and cooperation.

These criteria are crucial in identifying a proper partner, for they are the basis of a seamless corporation.

2. CONTACT WITH AND SELECTION OF THE PARTNER

After identifying several potential partners, the next step is to contact them, and finally to select one. First contact meetings with a Chinese organization, whether a factory, a commercial enterprise or a manufacturing group with many factories, habitually follows a set of patterns. Both sides will make a formal presentation of their company, their products and processes. However, much information may have been exchanged in advance through business intermediaries, written exchange or promotional materials. Even if the visitors are familiar with the ideas, it is discourteous to interrupt or attempt to shorten the presentation (Jonathan 1997, 215).

In the context of a Joint Venture discussion, where both parties are aware of the purpose of the contract, the foreign visitors may refer to the general objectives at the outset and its supporting logic, but should not make an outline proposal. Attempts to "lay out the deal on the table" at a first session will probably meet resistance. The Chinese style of discussion and negotiation is to examine things step by step. They would rather make a slow decision than making an imprudent one.

Foreign corporate managers may find the process tiresome, but there are several reasons why this measured rate of progress works well in Sino-foreign business discussions. A Chinese negotiation team is large by Western standards, five to ten participants representing different operating companies or parent company functions are normal, at least in the early stage. Certainly, to deal with such a big group, with possibly each of the participants representing different goals, can be a rather time-consuming matter. Another reason for delay is language: as the parties do not share a common language, communication through interpreters will certainly be a time-consuming procedure. There is another reason why too rapid an expose of the foreign party's business proposal may lead to misunderstandings, even to a potential partner with strong international experience: most foreign parties do not know that there may be elements in its opening positions which are completely unacceptable to the Chinese side, perhaps because of restrictions imposed by the authorities, or because some aspects of the proposal is contrary to state policy. A detailed and lengthy initial presentation demands polite appreciation and a considered reaction which will probably be deferred until the next meetings. It is quite likely that the first session will end without underlying objections being raised.

The second session could start with the foreign party working under the impression that its stated proposal will be acceptable. The Chinese party would have to seek assurance on specific points which will overcome the intrinsic objections. If the assurances sought appear unreasonable or unacceptable, the foreign party may conclude that the basic proposal is unwelcome and that the Chinese party has rejected the business proposition. According to Chinese customs, they could not say "no" outright to strangers when faced with an insurmountable obstacle; so there may be misunderstandings between the two parties. But after familiarizing with its partners, the Chinese party will explain more frankly the government policies and reasoning behind each difficulty.

At this stage, one thing should be made very clear, that is: if one shares common goals, they may not necessarily be exactly the same, but they certainly should not be in conflict so as to destroy any hope of mutual cooperation. One needs to be satisfied that the success of the venture is as important to the partner as it is to oneself, and that both agree on the means to achieve it (Geoffrey 1994, 158). "More haste, less speed" is a good theoretical foundation.

Success in the early stage of contact and negotiation depends largely on establishing a reservoir of confidence and good-will between the partners. The Chinese party will want to satisfy itself by seeing their partner's sincerity and flexibility. Giving this impression is usually a more important objective for the foreign negotiation team than technical brilliance or market strength. This is a special aspect in the Chinese character. Most Chinese would appreciate you first, then appreciate your project. This may be not acceptable by the standard of the Western people. Some of them may develop the impression: "these strange Chinese, they have no reason to refuse me, because I bring advanced management experience and technology." If you really think so, throw the idea away totally, since Chinese will have a different idea. Without thinking that you are a person they can cooperate with very well, most Chinese will break the potential partnership, no matter what brilliant future you promise to give them.

Towards the end of this first series of discussions, it is often useful to provide the Chinese party with a summary, a checklist of the major points on the foreign company's agenda for cooperation, and to invite the Chinese party to declare its own agenda. By making a comparison of the agendas, one will find whether there is room for further discussion. If the answer is positive, then a memorandum of understanding should be signed. Normally, a memorandum of understanding is followed by a decision if both party want to chose each other as preferred partner. Once a formal memorandum is signed, it is considered to be a breach of good faith for a foreign company to enter into negotiation with another Chinese enterprises, unless the first terminated by the mutual consent after a feasibility study (Jonathan 1997, 216).

Conclusion: the above text was dealing with a part of the issue of finding a good partner. In practical application, many unexpected issues may emerge. At that time, one should compare one'' own standards and the standard of the partner; if one thinks the gap to be too big, one may be better of to terminate the negotiation: there may be other, more qualified partners available in China. In summary, sticking to one's principles and applying them with the appropriate flexibility may be helpful.

F. SETTING UP THE OPERATIONAL STRUCTURE

1. CHINESE-FOREIGN JOINT VENTURES

According to the "Regulation for the Implementation of the Law of the PRC on Chinese-Foreign Equity Joint Ventures" and the measures of its enforcement, the establishment of a Equity Joint Venture should follow the procedure listed below:

1) The Chinese Partner in a Joint Venture submits to its department in charge a project proposal and a preliminary Feasibility Study Report of the Joint Venture to be established with the foreign partner.

2) After the proposal and the preliminary Feasibility Study Report being examined and approved by the department in charge, it should be submitted to MOFTEC or entrust offices for final approval.

3) The parties to the venture then conduct work centering around the feasibility study, and proceed on this basis to negotiate and sign a Joint Venture Agreement, contract and Articles of Association.

4) When applying for the establishment of a Joint Venture, the Chinese Partner is responsible for the submission of the following documents to the examination and approving authorities:

    - a written application for the establishment of a Joint Venture;

    - the Feasibility Study Report jointly prepared by the venture parties;

- the Joint Venture Agreement, Joint Venture Contract and Articles of Association signed by representatives of the venture parties;
- a list of candidates for chairman and vice-chairman and directors, nominated by the parties to the venture;
- written opinions concerning the establishment of the venture by the department in charge and the people's government of the province, autonomous region or municipality directly under the control of the central government where Joint Venture is located.

The above mentioned *Joint Venture Agreement* refers to the document agreed upon by the parties to the Joint Venture, covering the major points and principles governing the establishment of the Joint Venture. *Joint Venture Contract* (JVC) refers to the document agreed upon and concluded by the parties to the Joint Venture on their mutual rights and obligations. *Articles of Association* refers to the document agreed upon by the parties to the Joint Venture specifying the purpose, organizational principles and methods of management of the Joint Venture in compliance with the principles of the JVC. Where the Joint Venture Agreement comes into conflict with the JVC, the latter prevails. The parties to the Joint Venture may agree to sign the JVC and Articles of Association only, without signing a Joint Venture Agreement.

The aforesaid documents shall be written in Chinese. They may be written simultaneously in a foreign language agreed upon by the parties to the Joint Venture. Both versions are equally authentic.

Upon receipt of the documents listed above, MOFTEC will decide to approve or disapprove them, within three months. If they are approved, then an Approval Certificate would be given to the venture.

Upon receipt of the Approval Certificate, the Joint Venture shall register with the State Administration for Industry and Commerce, or any of its local and regional bureaus, within one month.

In applying for registration, a Joint Venture must submit the following documents and materials to the State Administration for Industry and Commerce:

- a written application for registration signed and issued by the chairman of the board of directors;
- an Approval Certificate from the Chinese government;

- the JVC and Articles of Association;
- the Feasibility Study Report;
- the legal certificate of commencement of business issued by the country (area) of the Joint Venture;
- the approval documents for construction which are issued by the people's government of the town and country where the Joint Venture is located. These approvals cover: environmental protection, building approval and provision of water and electricity.

The Administration for Industry and Commerce approves or disapproves the registration within one month of receipt of these documents. When approved, the date of the issuance of its business licenses is the date of the formal establishment of the Joint Venture.

2. COOPERATIVE JOINT VENTURES

The law of the PRC on Chinese-foreign Cooperative Joint Venture and the detailed rules for the implementation of the law of the PRC on Chinese-foreign Cooperative Joint Ventures provide the legal basis for the establishment of Cooperative Joint Ventures.

a) Approval procedure

The establishment of a Cooperative Joint Venture will be examined and approved by MOFTEC or the local people's governments authorized by the State Council.

In the following circumstances, the department or local people's government authorized by the State Council may examine and approve Cooperative Joint Venture:

- the total amount of investment is within the authorization for approval as set by the State Council, by its departments or local people's governments authorized by the State Council;
- the capital has been raised by the applicants themselves, construction and production conditions do not need to be balanced by the state;
- export of the products of the Cooperative Joint Venture do not require export quota and licenses to be issued by relevant competent departments of the state; or if export requires quota and licenses,

the consent of the relevant departments has been obtained prior to submitting the application for establishing the Cooperative Joint Venture;

- other circumstances apply, in which the department or local governments authorized by the State Council may examine and approve Cooperative Joint Ventures as stipulated in laws and administrative rules.

To establish a Cooperative Joint Venture, the Chinese Partner has to submit the following documents to the examination and approval authority:

a) application for establishing a Cooperative Joint Venture accompanied by the examination and approval documents of the competent authorities;

b) Feasibility Study Report jointly prepared by all parties to the Cooperative Joint Venture, accompanied by the examination and approval documents of the competent authorities;

c) Joint Venture Agreement, JVC and Articles of Association signed by the legal representatives or representatives authorized by them of all parties to the Joint Venture;

d) business licenses or registration certificates, financial credit documents and valid certification documents of the legal representatives of all parties to the Joint Venture; where the foreign partner is natural person, valid certification documents on his or her identity, resume and financial credit has to be presented;

e) list of chairman, deputy chairman and members of the board of directors or list of directors, deputy directors and members of the joint management committee of the Cooperative Joint Venture as determined by all parties through consultation;

f) other documents as required by the examination and approval authority.

The documents listed in the proceeding paragraphs have to be written in Chinese with the exception of the documents in the paragraph d) to be presented by the foreign partner, each of the documents under paragraph b), c), e) may be accompanied by a foreign language version agreed upon by all partners.

Upon the receipt of all the documents as stipulated, the examination and approval authority shall decide whether or not to approve them within 45 days.

Once a Cooperative Joint Venture is approved by MOFTEC or by departments authorized by the State Council, a Certificate of Approval is be granted by MOFTEC. If Cooperative Joint Venture is approved by a local people's government authorized by the State Council, the Certificate of Approval is granted by the relevant local people's government, and the relevant approval documents have to be submitted to MOFTEC for filing within 30 days of the date of approval.

b) Registration

Upon receipt of the Approval Certificate, the Chinese Partner must register with the State Administration for Industry and Commerce where the Cooperative Joint Venture is located within 30 days. The registration authorities will issue a business license to a Cooperative Joint Venture registered as a legal entity, and a business registration certificate to a Cooperative Joint Venture not registered as a legal entity, within 30 days upon receiving the all the application documents.

The date of the establishment of a Cooperative Joint Venture is defined as the date of the business license or the registration certificate. A Cooperative Joint Venture must carry out tax registration with the tax authorities within 30 days of its establishment.

3. WHOLLY FOREIGN-OWNED INVESTMENT ENTERPRISES

"The Law of the PRC on Wholly-Foreign-Owned Investment Enterprises" and its implementation rules stipulate the establishment procedure:

A foreign investment has to submit a report to the local people's government at or above the country level at the place where the proposed enterprises is to be established. The report should include: the aim of the establishment of the proposed enterprise; the scope and scale of business operations; the products to be produced; the technology and equipment to be adopted and used; the proportion of the scales of products between the domestic market and foreign markets; the area of the land to be used and the related requirements; the conditions and quantities of water, electricity, coal, coal gas and other forms of energy resources required; and the requirement of public facilities. The local people's government at or above the country level shall within 30 days after receiving the report submitted by the foreign investor, give a reply in writing.

The application has to be submitted to the examination and approving organs through the local people's government at or above the country level at the place where the enterprise is to be established, together with the following documents:

a) the written application for the establishment of a wholly-foreign-owned enterprise;

b) a Feasibility Study Report;

c) the Articles of Association of the wholly-foreign-owned enterprise;

d) the name-list of the legal representatives or the candidates for members of the board of directors of the wholly foreign-owned enterprise;

e) the legal certifying documents and the credit position documents of the foreign investor;

f) the written reply given by the people's government at or above the country level at the place, where the enterprise is to be established;

g) an inventory of goods and materials needed to be imported;

h) other documents that are required to be submitted.

When submitting the above documents, language should be take into consideration. As required, a) and c) must be written in the Chinese language; documents b), d) and e) can be written in foreign language, but a Chinese translation should be added as attachment.

If two or more foreign investors jointly file an application for the establishment of a wholly-foreign-owned enterprises, they have to submit a duplicate of the contract between them to the examination and approving organs for the record.

The above procedures are rather complex in practice, therefore, the foreign investor may appoint a Chinese service agency for enterprises with foreign investment or other economic organization to handle the process on their behalf, but a contract of entrustment has to be concluded and signed between them.

The examining and approving organ would decide whether to approve or disapprove the application within 90 days. If some of the documents are thought incomplete or inappropriate, the applicants have to make up complete documents, or to make necessary revisions within a prescribed time limit.

After receiving the Certificate of Approval, the applicant has to file an application for registration with the State Administration of Industry and Commerce at various levels and to obtain a business license. The date of the establishment of the enterprises is the date at which the license is issued.

4. RESIDENT REPRESENTATIVE OFFICES

Many companies chose Beijing for their first Representative Office because of the access to government officials and key enterprises. However, it is possible for a foreign organization to establish more than one Representative Offices in China. Large cities such as ShangHai, GuangZhou, and TianJin are popular choices for the establishment of a second office. The establishment of a Representative Office requires three main steps.

a) Finding a Chinese sponsor

The Chinese sponsor will normally be a major Chinese foreign trade corporation, a foreign affairs service unit, or other enterprises with which the applicant has had prior dealings and which is located within the same region as the proposed Representative Office. The Chinese sponsor assists in the submission of the foreign organization to the approval authority.

b) Submission of a formal application to the relevant authority in charge

In order to form a formal application, the applicant has to submit the following certificates and documents for approval:

- an application duly signed by the chairman of the board or general manager of the foreign enterprises with such details as the name of the residential Representative Office, names of the person in charge, its scope of business, residential duration and its address;
- a legal business certificate issued by competent authorities of the country or region where the applicant is located;
- a letter issued by a bank which has business relations with the applicant testifying its financial and credit standing;
- a power of attorney issued by the applicant for the staff of its office and their curriculum vitae.

The approval authority will depend on the location where the Representative Office is being established: In Beijing, government agencies act as sponsoring organizations. In ShangHai, the approval authority is the ShangHai Municipal Foreign Economic Relations and Trade Commission. A banking or insurance institution which desires to open a resident Representative Office has to submit its application to the People's Bank of China, upon processing a successful application, the approval authority will issue a Certificate of Approval.

c) *Registration with the local Administration for Industry and Commerce*

With the Certificate of Approval and the documents referred to in section b), the applicant can register its residential Representative Office with the local Administration for Industry and Commerce. The applicant has to fill in a registration form, pay a registration fee and receives a registration certificate.

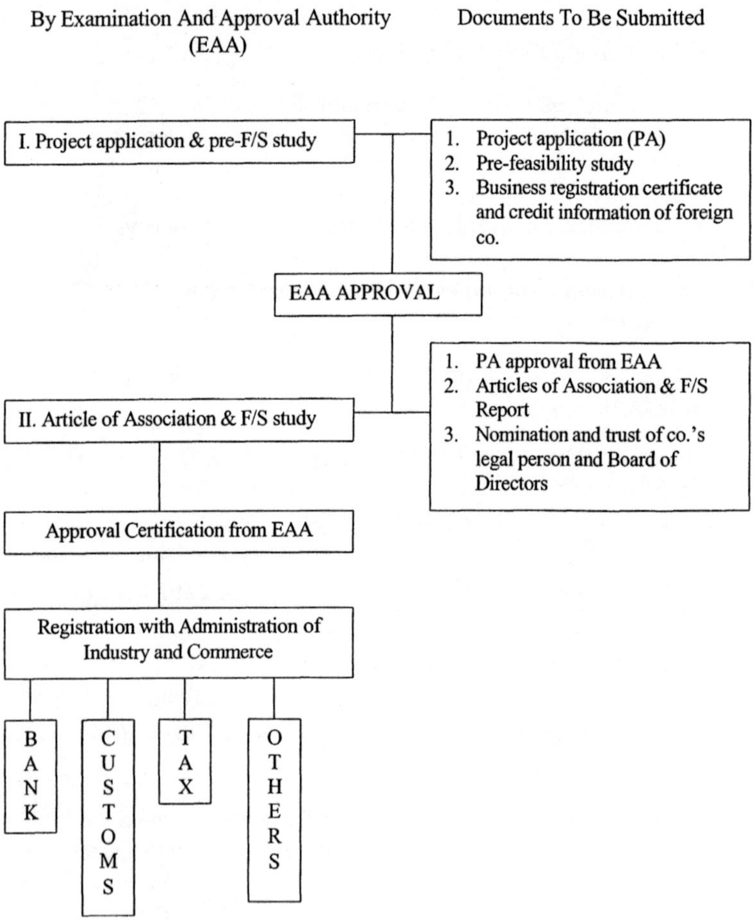

Illustration 1: Wholly Foreign-Owned Enterprise Approval Procedures

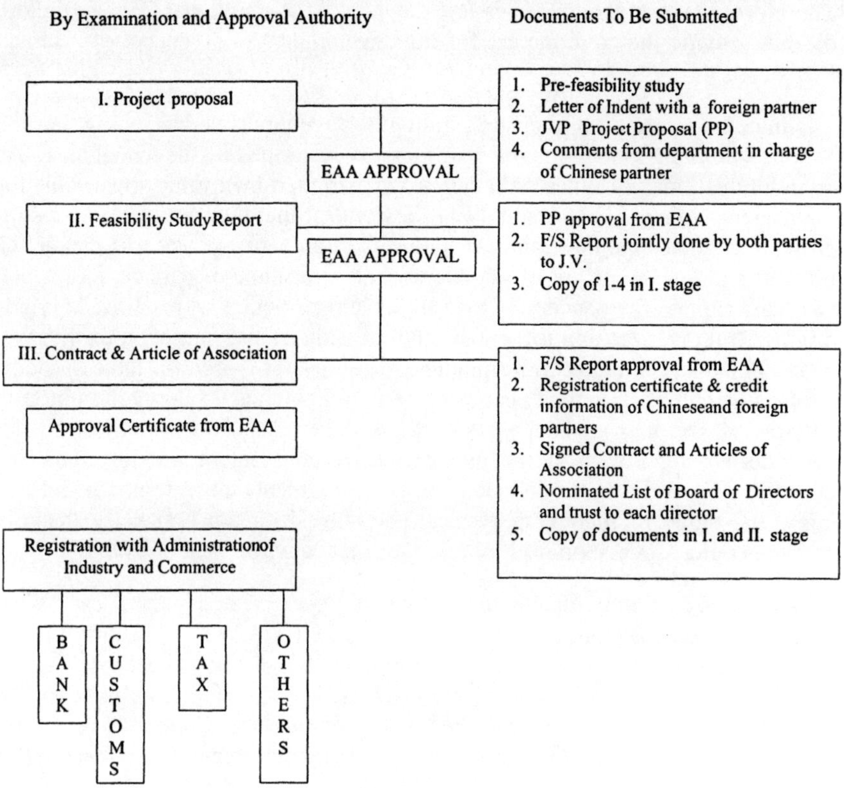

Illustration 2: Equity/Contractual Joint Venture Approval Procedures

G. DEALING WITH HUMAN RESOURCES ISSUES

1. HUMAN RESOURCES AND PERSONNEL MANAGEMENT

Reflecting about the literal meaning of the word, "Human Resources" or "HR" can be seen as a statement that "Human beings are a resource". In the perspective of most Chinese, HR is just a modern word, without any special connotations. The direct cause may be that Chinese are too familiar with the domestic expression "Personnel". More fundamentally, though, one will have to attribute the reason to traditional Chinese culture to some extent, which we have addressed so much in previous parts. In feudal society, Chinese were not treated as individual human beings; in fact, people functioned more as a tool for the governing of the emperor and did not have a high level of self-awareness. Without self-awareness, a person is not a resource that can be developed.

Therefore, in more general terms one may state: the traditional Chinese culture did not provide the environment for the development of a concept of "Human Resources".

Since the founding of the PRC, individual freedom was developing, but the people's thinking model remained still largely restrained by the feudal idea. As an individual, many Chinese still can not realize their own value, their value for the society. Many Chinese still share the concept that they are the more a subordinate of the social development, rather than an active power that can act or influence the development of the society. This attitude of passive acceptance has handicapped the concept of looking at human beings as resources. In addition, China was lacking the social environment for the formation of the concept: China had implemented a planned economy for more than three decades, before it switched to market economy. The old planned economy did not give enterprises free management power. State policies substituted almost all the decision-making power of the enterprises, so that enterprises lost their independence. Without the independence of judgment, the enterprises did not know the value of their employees. Therefore it is not a surprise that the concept could not develop itself within the social environment of China.

The concept of individual human beings has been created in the West. It has been developed for more than three centuries, from the late 17th century till the 21st century (Zhang JinGao 1999, 10). Are the Chinese ready to accept it, and is the social environment formed to accept it? Before having a discussion on this question, an introduction will be given about the Chinese "Personnel Management". Since SOEs are a major economic element in China, SOE Personnel Management will be discussed, for its representative function in the issues. Let us have a look at the origin of Personnel Management in SOEs.

(1) Labor contract

In the middle of the 1980ies, most Chinese thought that, if one can get into a SOE, then an "iron rice bowl" was guaranteed. That means, the SOE will provide a job for life and cradle-to-the-grave welfare coverage for their employee (Malcolm Warner 1999, 86). That means, the labor contract between employees and enterprises were life-long. The employee who worked under such a contract was called "public employee ". Then in 1986, Chinese enterprises begun to introduce fix-term labor contracts for new employees in some parts of China (Zhan XinMin 1995, 350). This practice spread to the whole country in the early 1990ies. The employee under such a contract was called "labor contract employee". Then in the later half of the 1990ies, the employees in SOEs were all made to sign a labor contract. By then, the life-long employment system came to an end.

But at that time, as an ordinary employee, not a lot of people knew the significance of the reform, until redundancy pressures built up. The enterprises were legally protected in laying off their employees, because of the existence of the labor contracts. Some of the enterprises drew up the policy of "redundancy compensations". According to the policy, certain amounts of money would be paid with regards to the number of service years of the employee. The principles of the policy stated that the employee chose redundancy out of their will, without being forced by anyone. As the inadequate performance of the SOEs had already upset many employees, and the employees often did not have much hopes towards the future of their enterprise, many employees chose to sign for redundancy. However, the process of decision-making was rather painful. Some young employees below 35 felt they were not well-trained in the SOE, and now they were lacking employability, which would be a significant challenge for them. Some middle-aged employee thought they contributed their working life to the enterprises, now being removed with a little compensation. Many people suffered from what they perceived as unfair treatment. The situation is quite clear: signing the agreement, one would get some compensation, and the future will not be ensured by the enterprises any more. Not signing the agreement, one had no compensation and was still facing the risk of being unemployment later on.

Obviously, the employees were caught in a dilemma. The above indicates that labor contracts in China's SOEs were a rather weak tool for the employees, when irreversible reform trends happened.

(2) Reward system

China adopted a grade wage system in the 1980ies, usually eight levels for workers. The difference in pay between each grade was 10 to 20 Yuan (Zhao ShuMing 1995, 173). So, there was not great gap between an ordinary worker's wage and a senior engineer's wage. Bonuses were given monthly or quarterly, varying from one enterprise to the other. Bonus rewarded to the employees did not vary a lot within an enterprise, however. Therefore, employees do not pay a lot of attention to it. Employees were thinking: "If working hard and working less hard are the same, then why should I work hard?" On seeing the inefficiency of the reward system in motivating people, China enforced a reward system reform, aiming at linking the employees wages to performance (Zhao ShuMing 1995, 175). The reform enlarged the wage gap between workers and academically trained staff, since academically trained staff was regarded as the major power to promote the development of enterprise. The wage was divided into several parts, including basic wage, yearly allowance, communication fee, book fee and so on. The reform motivated employee to some extent, but since the planned economy did not provide enough development room for the employees, the motivation function reduced, especially when the SOEs went into an economic downward spiral.

(3) Social insurance

Comprehensive social welfare coverage had for many years been the privilege of SOE employees in the urban sector. However, around one in six workers in SOEs is surplus, and retired employees account for over a third of the total SOE staff, forming a heavy burden. Total work-related insurance and other welfare costs amount to as much as 500 RMB per worker per year on average, excluding low-cost housing (Warner 1999, 88). This is part of the reason why SOEs lose money seriously. Now, the SOE reform is under way: under the new scheme, institutional and industrial employees pay one percent of their monthly salary for medical insurance, and three per cent for their unemployment insurance, whereas work units add another 20 percent for retirement provision and ten percent for medical care.

(4) Personnel management

Under the planned economy system, workers were assigned to enterprises by government bureaus, so there was no need to recruit employee by the efforts of the Personnel Manager. Similarly, retention was unnecessary, because no one would leave the company without a special reason. Training was a rather weak part of SOE personnel management: although all kinds of training plans were drawn up, lack of supervision and assessment systems meant that few plans were more than mere paper. In later 1990ies, the situation improved a little, as enterprises began to realize the importance of training in the overall performance of their employees.

For decades, Performance Appraisal (PA) has been a controversial and much debated subject in HRM for Western countries. Supporters of PA claim that it has worthwhile objectives, such as facilitating the implementation of organizational strategy, linking performance to rewards, enhancing communication between managers and their subordinates, as well as identifying training and development needs. On the other hand, opponents argue that PA may create more problems than it solves. For example, PA has been criticized for focusing too heavily on an individual's past performance, on comparison and other administrative practices, rather than on future goals and development aspects (Cherrie Zhu 1999, 115-116). However, in China, PA is in its infant stage.

The appraisal criteria for senior staff, which are currently used in Chinese PA, consist of four broad areas known as, "good moral practice, adequate competence, positive working attitude and strong performance record". Under these four major criteria, more detailed categories are set up, according to the organization's focus. Methods such as superiors evaluating subordinates and self-assessment are used. Nevertheless, subjective and objective factors in the PA system for cadres can sometimes influence the effects of PA. For example, questions are raised, whether the PA panel for the cadres is fair, or whether the criteria of PA are effective.

As to PA systems for workers, three approaches are commonly used. In the first approach, the appraisal is carried on the basis of job descriptions. Each position is described in detail, including quality control, technical requirements, tools and machine maintenance, labor discipline, caring for the working environment, team work cooperation, and safety of production. The second method is Management by Objective. PA is conducted within each working group, within which each individual has specific objectives to complete. The last method is internal sub-contracting, that is, the enterprise obtains a contract, and then the project or production work is sub-contracted to its internal departments or business units. Each unit is accountable for its profits and losses, and employees are appraised within the units, mainly for compensation purposes (Zhao ShuMing 1995, 151-157).

Form the above analysis it can be concluded, that Personnel Management in China is in the starting stage, scientific methods are not often used in PM. The purpose of illustrating PM in China is to let foreign business people prepare psychologically, if they originally assumed that China's PM is the same as Western HRM. Therefore, a foreign investor needs to realize that there is a tremendous difference to be covered. The following text will touch upon some practical problem in HRM that may be encountered by foreign enterprises.

2. HUMAN RESOURCE CHALLENGES FOR FOREIGN INVESTED ENTERPRISES

Of all the unknowns that organizations face when they venture into China, one of the most intriguing is the Human Resources environment. "Foreign companies face challenges in all aspects of HR management, ranging from traditional HR issues like recruitment, remuneration and dispute resolution, to "soft" issues such as 'face' and '*guanxi*'", this is a frequently heard comment. It has been pointed out that China's Personnel Management shares few common points with Western HRM. So one can ask: if the pure *Western* model is adopted, what will the consequences? The study of Child – an expert on foreign management in China – shows that this approach can cause considerable interpersonal conflict, and make the Chinese generally unwilling to cooperate. However, if the *Chinese* PM practice is accepted, and any changes are limited to financial and technical areas, will good results be produced?.

This approach might be suitable in lower technology industries, and when relatively short contract periods are under negotiation.

Putting these two approaches aside, the third approach involves the integration of Western and Chinese practice. It is easy to draw the conclusion through study, but it is rather difficult for foreign investors to find an effective way to put the theory to practice, for the great gap in culture can make it difficult for the foreign investor to understand many peculiar phenomena and the way of thinking of Chinese people. Therefore, communication problems appear, and the consequence can be that both sides do not trust each other. This kind of suspicion make the implementation of any presumed excellent HRM plan impossible. That is to say, the HR department of a foreign invested enterprise might risk lose the capacity to develop the human resources, and the company risks losing money. Therefore, finding the middle way (*zhong yong zhi dao*) appears of vital importance for FIEs. It is a Confucianism doctrine, and may be proper to describe the situation. It is commonly acknowledged that to learn from the other's experience is a shortcut to avoid making the same mistakes. Therefore, the following discussion is based on the experience of the others to deal with possible HRM issues in China.

a) HR problems in shaping the labor contract

Human Resource issues start with the negotiations to set up a venture. In law, FIE enjoy broad freedom to hire and staff a venture as they wish to. They can choose from the open market or among the staff available from a Chinese partner. "Both the enterprises and the workers and staff members shall, in accordance with the Chinese laws and regulations, conclude and sign a labor contract. Matters as employment, dismissal, salaries and wages, welfare and labor insurance shall be clearly stipulated in the contract", is stated in the Implementation of the Law of the PRC on Wholly Foreign-owned Enterprises. The law for Equity and Cooperative Joint Ventures have the similar regulations.

In the practical operation, considerable labor pressures are brought about to bear on a potential FIE asking for approval. The authorities can withhold approval until the labor contract is suitably adjusted, or else until management control is structured in a way that will permit the Chinese representatives in the venture to control decision-making on labor questions (Daniel Rosen 1999, 90). Moreover, the increasing unemployment rate makes the central and provincial governments wanting to get as many staff in FIEs as possible. The Chinese Partner firm (in the case of JVs) often has a similarly strong interest in maintaining employment levels and management control, even at the expense of performance. Chinese managers traditionally define prestige in terms of high head counts, even if that means lower output per worker (Daniel Rosen 1999,

91). In some SOEs, the staff in administrative offices do not have much work to do, but read newspapers and drink tea in the office. Even though, a manager can not remove them easily, because their complex relationship net (*guanxi wang*) may get the manager into trouble. To be exact: maybe one of his relatives or friends is a senior leader of the manager, and that leader may be unhappy about the case, and even more, interfere with the manager's work by administrative measures.

Therefore, the conclusion is: in China, where complex relationship nets tend to rule the society, be careful not to offend anyone. That is the safest way to protect oneself from hostile attitudes. That may make HRM, a work dealing with people, appearing complicated. But what has been addressed in this part are only the problems emerging at the early stage of negotiation.

b) Recruitment and retention

How do foreign companies go about finding staff in China? Traditionally, foreign enterprises had to hire either from their Chinese Joint Venture partner, or from the Foreign Enterprises Service Corporation (FESCO) or other state bodies. Currently, five state agencies provide such services: FESCO, China International Technology and Intellectual Cooperation Company, SIDA Company, China International Enterprises Cooperation Company and China International Talent Exchange Center. The companies will charge a certain amount of money for providing the recruitment service. Nowadays, with the opening of talent market in 1991, where foreign companies can set up booths to meet job-seekers, the ways of recruiting have expanded. Take BeiJing as an example: the talent market in the International Exhibition Hall runs once or twice every month, with more than 500 exhibition booth available. The talent coming from all over the country gathers around the booths, distributing their resume to the potential employers and trying to show how suitable they are for the available job. Normally, a recruiter can expect receiving more than one hundred CVs, although there may be only one or two vacancies. According to newspaper statistics, the success rate is below 10%, but that does not reduce the enthusiasm of the talent. The reasons for such low success rates are numerous:

- rapidly developing enterprises need comprehensive talent who are good at management and in certain technological fields, since enterprises now share one global market. The Chinese education organs do not always meet the requirement of training such talent due to the quality of teachers and education facilities. The problem is especially urgent in the booming electronics and information industries: e.g., new blood is needed to support the running of newly starting-up website and software companies;

- the employment policies for enterprises set barriers for the entrance of potential staff. For example, *HuKou* and *DangAn* problems still limit the free mobility of some talent. This issue will be addressed separately later;

- the talent market system itself has shortcomings. Just imagine, with a crowd of people before a small desk, try to promote themselves, how can a recruiter form a judgment about anyone. There is a real danger to depend on a CV and subjective first impressions as criteria to choose candidates. In any case, the HR department is not X-ray that can detect the inside of a person immediately. Therefore, if a FIE is attending such a talent market, a careful investigation and selection work is crucial for the success of recruitment.

Apart from these two ways to find candidates, newspaper advertisement is another alternative. Popular newspapers include Career Post, which is the ideal place for prestigious companies to recruit white-collar staff. Talent market newspapers present posts at various levels from blue-collar to white-collar. Youth News Weekly features advertising the news of both companies and job-seekers.

In this information age, the Internet is challenging the traditional ways of recruitment. All kinds of recruitment websites have been established in recent years. Currently, it might be the most convenient way for those using the Internet. Authorized recruitment websites in China include 51job.com and zhaopin.com. Certainly, this channel can only reach those who have access to the Internet. According to the statistics of the China Internet Information Center, there were 4,000,000 Internet users in China in 1999, and the number is increasing rapidly. Therefore, with the expanding of the network, there is an enormous market in on-line recruitment. Due to its convenience, rich information and quick response it has become widely accepted. If a job opportunity is just a few clicks away, almost nobody would refuse to have a try. That is exactly the reason why so many recruitment websites are set up in China. Both the suppliers and the demanders of the HR market support the appearance of a third channel which can link them together.

While recruitment is a challenge to FIE, how about retention? This is a new issue produced with more opportunities provided for talents. "The prosperity of younger Chinese staff to job-hop has been funned by foreign companies competing with each other, causing a wage spiral that would be unacceptable in many other countries . As a result, this has created the need for frequent reviews of the compensation, terms and conditions of employment", comment some foreign investors. In a market where the demand for talent exceeds the supply, finding what your employees need and try to meet their expectations seems the only way to solve the problem.

One of the efforts that some FIE make is home financing programs. Under these programs, the employer uses its financial power to finance low-cost, typically 10-year mortgages for employees; in some cases only for the best employees, in others for all employees. This creates a disincentive to leave the firm, because doing so would lead to foreclosure (Daniel Rosen 1999, 99). This move obviously satisfies those employee who are keen to own their own home.

Another intriguing way of retaining talented employees would be to provide training programs that will help employees grow personally and professionally (Yan XiaoYun 1999, 265). Top talent will stay as long as they pick up more skills and their market value goes up. Training helps to reinforce their self-image, their self-worth, and their ability to work as a team player.

Since everyone has different needs, to identify employees' needs and to meet them becomes an imperative task of Human Resource Management. In the overall program of recruitment and retention, the recruitment and retention of managerial staff might be the most important stage for the double role of managerial staff: on the one hand, the managerial staff is the object of HR programs of a company, on the other hand, they play an creative role in formulating and supervising the implementation of these programs. Therefore, the issue of recruitment and retention of management staff in China will be dealt with more specifically in the following parts.

c) Recruitment and retention of managerial staff in China

The awareness that FIE need a long-term management strategy became stronger and stronger when FIEs saw challenges arising in their management. The original idea that China can be managed in a similar way as other overseas operations has often proven to be wrong, due to the unique business environment of China, which has been discussed in earlier chapters. Under such circumstances, identifying, recruiting and training managers who can help FIE establishing a long-term presence appears a crucial issue related to business success. In this part, several potential ways of recruiting talented managers and possible issues related to recruitment will be addressed.

Initially, most firms will send a manager from their domestic operations to oversee the establishment of a new venture in China. In many cases, this manager will see the appointment as a short-term activity, and as an interruption to his or her normal career with the company. The perception of China as a hardship posting still exists in many companies. According to the study of Tung and Wang, the hardships comes from three aspects: lack of cultural knowledge, communication problems and isolation. The three hardships are highly interrelated. Lack of cultural knowledge leads to communication problems, which in turn result in isolation abroad. Normally speaking, a foreign company has three reasons to send expatriates to manage the business: first, to get things done; this occurs when qualified host country nationals are not available or are difficult to train. The second reason for expatriation is management development; giving managers international experience, preparing them for future important corporate tasks. A third motive for expatriation concerns organizational development and presumes that frequent and large-scale international transfers of managers will create international communication networks, thus allowing for more decentralization than available through traditional bureaucratic means (Jan Selmer 1999, 153).

The policy of using expatriates assumes that all expatriate managers sent to China will be able to operate effectively in the environment. But the case is not so promising as is assumed to be. Some expatriates are unable to cope with the demands of an alien work environment or face personal and family pressure. So what type of management recruitment strategy should be implemented to support a successful long-term pressure in China?

The chance is twofold. One is to recruiting outside the Chinese market. For example, recruiting "in house", which involves identifying those within the company who have a potential to succeed in China. The advantage of this policy is that the person chosen is already familiar with company policies and operational procedures. Moreover, in reporting valid and accurate information, the parent company often reveals a greater degree of confidence if the information emanate from an expatriate manager than if it came from a local employee. Foreign companies have a certain tendency of suspecting the loyalty of their local manager.

The disadvantage of pursing an "in house" recruitment policy is that the new manager has no operational experience in China. The culture, operational, structural and social challenges of separation in the Chinese business environment throw the newcomer in a pool of dense fog. Moreover, if the new manager assumed that accepted standards of business behavior apply universally, then he may risk failure in China. Another drawback of the policy can be reflected after the failure of expatriates. It is can be perceived a "loose-loose" strategy: the expatriate, looses confidence in himself, and the company looses a potentially good manager in the parent company, and has to choose more carefully another person to fill the position (Robert, McEccistor 1999, 100-103).

On seeing the risks of designating an expatriate manager, the company may be considering to select some other possible alternatives. Recruiting potential managers from the overseas Chinese communities is an alternative many choose, for they hold the belief that well-trained, ethnic Chinese expatriates sharing common cultural heritage with the hosts will benefit them (Tung and Wang 1999, 139). This is not necessarily true. Jan Selmer pointed out in this book, that ethnic Chinese expatriate managers from HongKong assigned to Bei-Jing and ShangHai experienced severe difficulties, comparable to the worst ordeals ever reported in the literature on expatriate management. It was found out that while the Western expatriate manager experience a greater cultural distance from China than the ethnic Chinese expatriate, they experience a higher degree of adjustment, especially compared to ethnic expatriate Chinese. Then, the possibility may exist that it could be as hard, or even more difficult for expatriates managers to adjust to a close than to a distant culture. Furthermore, according to the research of McEllister, there was a perception in senior management in many head offices of Western firms that many of these overseas Chinese lacked loyalty and would only work for them long enough to learn their operation and identify their market potential, before returning to their previous home to set up a rival operation. Through the above analysis, it can be seen, to have an overseas Chinese expatriate may not be the best choice.

The second alternative is to identify elite students from the PRC studying abroad. The company identifies the better achieving PRC students in the country's universities system, then offers them incentives to remain and undertake postgraduate studies. While doing this the company looking to recruit them involves the students in a program with a mix of work experience and management training. At the same time, their postgraduate study is tailored to complement the in-house program. The end result, hopefully, is a potential manager skilled in Western management theory, with some practical experience and company indoctrination. Once some of these managers begin to appear in very senior positions within these Western firms they may provide role models for other Chinese graduates to follow, and this policy may gain further acceptance among both Chinese and Westerns (McEllister 1999, 105).

The recruitment methods analyzed here have advantages and disadvantages, and the assessment given above can not be taken as an absolute standard when it comes to cope with real problems. In practical operation, the FIE can choose between these forms, and the criteria would be how the management of the Chinese operation fits in the overall development strategy of the company.

Are the managerial talents available in China's labor market? The answer is, three main pools exist for FIE to find them: existing expatriate population, Chinese management ranks and Chinese graduates (McEllister 1999, 106). Normally speaking, existing expatriates have already lived in China, so will have demonstrated an ability to operate in the environment. Nevertheless, the disadvantage might be they lack loyalty when a more attractive offer arises. – Foreign students studying in China are also a potential pool of managerial talent. A lack of managerial and working experience can be compensated by a comprehensive training program.

Recruiting from Chinese management ranks, such as SOEs or government departments can also be beneficial when these recruits bring with them their business networks. The *guanxi* can be extremely helpful when access to, or favorable treatment by the government is required. –. Chinese graduates serving as a recruitment target group of management talent have their own characters. Since the university system in China is of a uneven standard and many courses fail to produce graduates able to meet the demands of modern Western management, identifying suitable institutions and attracting the talent of graduates able to progress through management ranks will be a task that FIE have to perform attentively.

Recruitment and retention of managerial talent is rather a professional subject, and in-depth analysis could only be performed according to a specific situation. All the discussions above based on the earlier experiences of FIEs and the suggestions mentioned can be used as reference only. A checklist will help a FIE having a quick reflection of their managerial recruitment and retention policy:

1) audit a company's Human Resources, be aware of the staff's previous overseas experience, language skill, and particular cultural knowledge;
2) be aware of existing talent pools in the region for choosing managers;
3) get involved in overseas student programs, sponsoring suitable candidates to carry out in-country study providing them with work experience both in the domestic facilities as well as the Chinese venture;
4) select role models who can then be identified to demonstrate possible career paths;
5) ensure the China operation is viewed by head office as a legitimate equal to other operations, and not as a hardship posting or necessary penance;
6) expatriate managers in China should familiarize themselves with the local business community so that potential sources of managerial talent can be identified;
7) provide further education to Chinese manager in the head office.

d) Training

For the Chinese side, one of the main purposes of setting up FIE is to introduce new technology, which the SOEs are lacking. The laws relevant to the operating of FIEs state this purpose clearly. For example, in the "Detailed Implementation for the Equity Joint Venture Law of the PRC", Article 92 states: "Joint Ventures shall make efforts to conduct professional and technical training of their staff and workers, and to establish a strict examination system so that they can meet the requirements of production and managerial skills in modern enterprises". Why do Chinese pay such attention to training? Can the market not supply enough competent employees for FIEs? The new-comers in China may have this kind of questions. The answer is: the Chinese education system is different the one in the West. Therefore, both the quality and quantity of JV employees may not meet the needs of FIEs. Training can serve to remove performance deficiencies, to update technical knowledge and skills, to increase the adaptability of the workforce, and to increase commitment (Chorrie 1999, 345). As to FIEs, since cross-cultural issues exist, the function of training should contribute to cover the gap between different cultures. This makes training a most crucial step in the successful operation of FIEs.

As far as the enterprises are concerned, many are aware of the importance of training, and various training courses have been designed for different purposes. If the awareness was only on the side of enterprises, training would have less effect, without the reaction of employees. But in today's China, most employees realize how important training is, and they like to take an active part in it. The booming training industry in China is an evidence of such awareness.

All kinds of training courses are on offer. A popular greeting among the Chinese young people is: "What are you learning now?" It can be observed that the booming of Chinese training industry is not a coincidence; it is a reflection of the fact that people need it. To catch up with the rapid development of society is a common idea embraced by many Chinese. The episode of the greeting shows that Chinese are taking initiative to train themselves. In FIEs, if training is provided, and for free, the employees would certainly grasp the opportunity to update their knowledge or skills and thus pave the way for further personal development. Many Chinese will take training opportunities into account when selecting among potential employers.

Having realized the necessity of training, the next step is how to organize training in China. According to the experience of many Western managers, orientation programs are rather helpful to integrate employees into the company. In the orientation course, a range of subjects can be introduced to the employees, including the history, the business scope the enterprises is engaging in, the management systems, the values important to the company, the mission, the vision and the culture of the enterprise. A good orientation design should help employees build confidence about how the enterprise can assist them in gaining knowledge and skills, and how they can contribute to the enterprise. A consensus towards the mission of the employees and the target of the enterprise can be reached based on effective communication between the employees and the trainers.

If the employees are from a SOE, the mindset they formed in the SOE may be an obstacle for them to accept a modern management style. Therefore, to emphasize the importance of working within deadlines, in high efficiency and doing work according to plan will be a long-term training task that has to be performed consistently. Since Chinese employee are used to obey the orders of leaders without considering if they are right or wrong, they would not point out directly any problems directly, in order to protect the face of the leader. Therefore, if interactive suggestions are required, the reaction might be rather passive and less-co-operative; consequently the training should be organized to adjust the attitude of passive acceptance by the employees to an attitude of active participation.

This kind of training might be a formal class, telling the employees how important their participation is. Or, it can be a kind of change exercise by repeatedly practicing in the working process and thus encouraging the employees to practice it by imitating role models. It is essential to let the interaction between employees and employer become a part of the corporate culture. That is the requirement of modern HRM, and it is needed for management levels that is sought after by entrepreneurs (Fu YaHe 1999, 6).

There is not a rule set as to what kind of training should be organized and how it can be organized. The principle of any training is to let it conform with the HR plan and the overall development of the enterprise. Training may involve all levels from the managerial staff to common employees. Whatever the training form is, and whatever the target group is, training must be closely related to the working practice. Only then, lasting effects can be perceived. Any formalism goes against the principle to great impact and should be avoided. In general, training is a tool that paves the way for development, and it can not be over-emphasized, no matter how much attention is paid to the subject.

e) DangAn and HuKou system

DangAn and *HuKou* are two special issues in China; therefore some information about them will be mentioned here to help HR professionals have a primary understanding of the issue.

DangAn *is a personal file, a dossier on each employee, established as early as primary school, and maintained by employers. It tracks an individual's political and professional record from academic grades to performance reports, problems with authorities to marriage and child-bearing. This dossier is an essential record needed before an employer to hire or provide pension and insurance to an individual.*

HuKou *is a residence permit, entitling the bearer to social services and rights available to a local resident only. Without this permit, an individual has no access to subsidized housing, medical care, schooling for dependents, and social security that urban China was organized around over the past 40 years (Daniel Rosen 1999, 102).*

The *DangAn* and *HuKou* system involves many aspects of Chinese citizens, from employment to social security. Therefore, they are the two vital private social identities. Since the local governments worry about the heavy population burden, strict regulations have been promulgated to restrict the mobility of *DangAn* and *HuKou*, especially for big populous cities. This set of regulations, on the one hand, restraints the mobility of talent, for fear of losing the related benefits. On the other hand, it adds trouble to the HRM. If potential employers do not produce the two identities, it will lead to an uncertainty factor in recruitment, since the chronological history of the employee can not be obtained. Furthermore, the design of the compensation package is hard to be perfected, for insurance and housing allowances can not be given to employees without *HuKou* and *DangAn*. This is the regulation of the state. Normally speaking, the FIEs are required to employ local residents for the purpose of convenient management and a solution for employment. On condition that competent or higher level talent can not obtained in the local market, exceptions are allowed. The FIEs would add in their advertisement "*HuKou* and *DangAn* problems can be solved" as a way to attract talent.

In recent years, the restrictions of the employers related to *HuKou* and *DangAn* have been reduced to some extent. But the removal of the restrictions can only be performed gradually before a new social security management system established. The establishment of freelance service companies was seen as an alternative way for the regulation that FIEs are not permitted to hold *DangAn* and *HuKou* for Chinese workers directly. They can help the FIE to keep their employee's *DangAn*. For some staff, temporary residence permits are supplementing the *HuKou* during assignments away from their home municipality.

The above analysis indicates that some flaws exists in China's social management system. FIEs face the challenge to formulate a HRM plan that is adapted to the current situation.

f) Reward systems

A reward system includes the salary, housing, bonus, medical care, insurance and many other components. These compensation components are significant in attracting and motivating employees; therefore some information will be presented here to explain the relative importance of the different compensation elements in recruiting, motivating and retaining local employees.

According to the investigation results of Vivienne Luk, base salary, merit pay and year bonus were the three most significant items, as perceived by employers, for managers, supervisors and workers. The fourth and fifth position were occupied by housing provisions, annual leave, cash allowance and individual bonus. It can be found that all top five ranks were basically occupied by cash-form types of reward mechanisms. Salary, as a powerful incentive, has a substantial impact on performance motivation. But since egalitarianism is challenged, other cash-forms of rewards are also considered important by local Chinese. Then come merit pay and year-end bonus. Those two forms of compensation rewards have been widely practiced in Chinese enterprises to reflect the philosophy "work hard, get more".

Why do cash-form rewards occupy such a vital position in the view of Chinese employees? It may be explained by the following (Vivienne Luk 1999, 146):

1) Chinese culture encourages financial independence; the amount of cash one possess can reflect the independence status of a person;

2) the equity theory drive the employees expecting a dollars pay for a dollars work;

3) employees do not trust their employers, therefore, the indirect forms of reward, like social benefits – such as children facilities and holidays – were perceived as less dependable than the cash in one's pocket;

4) some want to save enough money to start their own business.

In the light of these findings, employers are recommended to design their reward systems to provide employees with take-home cash as the highest proportion of the package. Furthermore, with the perfection of Chinese social security system, various types of insurance and housing allowances and so possess a more and more important position in Chinese people's minds. Thus, in designing rewards packages, the principle should be: meet the needs of the various levels of employees, and keep a balance between the different components.

3. CONCLUSION

The text examines the current state of China's Personal Management and some aspects of FIE Human Resource Management, based on the experience of early FIEs. From the above analysis it can be concluded that China's Personnel Management was built on the planned economy system, and it does not always function efficiently under current market economy conditions. In light of the competitive principle of market economy – "survival of the fittest", PM, as a crucial part of enterprises management, needs to modify itself to meet the needs of the economic development. Compared to China's PM, Western HRM is more advanced in terms of market fit.

FIEs, as a mixture of Chinese and foreign economic elements, operating in the Chinese environment, undoubtedly will meet problems in their HRM. Under such circumstances, what HRM strategy should FIEs adopt: Chinese PM practice or Western company's HRM style, or rather, to formulate a new HRM that would be designed to introduce Western advanced HRM experience and possess strong adaptability to China's specific management needs? Or, in other words: is it necessary for FIEs to create a new HRM theory and practice that is specific to the Chinese market? The answer is probably 'yes'. The theoretical basis of the answer lies in the range of aspects which are closely connected with the questions discussed earlier:

1) the comparatively backward Chinese PM needs fresh blood;

2) the market economy in China welcomes new adaptable HRM;

3) the special basis of society, such as culture, people's ideas and concepts, demands the formation of a new HRM;

4) Western HRM needs a high degree of flexibility in order to succeed in the Chinese market.

The purpose of talking so much about the need to create a new HRM is, to indicate that the FIEs need to take initiative in their practice. Only on the basis of such initiative, problems can be detected, and the way of solving the problems can be found, too. What has been discussed in the text is only a small fraction of the problems. The next level of research can only be performed by the FIEs themselves, just like a Chinese proverb indicates: "hearing one hundred times is not as good as seeing once."

H. CREATING RELATIONSHIPS

One frequently used word in China is *guanxi*; not long after one arrives in China, one will hear this word. There are many words related to *guanxi*: to *la guanxi* (literally to "pull" *guanxi*) means to get on the good side of someone, to store political capital with a person; it carries no negative overtones (Arne de Keijzer 1992, 156). To *tao guanxi* (literally to "coax" *guanxi*) means to find a relationship with someone through somebody else's relationship, and to show good desire to built a friendship. *Guanxi zheng*, *guanxi* "tie", refers to a situation in which a relationship is as solid as iron and as good as from one's own family. *Guanxi hu* means a person, organization, even government department, occupying a key position in one's *guanxi* network. *Guanxi wang* means the whole network of *gunaxi* through which influences is brokered. – These are only a few examples of *guanxi* terms; in fact, it is only a small fraction of all the related terms. From the high using frequency, one can gather a primary impression: *guanxi* is of high importance in China. That is right: Chinese live in a huge *guanxi* network and have to deal with *guanxi* everyday. Then, one may ask: what does *guanxi* mean in China, what kind of *guanxi* exist in China, and why is *guanxi* so highly valued?

Guanxi means interpersonal relationship; it is a kind of psychological feeling of people, and it can be measured in terms of distances. Therefore, if people's psychological distance is far, then their relationship is unfamiliarity; in the inverse case, it is intimacy. In one's life, one has various relationship with others, because one contacts people every day. – A hypothesis can be made: each person is a node, the *guanxi* a person has is just like a line connecting him with other people, and the line can be short and long. Through such links, a net is formed. In this case, people interact with each other. This net is referred to *guanxi wang* in China. It is not difficult to imagine a comparison with the modern Internet: one will find they share the same principle; it is just that the Internet is a modern phenomenon, while the *gunaxi wang* has already been in effect for thousands of years.

Similar to foreign countries, there are various relationships: work relationships, classmate relationships, teacher and student relationships and many other varieties. The difference lies in the link method and contexts. One may say that the line between Chinese people is stronger and more sensitive than that between foreigners, that means, Chinese are influenced and regulated more strongly than foreigners. Therefore, it is not strange that Chinese value *guanxi* highly.

In the chapter on culture, Chinese culture has been defined as agriculture culture. Agricultural production required people to cooperate with each other closely, due to the rather low production capacity in ancient China. The smallest production unit in China was the family. The family members were connected by blood relationship. The "clan" was the larger family; it was formed by several families. Of course, these families had blood relationships. The "patriarchal clan" was the highest organ of clan, several clans formed a patriarchal clan. Therefore, one could say that China was a patriarchal society: the emperor was the biggest feudal father; below him were feudal fathers at different levels.

Starting the analysis from there, China could be described as a status society with blood relationships as its tie. In the status society, the role of each person was strictly regulated by ethics. Here "ethics" refers to the Confucian ethical idea. Confucius said: "father and son should be intimate, subjects should be loyal to their emperor, husbands should be distant from their wives, elder and younger should be in order, friends should be trustworthy (Jia YuXin 1997, 161). This is just the basic principle of interpersonal relationships in feudal China. It helps to explain why Chinese obey and respect authority, and why there are so many relationships of leader and subordinate in China.

Confucius emphasized that a benevolent person loves the others, that means people were encouraged to love each other. However, this love is different, depending on the different relationships between people. In Confucius's idea, love and social status did not contradict with each other; love had to conform with the requirements of the social status system, while the social status system was maintained by love. In general, whether looking at the patriarchal social system or at the feudal ethics of Confucius, what they are emphasizing and regulating is the relationship between people. People lived in a relationship society. Naturally, relationships were highly valued. Therefore, the conclusion would be like this: *guanxi* is the product of Chinese culture.

In the *guanxi* of China, many emotional elements are part of the equation. Therefore, when people talk about *guanxi*, naturally they would think about the corresponding responsibilities and obligations. If two people have a relationship, then they are required to show empathy to each other and take up the corresponding duty. If a person has many relationships, then there are many people feeling responsible for and taking care of that person. Certainly, this relationship makes one feel comfortable. Just imagine, when one travels to a place, where one has friends. The relationship one has will give one's friends the feeling that they should take up the responsibility to look after the traveler. Thus they will arrange a hotel, meet and greet, perhaps serve as tour guide. And in return, perhaps one will buy a gift for this consideration. In this way, the relationship is strengthened.

Now, you form a primary impression of Chinese *guanxi* and its character, and you will understand: as a foreign business person, if you really want to merge into the society and become successful here, it is important to be a nod in this *guanxi* society and to create active and effective links with the others. Then you may ask what *guanxi* you have to create and how to create it.

Depending on your business model, the *guanxi* you will be involved in may vary. Therefore, a specific guidance on what relationship you should create is impractical. The discussion here is not intended to provide a panacea for dealing with various types of relations, but rather the general rules that foreign business people should pay attention to in getting along with the Chinese. Here a foreign enterprise will be set as an example to illustrate the *guanxi* issue.

No matter whether you are representing a Chinese or foreign enterprise, dealing with government is the necessary course you have to learn. It has been pointed out in earlier chapters: Chinese government plays a special role in business activities. Generally speaking, foreign enterprises have to deal with the following department (Li KePing 1999, 24-25):

- the local government, which is responsible for promulgating local foreign trade and economic policies;
- public security and judicial organs, which supervise and examine among others: the maintenance of public security, road occupation, means of transportation and economic litigation;
- custom offices and commodity inspection bureaus, responsible for clearance of goods through customs, customs inspection and health quarantine;
- the tax bureau and the financial bureau, responsible for collecting tax, supervising and examining financial activities;
- the audit and statistic bureau, which conducts official examination of financial and tax work to the company;
- the industry and commerce bureau, and the healthy epidemic prevention station, which is in charge of company registration, trademark registration, contract management and resolving contractual disputes. Enterprises producing food and medicine, as well as re-

lated products and equipment, have to accept the examination of the production process and the products by the health epidemic prevention station;

- the state license issuing department and patent bureau also provide services related to enterprises;

- foreign enterprises may have to deal with some other departments, such as the environmental protection bureau and the quality supervision department.

On seeing so many departments on the list, perhaps you will feel puzzled. Never mind, so long as your *guanxi* is properly disposed, these departments would provide adequate service to you instead of becoming a barrier on the development road. Then what is the proper way to build relationships?

First of all, you should abide by the various regulations of the government and get a clear understanding of what has government support and what is forbidden, and adjust your company's policy accordingly. Take the employment and welfare system as an example: the Chinese state and local governments all have their rules to regulate the enterprises' operations. Some local government does not allow foreigners to recruit the residents of other provinces, so that the employment of their province could be ensured. If this policy contradicts with the employment policy of your company and you have adequate reason to insist on your policy, make a statement to the department in charge and you can expect a considerate reply from them. In coping with contradictions, public confrontation should be avoided. Chinese people appreciate harmony, and they will contribute efforts to keep such harmony. And you are expected to maintain harmony, if you are acting according to what you are expected to do, then government officials will feel that you give face (*gei mianzi*) to them and they will give you face in return.

Therefore, adopting an indirect way of negotiation with Chinese government officials is recommended here. For example, find a "China hand" who may be an experienced consultant that is familiar with your issue, entitle him to cope with it for you or visit the official yourself, express your view sincerely based on adequate reason and using polite attitude (*keqi*) to make them feel they are respected, and your problem may be resolved. At the same time, you can try to find a *guanxi* with them: maybe one of your friends or employees who claim to have a good *guanxi* with the official. You can ask them to introduce you to the official. By looking after the *mianzi* of his acquaintance, the official will pay more attention to your problem.

At this stage, a warning should be given. In the process of choosing the right introducing person, you need to make sure if the person has enough *mianzi* to gain the empathy of the officer. Otherwise, the interference of the mediator can make the problem more complex, instead of bringing hope to resolving the problem. After being introduced, you can contact the officer actively and find a proper opportunity to discuss the problem. Furthermore, do not try to find relationships with the officials only when problems happen; in normal times, you should try to establish a relationship with them through various ways. This is exactly what Chinese call "flexible", and this ability is appreciated by everyone. The above is only an example of dealing with Chinese government officials. In the process, public and personal relationships are mentioned; if you really can command the subtle *guanxi* between public and personal *guanxi*, then you can be called a "*guanxi* scholar". One thing you should always keep in mind: your action of *la guanxi* with officials must be reasonable and legal.

In dealing with government departments, other than regular communication, you can also seize advantageous opportunities to contact them so that your prestige and influence are enlarged. For example, you can invite government officials to participate in ribbon-cutting ceremonies, news conferences, major corporate events, inspection tours, seminars, exhibitions, etc. Sponsoring government initiated community projects and civic affairs can also be a good way of initiating closer relationship with them. You can take advantage of such opportunities to send gifts to the officials. In general, in dealing with government departments, an active, cooperative and sincere attitude can be helpful to create a close and harmonious *guanxi*.

Except for government relationships, creating *guanxi* with your cooperative partner is also very important. Here, cooperative partner is not limited to your partner in one company, but also refers to your raw material suppliers, your distributors, your authorized agents, your advertisement agents and those entities with which you have business relationships. It has been mentioned earlier: you are a nod in a network, and you can treat these partners as other nods in the same network. The common benefits connect you together closely. It can be described by a Chinese saying: "a slight move in one part may affect the situation as a whole".

In the end, you and your partners share one motivation: generating profits. Therefore, you should hold the belief that your partner embraces the same good wish as you do. With this belief, when contradictions build up, you will have the patience to negotiate. Chinese stress collectivism and possess a very strong collective awareness. This may be different from the West. A Western person is comparatively more independent. Thus, when trying to build relationships with Chinese, Chinese will ask you to put more energy and enthusiasm in maintaining relationships. Perhaps you would think that Chinese are demanding, and the Chinese would think you lack sincerity to build good relationships with them. Thus, avoiding such misunderstandings is a crucial step in creating relationships.

Chinese people often say, "if one man is helped by three the others, he becomes a true man". Nevertheless, in order to win the help of three other men, what does the would-be true man have to contribute? Here are some suggestions (Li Yong 1995, 252):

- Be honest and keep your word. In a business operation, this is the top principle to win the others' confidence. Without this confidence, your partner will look at you with suspicion, they will wonder if you are cheating them. A Chinese saying speaks vividly about this problem: "once bitten by snake, one shies at a coiled rope for next ten years." Therefore, do not take the risk of going against this principle. Furthermore, every Chinese business person has a large group of *ganxi hu*, if your bad behavior is known by one of them, then your name will be ruined. Do not expect anyone to show mercy on you; Chinese have the habit to spread rumors, just like a Chinese saying goes: "Good deeds are never heard of outside the door, but bad deeds are proclaimed for three hundred miles."

- Share benefits together. Making money is what every business person seeks after. Therefore, the ultimate goal of your partner is to get common opportunities with you to make money. Thus, do not try to maximize your profits by minimizing the other's profits. Without common profits as motivation, nobody will help you.

- Show empathy with your partner. Chinese stress emotional communication with the others. If you always mind your own business without showing consideration to your partners, he will feel you are far away from them and do not belong to the same group. The next time, when you have problem, he will not show sympathy to you because of lack of empathy. Chinese pay attention to "exchanging one's heart with the other's heart". So long as you provide your true heart to the others, you will get a true heart back in return.

- Warm the threshold. Even if your business with the Chinese Partner is quite sporadic, keeping warm the relationships with them should be considered as a part of the long-term strategy: a Christmas and New Year card may remind them of your existence,

> and that they are remembered. Occasional phone calls will give the relationship a little personal touch. When you travel to China for unrelated business, having a chat over lunch or dinner would bring the relationship even closer. When the paths of your business do cross some time in the future, you will still be treated as an old friend.

In China *guanxi* rules; *guanxi* with media can not be neglected. A good working relationship with the media in China is imperative for successful public relations. The Chinese media are not only the mouthpiece of the government, but also an avenue of public relations. In recent years, media have developed rapidly in China. All kinds of newspapers, television station, journals and radios carry abundant information for people to choose from. Since public media in China are owned by government, they have a special position in the minds of Chinese people. People tend to believe that what the media say is true. Therefore, setting up good relationships with the media appears valuable for an enterprise that wants to be publicized by media. Because of the free character of news reports, developing personal relationships with reports seems rather crucial. The competition for good personal relationships with them has resulted in the abnormal practice of paying for news reports (Li Yong 1995, 256). Some news reporters have taken advantage of the opportunity and became rich quickly, disregarding professional morality to provide impartial reports. Excessive publicity on the good aspects of enterprises are a common phenomenon. Under such circumstances, dealing with media becomes a complicated task.

Maintaining a good relations requires a lot of understanding about the media business. You need to know that news media need; what news will produce good publicity effects. Being responsive and cooperative is the key to good media relationships. It always pays off to build good personal relationships with journalists and reporters.

Conclusion: apart from the relationships mentioned above, there are others which can not be ignored in corporate public relations, such as industry experts and research professionals, community staff and competitors. Not too much has to be said here about how to develop relationships with them, because the principle of creating *guanxi* in China is always the same. What you need to pay attention to is some details in different situations, and no one can teach you that. Furthermore, when dealing with Chinese, do not always think of them as different from you and do not worry too much what tactics should be applied to treat them. Anyway, Chinese are not more special than others; therefore, being considerate and keeping an unassuming and approachable attitude are enough to create good *guanxi* with Chinese.

I. PROMOTING PRODUCTS AND SERVICES

1. CHOICE OF MARKETING STRATEGY

It is commonly recognized that the realization of value must be performed through the commodity market; the process of market exchange is reinforced by marketing, or more accurately, marketing is the process of planning and executing the conception, pricing, promotion and distribution of ideas, goods and services to create exchange that is satisfying individual and organization goals (international marketing 1999, 23). With the development of the commodity economy, the exchange has freed itself from the limitation of national boundaries. Thus, a corresponding kind of marketing has evolved: international marketing. As different countries have quite different market environments, such as consuming habits, purchasing power, market distribution channels and so on, a challenge has built up for those market participants: What strategy should they adopt, a standardized marketing strategy, or an adaptable marketing strategy? This might be the first question any international business person has to ask.

To solve the problem, a question that that is closely related to the question must be mentioned here in order to make the answer of the question and the other related questions reasonable. This related question is: what is the objective of choosing a marketing strategy? The question may appear meaningless to a business person, but as the starting point of a series of questions, this question is extremely significant. The correct answer of this question can only be: maximizing profits. This conforms with the essence of the commodity economy, and it is also the reason for the existence of the commodity economy.

Having defined the objective, the next question is: where to find the maximized profits? Common business sense would state: from customers. That is to say that the customers ensure the maximized value. In this sense, customers are the ones that possess the biggest value to the realization of profits, and as a consequence, to the marketing strategy. Through this analysis, the core of marketing strategy is defined: the customer. Therefore, any marketing strategy must be developed with the customer standing in the center. That means, the marketing strategy must focus on understanding customers and environments, creating superior value for customers and building long-term relationships when appropriate (international marketing, 1999, 23). Obviously, in dealing with the relationships between customers and marketing strategy, the customer is in the dominant position, while marketing strategy is in a subordinate position. Therefore, the conclusion can be drawn like this: a successful marketing strategy should be a course that brings values to customers and thus bring profits to the firms. This conclusion provides a criterion for the international business person in choosing between global strategy and adaptable strategy.

Having understood that customers are the core of marketing strategy, then the strategy choice should be made according to the value concept of the specific customers. Nowadays, the world is experiencing an unprecedented globalization wave. Will the world be integrated by it? Will the value concepts be integrated through this movement? The answer is "probably not": first of all, the globalization is limited to the economy. The economic system and development model were influenced greatly by the economic globalization. But the effects can not be exaggerated too much, for no matter how strong it is, the differences in economic development models and value tendencies can not merge into the same one. Therefore, it can be seen that economic globalization can not bring economic integration (Li ZhongKui 1999, x). This judgment proves the existence of the various economic feature in different countries.

Value concepts, as a deep-rooted reflection of culture, can not be changed overnight, even if the wave of economic globalization is strong. This has been determined by the characteristics of culture: culture is a historical concept, and it tends to be handed down from generation to generation. The people all over the world have lived in their respective countries, worked together and therefore formed many common cognition to the world, such as common beliefs, art, morality, laws and customs; these common phenomena reflect the people's collectives way of thinking, value concept, ideal personality and ethical concept. This deep-level contents of a specific culture is fortified through a long time, possibly thousands of years; so it is deep-rooted in the people's mind, and it is very difficult to change.

This is certainly true in China, a country claiming to have 5,000 years of history. The Chinese people have their unique value concept in judging what beauty is and what not, what good is and what evil is. But this is not only true in China but also in other countries that share some common cultural background, such as the United Kingdom, the United States, Canada, Australia and New Zealand (Herbig 2000, 53).

It should be noted that the deep-rooted value concept was strengthened by economic globalization. It can be explained like this: people need to have a community recognizing their value concept. Only by living in such a community people can gather self-awareness and be identified as a valuable person. Nevertheless, economic globalization introduces new value concepts into many countries; that means the old value concept might be denied. On observing the danger of the loss of the soil that their values are rooted in, they may rebel against the invasion. Actually, the process of defending value concepts is aimed at maintaining their original value. Therefore, the conclusion here can be illustrated in this way: no matter how strong the economic globalization is, the integration of value concept can not be achieved in the short term. Therefore, a strategy of absolute standardization can not be realized, since it requires cultural integration and advocates standardized marketing strategies in the world market.

Neglecting the specific features of a group will probably not please its members. In fact, an absolutely global marketing strategy is doomed to be a failure. Take Nike as an example: Nike has formulated a centralized marketing strategy, and the activities of their global marketers were standardized in the headquarters. The company chose one advertising company as agent to promote the products. The promotion slogan and picture was the same world-wide, and the result was not satisfactory. This is an example to show the shortcomings of absolute standardization. Nevertheless most successful global companies, such as McDonald's or Coca-Cola were respected as the role models of standardization. But it should be noted that the marketing standards of these company are quite far from absolute standardization (Herbig 2000, 53). McDonald's provides a standard menu, but still adjusts it according to the local environment: they supply a kind of berry beverage in Brazil, have introduced a kind of fruit juice in Malaysia, Singapore and Thailand, and sell Chinese food in Japan. Therefore, an absolutely standardized strategy will not be suggested for China. Just like what has been mentioned before: the great discrepancy in economic developing models and value concepts would pose a challenge for the implementation of the strategy.

Then can an adaptable strategy be forcefully implemented in China? It should be noticed that adaptable strategies come with high costs. It is time- and capital-consuming to formulated a whole set of marketing strategies specially for China. Furthermore, the implementation of an adaptable strategy has the risk of neglecting the common aspects between the Chinese market and other markets. For example, Chinese young people embrace the same love for MTV, American movies and sport jackets. Chinese people need highly efficient services of high quality as well. Therefore, if an adaptable strategy exaggerates the differences between Chinese consumers and those in other countries', the result may be both high cost and low efficiency.

Having seen the disadvantages of both standardized strategies and adaptable strategies, a type of strategy has been developed that tries to overcome the disadvantages of both of them whilst combining their respective strength, which is "global localization" (Herbig 2000, 56). This kind of strategy emphasizes global thinking and local implementation. For example, Sony drew up a long-term strategy in Tokyo, while the local managers all over the world make their own product decisions. It has been proven that the consumers have began to adopt some similar life styles, but that their traditional value concepts do not disappear. This is exactly the theoretical basis of the usefulness of "global localization".

The strategy may be accepted in China since its essence conforms with the Chinese way of doing business. Chinese admire the unification of sticking to principles and adopting flexibility in their action, which can be seen in many things. For example, in Chinese "*qigong*" which advocates the combination of hardness and softness. Or in China's policy to HongKong and Macao and one country, two system principle. These are good examples of the unification of firmness and flexibility. Therefore, it can be observed that the strategy of "global localization" may be accepted by Chinese theoretically. In practical operation, the feasibility of the strategy has been proven by many successful multinational companies, such as P&G, which almost monopolizes the Chinese shampoo market. Furthermore, the original purpose of the "global localization" strategy gives consideration to both the unification of demands of the consumers, and the peculiarity of value concepts of different consumer groups. Therefore, the answer to the question raised about the marketing strategy choice can be given: adopt "global localization" as a strategy in China.

2. PROMOTING PRODUCTS

After examining the marketing strategy from a higher level, now "promotion" is chosen as the topic for further discussion. The reason for choosing promotion as the topic is that promotion is more rich of cultural context than the other stages of marketing (Herbig 2000,19). Promotion, as the last stage of marketing, takes the responsibility of propagating and displaying the products, thus letting the consumers understand the enterprise and its products, and finally being motivated to buy the product (Gan BiQun 1999, 450). From the responsibility and aim of promotion, it can be seen that actually promotion is a process of propagating a kind of value and trying to get it accepted by the consumers. Therefore, promotion makes direct contact with consumers, is examined by consumers directly, and the criterion of the consumer in examining is exactly their value concept. Thus, whether a promotion works or not is determined by the extent to which the organizer understands the culture of their target consumers. In understanding the significance that culture plays in promotion, the implementers of a promotion strategy hold the key to the communication with their customers.

Then, how does difference in culture influence the operation of promotion in different cultures? An example can illustrate this: an American company put up a huge advertisement, in which a Japanese woman was wearing a kimono. The position she took was one that in Japan is reserved for prostitutes. One can imagine the effects of that advertisement (Herbig 2000, 162). Such examples are numerous; the basic reason of the phenomenon is the lack of proper understanding of the target consumer's culture.

With respect to the characteristics of Chinese market, what should one pay attention to? Chinese culture highlights harmony, the harmony between organization and individual, the harmony between people and so on can always stimulate the sympathy of Chinese. Therefore, in promotion strategy, one should pay attention to this subject. For example, in order to get feedback from Chinese customers about the recognition degree of products as a basis for a marketing plan, some investigation is needed. But it must be considered carefully what questions should be asked and in what manner. If it is a verbal investigation, then most likely, Chinese will give a positive response. This will make the other happy, thus keeping a harmonious atmosphere (although sometimes a superficial one); this is just what the Chinese seek after. Therefore, one should not expect that the result of such investigation is true. If it is an investigation in written form, one should not ask the Chinese to compare one product with another. Such comparisons give Chinese the impression that someone is trying to draw positive comments on his product. If one tries to break the balance in their concept by letting them compare, one will face resistance. Many Chinese think: to keep balance is beauty, while Westerners think: distinguishing things is beauty.

As mentioned before, China is a relationship society, and Chinese people live in a complicated *guanxi* web that asks to abide by strict rules. Certainly, such rules will not be seen from the surface, even though some of them have been put in law. The reason for emphasizing the relationship between Chinese here is that such relationships will be involved in promotion rather often. For example, in Chinese advertisements, family situations are frequently used (Wang LuChang 1998, 5). In promoting health caring products, a young couple presenting it as a gift to their father or mother always will evoke the sympathy of Chinese, for in the Chinese value concept, filial piety is highly appreciated. There are also parent's love for children, the true consideration between sisters and brothers, husbands and wife's true love and so forth. Love and dedication to each other dominate family relationships. It would surely be accepted, if such subjects are used in the promotion process to highlight the value of these relationships. Take another example to illustrate the theory: in a air-conditioner advertisement, a mother puts her baby in an air-conditioned room, and the baby is soundly sleeping. The love of mother to the baby is strengthened and shown by the use of the air-conditioner. The function of the air-conditioner is revealed through such a caring situation. Thus the air-conditioner becomes the symbol of tender love. The value of the air-conditioner is fully revealed in the advertisement.

From the advertisement, it can also observed that Chinese adopt an implicit way to express their thoughts. They did not use clear, positive words to reveal the characteristics of the product. How excellent the products are can sometimes only be learnt from the implicit picture of the advertisement. Actually, this is exactly the feature of Chinese culture. The Chinese language is implicit, the Chinese way of expression is implicit, and this can be found in many situations. For example, the smile of Chinese girl. In the traditional Chinese culture, the most beautiful smile of a girl is not to show her teeth while lowering the head a little. Certainly, the criterion has slightly changed, but the criterion to judge beauty does not disappear. For many Chinese, being implicit is a virtue of people, and the things embodying such implicit statements are beautiful. For example, no matter how successful a man is, he should not express it too clearly in his words and his behavior. He would better keep silence and behave as a common person. Only in this way, if one day, his merit is discovered by the others, its beauty will appear convincing. With respect to the value of being implicit in the Chinese concept, one should embody and respect this kind of implicit statements in one's promotion, especially in advertisements and public relationship campaigns in order to gain maximum acceptance.

In the above text, three aspects of the Chinese value concept and its effects on the characteristics of promotion in China have been discussed. These three aspects, *harmony*, *family relationships* and *being implicit* are only a rough profile of Chinese value concepts. It should be noticed that these three aspects belong to the macro-side of value concepts. As to how the harmony is defined in daily life, what kind of family relationships are best and what the specific ways are to show implications belongs to the micro-side of the study. Corresponding to the macro-side of value concepts, there are macro promotion strategies. Corresponding to the micro-side of value concepts, there are specific promotion plans, which must combine the detailed information of products and the characteristics of the target consumers. That is to say, they have to be connected with the specific situation of promotion. Therefore, the answer of the questions will not be given here, and the study will only be developed on the macro-side. It only tries to help one understand some characteristics of the Chinese value concept and to formulate a corresponding macro promotion strategy.

Value concepts embody many aspects. They range from judgment on social hot issues to color preferences. It has been pointed out that different cultures teach people different value concepts. Nevertheless, there are some common value concepts among people all over the world: one may think of the appreciation of health, energy, strength and youth, the love for clear air and beautiful flowers, the love for modernization and convenience brought by hi-tech and so on. These are the common concepts existing in different nations.

Based on these common value concepts, common demands have built up, and the economic globalization has become possible. Therefore, promotion strategies should not neglect such common aspects. In fact, only because of the existence of common value concepts can global marketing be realized and can a global promotion strategy be formulated. Without such common demands, globalization would lose the foundation that it based on, and the related marketing and promotion would loose their value totally.

Because of the existence of commonly shared value concepts and demands, Chinese companies use many similar promotion methods, such as sending samples, delivering lottery tickets, onsite consulting, exhibitions and so on. How these methods were developed and if they are introduced from overseas is not important; the significance lies in the fact that it demonstrates that common promotion methods can be realized in the Chinese market. That indicates that in drawing up a promotion strategy in China, one should not over-emphasize the disparity of Chinese value concepts with the foreign ones. The formulation of a promotion strategy must consider the two sides of Chinese culture: one side is the common points and the other is special points. Fully understanding the common points is the starting point of stressing the special points. Furthermore, the cultural contents of the products one wants to promote is often crucial when choosing promotion channels (Wang LuChang 1998, 17).

For example, sports products represent health and energy, and these two characteristics are welcomed in any culture. Thus sports products have relatively little cultural content. Food, on the other hand, varies greatly from country to country, and what is considered delicious food in one country may be thought terrible in another country. Therefore, food has more cultural content than sports products. People accept products that have little cultural contents more easily than those having more. According to this characteristic, when formulating the promotion strategy of products with little cultural content, one should highlight the common value concepts and use a standard promotion strategy. On the other side, diversified promotion should be adopted to conform with special value concepts. This can be taken as the principle of promoting products in China. The core of the principle is to balance the relationship between the cultural contents of products and Chinese value concepts, thus gaining maximum acceptance by the Chinese consumer.

3. ADVERTISING IN CHINA

In the earlier parts, marketing strategy and promotion strategy in the Chinese market were dealt with in combination with the characteristics of the Chinese culture. Advertising, as a popular promotion method, will be discussed in this part for the purpose of providing some practical information on how the

Chinese advertising industry works and how should go about doing advertisements in China. The discussion will begin by introducing the Chinese advertising industry.

Before the opening up in 1979, there was hardly any commercial advertising in China. The advertising industry in China did not start until 1981, when advertising revenue totaled only 118 million RMB. In the past ten years, however, the industry developed very rapidly. The revenue of 1996 reached 36,660 million RMB, which is 311 times that of 1981 (Li Yong 1998, 247). From 1992 to 1995, business income has risen at a rate of 97 percent, 49 percent, 36 percent from the previous years respectively. The speed with which the industry has taken off has made advertising a very important sector of the Chinese market economy (Zhang HePing 1998, 6). By the end of 1999, there were 64,882 advertising units, including advertising companies, television stations, broadcast stations, newspapers, journals, wire broadcast stations and some other units. Professional staff in the field reached 579,000, and the total advertising turnover reached 62 billion RMB. The detailed statistics can be obtained from the table below.

Name of the Advertisement Unit	**Advertising Unit**		**Professional Staff**		**Turnover (billion)**	
	Number	Ratio %	Number	Ratio %	Number	Ratio %
Advertising Company	36132	55,7%	368638	62,7%	27,78	44,7%
Television Station	2982	4,6%	266693	4,5%	15,61	25,0%
Broadcast Station	763	1,2%	6469	1,1%	1,25	2,0%
Newspaper Office	2252	3,5%	20689	3,5%	11,23	18,0%
Journal Office	3943	6,1%	18129	3,1%	0,89	1,4%
Cable TV Station	316	0,5%	1801	0,3%	0,05	0,1%
Other Units	18464	28,4%	145028	24,7%	5,37	8,6%

■ *Table 1: Promotion in China 1998*

Among the advertising units, there are advertising companies having absorbed foreign capital and those monopolized by stated-owned media. According to the statistics of the Chinese Advertising Association, there are 23 Joint Ventures, 20 state-owned companies, 5 collective companies and 2 private companies among the top 50 advertising companies in China according to turnover. One appealing phenomenon is that the first six places are all occupied by Joint Venture companies. From this fact it can be seen that the development of the Chinese advertising industry is inseparable from foreign support. China's advertisement units inevitably learned the advertising concepts, management and techniques from their foreign partners. This is one of the reasons behind the rapid growth of China's advertising industry, which conforms with the economic growth of China.

China's advertisement industry has developed to different stages in different parts of the country. Nine of the top ten provinces in advertising income concentrate in coastal areas. Those with turnover exceeding 1 billion RMB are all in coastal areas. BeiJing, TianJin, ShangHai, JiangSu, FuJian, ShanDong, GuangDong and SiChuang account for 82% of the total turnover. Beijing, ShangHai and GuangDong alone account for 46% of the total national turnover, while the Western Region takes up only 9% of the total *(modern ad 2000, 14)*. The unbalanced situation between various regions reflects the relationship between the advertisement industry and the market economy in general: the more the economy is developed, the more the region has already adopted the market economy, the more developed the advertisement industry is. Therefore, market and advertisement industry interact as both cause and effect.

The role of advertisements has changed from simply promoting products to helping enterprises promoting their image, propagating corporate culture and leading the formation of value concepts of people. Therefore, the operation state of an enterprise is determined largely by how their advertisements fulfilled their role. To put it simple: it depends on how successfully they communicated with their customers. For a foreign enterprise, such communication appears challenging work, for their new image and new products have to undergo a process of recognizing and acceptance by the customers. Then what should a foreign enterprises pay attention to in their advertisements, and how to find an effective way to communicate with Chinese customers? The following are some indications that might have reference value.

a) Understanding the consumer

First of all, an accurate division of consumer groups has to be defined; an example will be presented here. This will answer the question of what kind of consumers will a foreign enterprise face. According to different value concepts and life styles, China's consumers could be divided into different groups, which are strivers, pressured, adapters, traditionals and unassigned (Xiu ZhiMing 1997, 172):

- *Strivers* refers to those young people who strive to go upward in life. This group accounts for a large proportion of the young people, aged eighteen to thirty-five. Achievers are those that have success in their career and are admired by strivers. This group represents high level consumption; its members are the mainstream of luxury life.

- *Pressured* group means the female consumers; they have to share family and economic burden together with their husband. The reason that they were defined as an independent group is that they represent a new group that came into being in the twenty years of reform. In the traditional Chinese concept, the female's duty was to look after the family. They depend on their husband economically. Nowadays, with the enhancement of the position of women in society, many Chinese women participate in social life directly and have achieved their economic independence. Normally, people say that rights and duties exist on a reciprocal basis. That indicates that woman must take up duties when they ask for equal social status. Women may have greater demands for some commodities like clothes, cosmetics and so on. Therefore, it can be seen that women's economic pressure comes from two sides. One is from family duties, the other from personal needs. Another point worth noticing is that this generation of women is in a transformation period from traditional ideas to modern concepts. They were caught in middle between these two concepts. The resulting contradictions make the pressure appear even more heavy.

- *Adapters* refers to those older consumers that are satisfied with their current life. This might be the philosophy of previous generations: "contentment brings happiness".

- *Traditionals* are those that maintain intrinsic value concepts and are relatively conservative.

- *Unassigned* do not belong to any of the other groups above. So it is hard to define their characteristics. But this group does not possess a leading position in the consumer market.

Understanding the characteristics of Chinese consumer groups will help one identify the consumer target group and aim directly at them when designing advertisement. The above discussion describes the differences of Chinese consumers. Now, it is time to find out the common characteristics of Chinese consumers. The following is based on the investigation of China on-line and China Base.

One can differentiate three stages in the development of the value concepts of the Chinese consumers. The *first* stage can be called: "The Confucian moral concept judges me". That means, Chinese took Confucianism as a value scale to judge their own behavior (Cheng YiTong 1999, 9). In this stage, Chinese consumers did not have an independent value concept. The *second* stage is referred to as "selfless me". That is to say, communism controlled people's ideas, and people's individual values were absorbed largely by the communist value concept. The *third* stage is called "individual self", which means that after the long time that personal values were submitted to social values, the modern

Chinese at last begin to realize their individual value, and they eventually form their own independent value concept.

Obviously, the alteration of the Chinese value concept does not only manifest itself in the consumer field, but also in many other fields like scientific research, literature and art, business management and so forth. But concentrating on the consumer field, what needs to be paid attention to is the alteration of *consumer value concept.* Based on this current value concept of the Chinese consumer, the advertising should represent, reflect and support this kind of value concept. An example here would give an explanation of this question. Originally, the advertisement sentence of Sprite was "sparkling as it is, it is cool to the heart". Later on, it changed to "sparkling as it is, I am myself". Actually, what "I am myself" reflects is exactly the more independent mindset of modern Chinese, and it stimulated the sympathy of consumers. Another example is rather convincing from the sale merit it achieved. Twin Bridge is a brand of monosodium glutamate. It emphasized the 99 percent degree of purity, and the packaging repeated the theme of the crystals in their advertisements. The advertisements satisfied the needs of consumer for beautiful things, thus the sale went up 70% within just two years (Xing He, 2000,12). There are numerous examples of this kind. Therefore, it shows that understanding your consumers and understanding what they want is always the first step of communicating with them effectively, and eventually being accepted by them.

Value concept alteration is one of the features of the modern Chinese consumer. Another feature is an optimistic outlook, combined with a feeling of disorientation. This kind of psychology can be called "security paradox" (Cheng YiTong 2000, 9). On the one hand, consumers are quite optimistic about the future of China, on the other hand, because of social welfare reform and the rapid changes in the economic situation, this group is worried about their personal development and is afraid of being left behind the social development. In order to illuminate the feeling of insecurity, and to confirm their value, Chinese consumers strive very hard to enhance themselves. Nevertheless, the negative part of such psychology can be described as "goat flock psychology" (Cheng YiTong 2000, 10). Others buy a product, so everybody else will follow, if the other do not buy, they would not buy. This is perhaps a phenomenon of running after the fashion of the time. It may indicate that the Chinese consumer markets are immature. Understanding the psychology of the Chinese consumers will help one understand the unstable factors in the Chinese market. "Goat flock psychology" as one of the factors adds to the instability of the market. Furthermore, it shortens the market cycles. That means that a product experiences a short period from producing to marketing. Certainly, as a method of promotion, advertisement must conform with such rapid circulation.

From the examination of these two common characters of Chinese consumers, the conclusion is: in view of establishing a good communication with customers, effective advertisement promotion should take the complex but relevant value concepts and the consumer psychology into consideration.

b) Cultural factors in advertising

Since culture plays a rather important role in promotion, how should one pay attention to it in advertisements so that cultural connotations are accepted by Chinese consumers? This question has been dealt with to some extend in the earlier part, addressing the family concept, harmony, implication. The emphasis in this part is how these cultural connotations are merged into advertisement. It should be observed that cultural connotation is not an attachment that one creates or adds to advertisement; it should rather be implied in the product. The creator's task is to find, reveal and show the cultural connotation (Wang LuChang 1998, 17).

Take the golden award winner of the Chinese advertising prize as an example, the GuangDa garden health auction series. The advertisement words are: "GuangDa garden, today health is up for auction". The implication is: what GuangDa sells is healthy, or in other works: GuangDa garden equals health. The advertisement words reveal the cultural implications of the product, that is: health.

The whole series was composed of three pictures. The first picture shows four little transparent bottles. The first bottle shows a green forest, the advertisement words are: "why do you not live in GuangDa to enjoy it forever". The second bottle contents soil with new flowers on it, the ad words are: "why do you not live in GuangDa to be with it forever". The third one put moon and stars in it, the ad words are: "why do you not live in GuangDa and share it forever". The fourth bottle is fresh air, the ad words are: "why do you not live in GuangDa and breath it forever".

The four bottles reveal the contents of health by resorting to four natural materials that are rarely found by modern Chinese. Therefore, they embody the needs of modern Chinese. Certainly, forest, soil, moon and stars as well as purified air have the authority to represent health.

The second picture shows five bottles. The first bottle contents GuangDa garden buildings and gardens, the other four are the originals. In the picture, the reader sees the real product for the first time. With the impression of the first picture, the reader will strengthen the feeling that "GuangDa can provide such healthy things".

The third picture has the same bottles, but GuangDa is put in a remarkable place, thus further highlighting the product.

After seeing the advertisement, the readers have a positive feeling, and certainly will have a deeper impression than of other house selling advertisements. The success point of this advertisement is exactly that it reflects the health connotations of the product as well as the cultural connotations of the product and in the same time stimulates the sympathy of the reader. Thus, a good advertisement should be a combination of the cultural connotation of the product and the perfect illustration form.

Female images are an ever-lasting subject of advertisements, but what women would be appreciated by Chinese? If the ad has some sexual contents, what degree would be proper? A lovely young girl, happy and pretty; a family housewife, dignified, diligent and tender; an aged woman, kind and caring for later generations will surely be appreciated by Chinese. However, if the ad image is too seductive and lacks elegant beauty, then it may be less welcomed.

Here are two examples to illustrate the question: the famous Chinese actress Zhang ZiYi acts as the ad image of Legend. She smiles brightly in the picture, the silk cloth make her extremely outstanding by implying the elegant beauty of Chinese girls. It can be seen that the youth, health and beauty full of Chinese flavor will help the consumer understand the features of the product.

Another ad shows an extremely mature and sexy actress promoting cosmetics. Since this actress has been remembered as a sex star, and many Chinese reject the idea of native sex actresses (overseas stars are a different matter), the result of the ad was not so desirable, although the woman is very beautiful. – One may find an explanation in Chinese traditional culture. The traditional Chinese culture defines the beauty of women as being elegant, tender and implicit, while sexy appearance belongs to the culture of other countries. Therefore, the imitation of the Western style in the ad made people feel uncomfortable.

There are people who have done investigations about the sex contents in advertisements; it is said that more than 50% have such contents (international ad

2000, 8). However, in China, in such a conservative society, too explicitly using such contents may be dangerous. Thus, commanding a proper degree in using such contents is extremely crucial.

An interesting story which has condensed into a proverb (*Dong Shi Xiao Pin*) would be quite forceful in explaining the situation. In the late Spring and Autumn Period, there was a beautiful woman called Xi Shi in WuGuo. Since she always had stomach pain, she had to put one hand on the stomach, and she had to lower her head a little. Another, rather ugly, girl named Dong Shi, envied the beauty of Xi Shi. For the purpose of making herself looking as beautiful as Xi Shi, she imitated the walking position of Xi Shi, but that only made her uglier than before. Therefore, when dealing with sensitive issues, commanding a proper degree is crucial, or one may end up producing the effect of "*Dong Shi Xiao Pin*".

Moral standards are quite different in each culture. A widely practiced behavior in one country might offend the people of another country. The difference in moral standards applied to advertisements can become a sensitive issue (Cheng YiTong 1999, 10). For example, an American ad of Levis jeans tells the story of a female prisoner running into a male restroom for avoiding the pursuit by a policeman. The traitor image of the actress did not stimulate sympathy of Chinese: Chinese people thought that committing crimes is evil behavior; the Levis ad is not suitable in China. An advertisement must conform with the social norms, even if this appears to be complicated.

c) Advertising regulations

China has some regulations on the advertising industry. Some significant articles are chosen here for reference:

1) advertisements should be true, legitimate and conform with the requirements of the socialist culture and the ideological progress;

2) the following contents shall not be allowed in advertisement:

    - national flag, national emblem or national anthem of the PRC;
    - terms such as "state level, supreme, very best";
    - names of any state organs or state personnel;
    - content which may adversely affect social stability, endanger the security of persons or property, or harm the public interests;
    - content which may jeopardize the social order or go against the prevailing social custom;

- content which may contain ethnic, racial, religious or gender discrimination;
- content which may obstruct protection of environmental or natural resources;
- content which may contain obscurity, superstition, horror, violence or social evils;

3) should advertisements indicate that gifts will be included, than the gift item and quantity shall be explicitly expressed;

4) content which makes comparisons in effect or safety with other pharmaceuticals or medical appliances;

5) content which provides proof by making use of the name or image of pharmaceutical research institutes, academic institutes, medical units, specialists, doctors or patients;

6) tobacco advertisements shall not be allowed in radio, movies, television, newspapers or magazines. Tobacco advertisements shall not be placed in public places such as waiting rooms, cinemas, conference rooms and sport venues. Tobacco advertisements shall explicitly indicate that "smoking is hazardous to health";

7) advertisements for pharmaceuticals, medical appliances, farm chemicals and veterinary drugs shall not be published without prior examination and approval;

8) food advertisements should not have words as "latest science, latest technology and latest processing technology".

The above articles should be paid attention to. It should be observed that the Chinese advertising market is still not standardized, and illegal cases emerge rather regularly. China examined 8100 cases of false advertisement in 1999.

Here is an advertisement checklist for the convenience of reference.

1) information should be significant to the past experience of Chinese people;

2) information should stimulate the sympathy of the expected and aspired target audience;

3) information should not touch sensitive problems;

4) understand Chinese ad regulations and their influence on advertisement;

5) do not think that an advertisement successful in another country will attract Chinese people;

6) pay attention to cultural influence on advertisement strategies;

7) define target consumers in the Chinese market.

Conclusion: the text discussed three big issues, which are marketing strategy, promotion strategy and advertising in China. Many cultural issues are involved, however, because of the rich connotation of culture, this text can not cover all cultural issues. Furthermore, every person has a different understanding of cultural connotations, thus the text above can be used as a reference only. As a theoretical basis of promotion in China, it will serve its purpose. In the practical operation, a strategy of Chairman Mao might be helpful: " despise the enemy in strategy and think highly of the enemy in tactics". If one takes marketing in China as a war, its seriousness should not be neglected at all. When the enemy is quite strong, adopt guerrilla warfare tactics, when the enemy is relatively strong, adopt movement warfare tactics, when enemy and one's own forces are equal, adopt positional warfare tactics. By adopting different tactics according to the different situations, the war will surely be won.

J. BUILDING UP A GOOD REPUTATION

Reputation is an abstract concept, which can be used to describe human beings and the activities that people participate in. Therefore, the activities of enterprises, being performed by people, naturally will involve the question of reputation. Then, how to define the reputation of an enterprise? What is a good reputation to a enterprise? The general public has an absolute authority to answer the question it is the public that uses products and services of enterprises, and that is affected by the activities of enterprises. Thus, enterprise reputation can be defined like this: a reputation refers to the image of identity commonly recognized by the public, and an image results from the special characteristics of an enterprise that make it outstanding from other enterprises. The special characteristics can be excellent quality of products and services, enterprise ideals that are accepted by the public, or some other characteristics that can meet public's material and spiritual needs. The process of building up a good reputation is not an independent process; it should in fact penetrate the whole marketing process. That is to say: the process of product, price, place and promotion is also the process of establishing a good reputation.

China is not the origination place of market economy; Western developed countries have been market economies for a much longer time than China. Western countries have more completed market systems (commodity markets, financial markets) and market self-regulating capacity (sector regulations, laws). Therefore the market economy systems of Western countries are in a more mature state than those in China. Many concepts that are new in China have been developed in the West, for example green marketing, enterprise culture construction, culture marketing and so on. These concepts have been introduced to China through academic exchange and foreign enterprises in China. Nevertheless, since the background against which these concepts were developed is different from China, they were given new meaning to fit into China's political, economic and cultural state of development. Corporate Identity (CI) is one of these concepts.

CI originated in Germany in the 1940ies. AEG used a unified trademark for the electrical appliances they produced (Peng XingLu 2000, 266). But it is IBM that is regarded as the role model of promoting the strategy. Then in the 1970ies, CI was introduced into Japan. The Japanese combined CI concepts with their own cultural characteristics, creating Japanese CI. Then what is the difference between American CI and Japanese CI?

First of all, three levels of CI will be introduced here. *Mind* identity (MI) is seen as the core and motivational power of CI, which includes the operational philosophy and concepts, corporate culture, the enterprise's operational style, the enterprise's development target and the enterprise's marketing strategy. The applied forms of MI are enterprise operational principles, beliefs, advertisement words and so on. – *Visual* identity (VI) includes the enterprise's organization, education, management, research and development, employee benefits, working environments and so on, which belongs to the internal operation of the enterprise. Visual identity also has external activities, such as market research, public relations, social benefits and so forth. VI realizes an enterprise's operational concept and culture. Visual identity embodies an enterprise's ideals and concepts in an external, superficial form. For example: enterprise name, promotion slogans, clothing, communication signals and so on. Compared to MI, which is regarded as dynamic system, VI is more of a static system.

American CI emphasizes VI, but American VI does not depend solely on VI. That means, VI embodies MI. In America, ideals and concepts, as well as the behavior of the enterprise have become comparatively clear after a long period of seeking and regulating. Enterprises have their culture which feature national characteristics. Therefore, MI and VI do not need to be emphasized in America. VI, as the signal of enterprises, content a good portion of national culture. It can be seen that American VI reflects the mature state of the American market economy and enterprise culture (Yu YangMing 1999, 28).

As to Japanese CI which highlights MI, it can find its source from the Japanese culture. Japanese culture benefits a lot from Chinese Confucianism. For example, loyalty and harmony which are the spirits of Confucianism now are the core spirit of Japanese culture (Zhang De 2000, 50). Consequently, this spirit penetrates in Japan's corporate culture. Collectivism and harmonious features of the Japanese enterprises culture make them pay more attention to people's awareness and thinking, rather than behavior and external forms.

From the above analysis, it can be observed that no matter what aspects American and Japanese enterprises pay attention to, their CI has integrated the respective social culture. As their CI are nationalized CI, the national features of the CI make them appear attractive and effective. Coming back to Chinese CI, it seems needless to say, that CI in China should integrate China's social culture.

When talking about social culture, morality must be highlighted. In the culture part, it is mentioned that Chinese society is a society combining etiquette and law. Etiquette contains law, law contains etiquette. Here "etiquette" is a series of moral regulations. Perhaps, one would think that is the feature of feudal China. However, in modern China, this feature has not disappeared; some morality reached the status of law and its function is reinforced by law. However, with the development of the economy, the relationship between people became even more complicated. Some relationships can not be regulated by law; furthermore the enforcement of law should be in accordance with the morality of people. Especially, China's legal system has not been completed yet, and this has left room for morality to maintain social order to some extent.

Therefore it is reasonable to say: China is still a society that highlights morality and rule of law. Rule of morality and rule of law do not contradict each other. On the contrary, they complements each other and function together. Certainly, the contents of morality has changed tremendously. Some traditional ideas, such as "men are superior to women" have less influence today. Some traditional morality standards have been kept for their progressive meaning to modern China. In light of the importance of morality in China, the first step a foreign business person is suggested to do is to include Chinese morality into CI strategy. Then, what is Chinese morality? The following text will give an illustration.

Confucianism doctrine advocates "respecting morality means expanding business" (Feng HuXiang 1998,7). That means the development of an enterprise should be given moral significance and targets. By comparing with the modern Western CI and Japanese CI, it can be found that Confucian ideas share some characteristics with them. For example, Johnson & Johnson writes in their corporate statements: "what we do must be fair and conform to morality, we take responsibility to the society and the whole world" (Feng HuXiang 1998,11). Panasonic holds the belief to be "dedicated to one's country".

Confucius also pointed out: "human beings can propagate beliefs" (Feng HuXiang 1998, 19). According to Confucius, the leader of a company should courageously propagate his belief and let them be recognized by his followers. Here "belief" equals to value concept. An organization should have a common value concept held by all members. Motivated by the value concept, work would be performed actively and creativity would develop. As a consequence, enterprises would develop, and so would society. Therefore, it is be no means an exaggeration to say that belief is power, that belief is the source of cohesive power, and that belief is the source of attractiveness.

Based on this, an enterprise must have its beliefs. Certainly, value concept vary from one person to another. Especially, the social environment plays a decisive role in the formation of beliefs. But it should be noted that common belief exists among all mankind. What a foreign business person should propagate in China is exactly these common beliefs. For example: "one should seek for the outstanding"; "practice makes perfect"; "where there is a will, there is a way"; "you will never know if you do not try"; "honesty and trustworthiness is beauty ". Through recognizing these beliefs, communication will be realized, trust built up and relationships will be harmonious. Once belief is built up, the operation of an enterprise will be self-regulated and a good public image established naturally. Therefore, propagating beliefs or value concepts accepted by Chinese function as crucial step in CI.

It is sometimes amazing to find the similarity of traditional Chinese Confucianism and modern advanced management ideas. This may lead to the question: why do Chinese enterprises have to draw from the experience of foreign countries in building CI while the essence of it has existed in China long time ago? An answer to this question can be found in Chinese attitude towards culture. Modern Chinese sometimes adopt a negative attitude to their culture. The culture revolution is one example. There is a Chinese saying: "a foreign monk prays more effectively than a Chinese monk". This explains very well that Chinese people sometimes lack confidence. The source of this perceived lack of confidence will not be explored here. The conclusion here is: in designing CI's, the morality of serving the society must be put in a central position, since it conforms with the essence of Chinese culture.

One of the concrete appearances of morality is virtue, which has been discussed in the culture part. Looking at this, one might think Chinese culture highlights virtues and neglects benefits. This is a wrong impression of Chinese culture. In fact, modern Chinese culture give equal position to virtues and benefits. There are idioms in China such as "seeking benefits while thinking of virtue", "seeking after benefits by resorting to virtue". In these proverbs, benefits and virtues are unified. Benefits are targets, and virtues correspond to the behavior to abide the reasonable regulations that lead to the targets; it is a kind of spiritual feature. Specifically speaking: "do not make poor quality products to cheat consumers' money"; "do not use exaggerate in advertisements to cheat consumer"; "provide secure products and help consumers to distinguish fake products"; "do not abuse monopoly prices". This is only a part of it; in general, a business person is always asked to remember the consumer when making money. Only in this way can he be trusted by consumers and make more money. In this sense, virtues and benefits go together well.

XunZi had a deep philosophy which can be used to describe the relationship between virtues and benefits: "everyone is borne with desires, like loving beauty, but human's desire would be better if it was the same as loving beauty, even if it was a little bit too much, it would not bring harm to others" (Jia Zeng-Jie 1999, 23). The Chinese combination of "benefits and virtues" and the words of XunZi share some features with Western customer satisfaction (CS) strategy. All three emphasize paying attention to the other's benefits while running after self-benefits. CS has been regarded as the more intelligent marketing strategy than CI for it attaches great attention to satisfying the customers. However, no matter whether one follows CI or CS, to deal with the relationship between virtues and benefits are the essential. Only if those two aspects are balanced can a marketing strategy succeed.

The above text has analyzed elements of CI in China from a cultural perspective. Some connections between Chinese culture and CI are discussed in the text. That indicates that China has a receptive environment to introduce CI, and some ideas of CI have already existed in China for thousands of years. The problem is, these ideas have not sufficiently been applied in business operations due to the economic state, the economic system and historical reasons. With respect to the current situation of management in China and the Chinese culture features (highlighting communication, relationships, the function of morality, collectivism, harmony and so on), MI should be the core of CI strategy in China.

The problem of how to integrate CI with Chinese culture is analyzed primarily theoretically. As to the practical operation of CI in China, one should apply CI theory according to the state of the respective sector and enterprise, and it is impossible to explore this here. However, a list of points to think of will be given for the convenience of reference:

- diversity of modern Chinese culture (combination of traditional culture, Western culture, elite culture, political culture and popular culture);
- diversity of value systems (traditional and modern, Chinese and foreign);
- combination of rule of law and rule of morality;
- appreciation of high morality;
- balance between benefits and virtues;
- importance of beliefs;
- diversity of levels of enterprise management;
- transformation of the economic and political system.

VI. CONCLUSIONS

I have evaluated this guide in the case of China, and I come to advice covering the following items: the negotiation, the contract and its implementation.

A. NEGOTIATION

In the area of negotiation, there are four Critical Success Factors to be considered throughout the process:

- the foreign party needs to **develop understanding** for the host country, in this case China. It may be considered an impossible task to try and do this given the limitations on time and resources that often apply. However, it is safe to say: the better the understanding, the better the own negotiation position, and the more subtle the negotiation process.

- It is crucial to **clarify the objectives**, asking questions such as: are you there to stay, or do you aim at short-term involvement; is the country you are dealing with only one of many, or is it the one that will determine success or failure of the corporation. In a wider sense, one has to understand the objectives of the other stakeholders – do you partners wish to establish a business relationship, or are they somehow forced to do so?

- Part of the stakeholders' objectives can be the implementation of certain corporate standards. It is essential to **keep a balance** between adaptation to local circumstances and sticking to principles that may constitute the very nature of a corporation, or in other words its reason for being in business.

- Understanding takes time – one should **have a lot of patience**. This is particularly true if the cultural gap between the partners is relatively large. It is important to build relationships of trust in order to bridge the gap.

B. CONTRACT

When it comes to drafting a contract, one needs to focus on the following two Critical Success Factors:

- In the interest of winning time, one may be inclined to defer issues on which the partners do not agree. This is a risky strategy – deferring means drawing a loan on the future. You should rather **work on the wording** until all parties can live with it.

- A contract can be seen as a cast-in-stone plan that only needs to be implemented – or as a snapshot at what parties think at the moment the contract is signed. You should be aware of the fact that you may need to **continue to negotiate after the signing**.

C. IMPLEMENTATION

Once a contract is signed, it needs to be implemented. In that stage, the following advice can be given:

- Developing an idea and putting it into practice are two different issues – the negotiation team may not be the ideal implementation team. It may be wise to **consider exchanging the key players** when it comes to making things happen.

- Implementation takes time – just as negotiations and writing contracts. In this stage it is crucial to **manage stakeholder expectations**, who may underestimate the effort that is required in this stage.

VII. APPENDICES

A. ABBREVIATIONS

e.g.	Example given = for example
FDI	Foreign Direct Investment
FIE	Foreign Invested Enterprises
FSR	Feasibility Study Report
HR	Human Resources
HRM	Human Resources Management
i.e.	Id est = that is to say
JV	Joint Venture
JVC	Joint Venture Contract
MNC	Multinational Corporation
MOFTEC	Ministry of Trade and Economic Cooperation
PA	Performance Appraisal
PRC	People's Republic of China
SOE	State Owned Enterprise

B. REFERENCES

ALASUUTARI, PERTTI 1995: "Researching culture"; London, Thousand Oaks, New Delhi: SAGE Publications Ltd..

ALSTON, JON P. / STEPHEN YANGXIN HE 1997: "Business Guide to Modern China"; East Lansing, Mich.: Michigan State University Press.

AN PING (ED.) 1997: "HuoYong SuZi BingFaYu JingShang (Apply the Arts of War of SuZi Following Your Inclinations in Business)"; Lan-Fang: Economics Daily Publishing House.

AN ZUOZHAN (ED.) 1986: "A Simple Edition of Chinese History (ZhongGuo Shi JianBian)"; JiNan: ShangDong Education Publishing House.

BAI YANG 1998: "ZhongGuoRen ShiGang (An Outline of Chinese History)"; BeiJing: China Friendship Publishing House.

BAO YUE / ZENG HONGLU (ED.) 1998: "Ding XiaoPing LiLun GaiLun (An Introduction to the Theory of Deng XiaoPing)"; BeiJing: Science Publishing House.

BLACKMAN, CAROLYN 1997: "Negotiation China: Case Studies and Strategies"; Australia: Allen & Unwin Pty Ltd..

BOND, MICHAEL HARRIS (ED.) 1996: "The Handbook of Chinese Psychology"; HongKong: Oxford University Press Ltd. (China).

BRAHM, LAURENCE J. / LI DAORAN 1996: "The Business Guide to China"; Singapore: Butterworth-Heinemann Asia.

BRAHM, LAURENCE J. 1997: "Sun Tzu's Art of Negotiating in China"; Hong-Kong: Naga Group Ltd..

BRAHM, LAURENCE J. 1998: "Zhu Ge Liang's Art of Crisis Management for China Joint Ventures"; HongKong: Naga Group Ltd..

BRAHM, LAURENCE J. 2001: "China's Century"; Singapore: John Wiley & Sons (Asia) Pte Ltd..

BRAHM, LAURENCE J. 2001: "Chinas Jahrhundert"; Weinheim: Wiley-VCH Verlag GmbH.

BUCKNALL, KEVIN B. 1994: "Culture Guide to Business in China"; Oxford: Butterworth-Heinemann Ltd.

CAI DINGJIAN 1999: "LiShi Yu BianGe (History and Reform)"; BeiJing: China Politics and Law University Publishing House.

CHANG JIANG 1999: "Fesco ErShi Nian (Twenty Years Fesco)"; BeiJing: BeiJing Publishing House.

CHAO FULIN (ED.) 1994: "ZhongGuo GuDai Shi (Ancient History of China)"; BeiJing: BeiJing Normal University Publishing House.

CHEN DONG (ED.) 1993: "ZhuXi ZheXue YanJiou (The Study of ZhuXi's Philosophy)"; BeiJing: China Social Science Publishing House.

CHEN QIHUA 1999: "ZhongGuo ShangGui (The Rule of Chinese Business)"; BeiJing: China Industrial and Commercial Publishing House.

CHEN ZHILI (ED.) 1999: "Deng XiaoPing LiLun ZhiDao Xia De ZhongGuo JiaoYu 20 Nian (20 Years Chinese Education under the Guidance of the Theory of Deng XiaoPing)"; FuJian: FuJian Education Publishing House.

CHENG DONGSHENG (ED.) 1999: "ZhongGuo QuYu FaZhan Kua ShiJi De (China's Regional Development Across the Centuries)"; BeiJing: China Regional Economy Association.

CHENG JINGCHUAN (ED.) 1998: "DiYuan ZhongGuo (Regionalism in China)"; BeiJing: China Archive Publishing House.

CHENG LIAOYUAN 1999: "Cong FaZhi Dao FaZhi (From Rule by Law to Rule of Law)"; BeiJing: The Law Publishing House.

CHENG MINGXIAN (ED.) 1999: "Xin ZhongGuo WuShiNian (Fifty Years New China)"; BeiJing: LiGong Publishing House.

CHENG SHIYING (ED.) 1997: "ZhongGuo GeMing Shi (A History of the Course of China's Revolution)"; BeiJing: Capital Normal University Publishing House.

CHENG WANGZHI 1998: "FaLu JiChu JiaoCheng (A Basic Course of Law)"; WuHan: WuHan Industry University Publishing House.

CHENG YITONG 2000: article in *International Advertising Journal*; BeiJing: International Advertising. 104, 8-10.

CHENG ZHILIANG 1996: "YaSheng SiBian Lu (Chinese Confucianism)"; BeiJing: Religion and Culture Publishing House.

CHENG ZHIMING 1999: "ZhongWai HeZi QiYe Zhong De XieTiao Yu KongZhi (Coordination and Control in Sino-Foreign Joint Venture Management)": XiangSu People's Publishing House.

CHURCHILL, GILBERT A., JR. / J. PAUL PETER 1998: "ShiChang YingXiao Xue (Marketing: Creating Value for Customers)"; BeiJing: Mechanic Industry Publishing House.

CORNE, PETER HOWARD 1997: "Foreign Investment in China - The Administrative Legal System"; HongKong: HongKong University Press.

DAVID, JONATHAN / LI YONG (ED.) 1995: "Doing Business with China"; London: Kogan.

DU PING 2000: "XiTu QuJin: XiBu Da KaiFa De ZhengCe BeiJing yu ShangYe JiYu (Find Gold in Western Areas: The Policies Background and Business Opportunities of Western Areas)"; BeiJing: China Honesty Publishing House.

DÜLFER, EBERHARD 1992: "Internationales Management in unterschiedlichen Kulturbereichen"; München, Wien: R. Oldenbourg Verlag GmbH.

DUO SHENGCHUN 1997: "MaoDu De ZhongGuo Ren (The Contradicted Chinese)"; BeiJing: China Building Material Publishing House.

THE EDITORIAL BODY OF CHINA FOREIGN TRADE AND ECONOMIC YEARBOOK 1999: "ZhongGuo DuiWai JingJi MaoYi NianJian (The Yearbook of China's Foreign Economic and Trade)"; BeiJing: China Economics Publishing House.

FAN QIAN / ZENG SANSHENG 1997: "SunZi BingFa JiQi YingYong (The Art of War and its Application)"; WuHan: China Geology University Press.

FEI HONGPING 1998: "ZhongGuo JingJi QuYu FaZhan (The Development of China's Regional Markets)"; BeiJing: Science Publishing House.

FENG HUXIANG 1998: "ZhongGuo ChuanTong ZheXue Yu XianDai GuanLi (China's Traditional Philosophy and Modern Management)"; JiNan: ShanDong University Publishing House.

FENG, PETER 1997: "Intellectual Property in China"; HongKong: Sweet & Maxwell Asia.

FEUCHTWANG, STEPHAN 2001: "Popular Religion in China - The Imperial Metaphor"; Richmond, Surrey: Curzon Press.

GAN BIQUN (ED.) 1997: "ZhongGuo YingXiao DaoDe (Enterprises Marketing Morality)"; WuHan: HuBei People's Publishing House.

GAN BIQUN (ED.) 1999: "GuoJi ShiChang YingXiao Xue (International Marketing)"; WuChang: WuHan University Publishing House.

GAN JUNQI (ED.) 1998: "ZhongCai Fa JiaoCheng (Arbitration Law Course)"; BeiJing: China Financial and Economics Publishing House.

GAO GUOBIN (ED.) 1998: "GuoJia QuanLi JiGuan GongZuo YanJiou (State Power Organs Work Study)"; HuBei: HuBei People's Publishing House.

GE JIANXIONG (ED.) / YAO DALI 1999: "QianQiou XingWang Yuan Dynasty (Rise and Fall of the Yuan Dynasty)"; ChangChun: ChangChun Publishing House.

GONG PEIXIANG (ED.) 1999: "DangDai ZhongGuo De FaLu GeMing (The Law Revolution of Modern China)"; BeiJing: Law Publishing House.

GRÜNEBAUM, BERTHOLD (ED.) 1995: "Marktchance China - Vom ersten Kontakt zum Joint Venture"; Frankfurt: Campus Verlag.

GU JIANHUA (ED.) 1998: "ZhongGuo ChuangTong WenHua (Traditional Chinese Culture)"; BeiJing: China Industry Publishing House.

GU YUMIN / SHI JIANSAN / ZHOU YAFEN 1994: "ZhongGuo BaoShuiQu (China's Bonded Areas)"; BeiJing: China Economics Publishing House.

GUO CHAOREN (ED.) ET AL. 1999: "ZhongHua RenMin GongHeGuo NianJian (The Yearbook of the People's Republic of China)"; BeiJing: Yearbook of the People's Republic of China Publishing House.

HE MAOCHUN (ED.) 1999: "ZhongGuo JingJi MaoYi BaiPiShu (The White Paper of China's Foreign Economy and Trade)"; Beijing: Economy and Science Publishing House.

HE XI (ED.) 1997: "Ding XiaoPing LiLun GaiLun (The History of the People's Republic of China)"; BeiJing: Higher Learning Education Publishing House.

HE XIAOMING 1995: "YaSheng SiBian Lu (The Lesser Sage Thinking Record)"; KaiFeng: HeNan University Publishing House.

HERBIG, P.A. 2000: "Kua WenHua ShiChang YingXiao (Handbook of Cross-Cultural Marketing)"; BeiJing: BeiJing Mechanical Publishing House.

HERMEL, PHILIPPE 1993: "Management Européen et International"; Paris: Ed. Economica.

HINKELMAN, EDWARD G. 1994: "China Business - The Portable Encyclopedia for Doing Business with China"; San Rafael California: World Trade Press.

HOFSTEDE, GEERT 1993: "Interkulturelle Zusammenarbeit"; Wiesbaden: Gabler Verlag.

HONG XIOUPING 1994: "ZhongGuo ChanXue SiXiangShi (A History of Chinese Buddhism)"; NanJing: NanJing University Publishing House.

HOU GUISHENG 2000: "ZhongGuo DuiWai MaoYi TongLun (On China's Foreign Trade)"; JiNan: ShangDong University Publishing House.

HUAI XIAOFENG (ED.) 1998: "FaZhiShi JiaoCheng (The History of the Legal System of China)"; BeiJing: China Politics and Law University Publishing House.

HUANG KEAN (ED.) 1998: "ZhongGuo DuiWai MaoYi JingJi (China's Foreign Economic and Trade)"; XiaMen: XiaMen University Publishing House.

HUANG ZUOPING 1998: "ZhongGuo JingJi QuYu XinLun (A New Study on China's Economic Regions)"; BeiJing: China Agriculture Publishing House.

HUANGYASHENG 1998: "FDI China: An Asian Perspective"; HongKong: Institute of Southeast Asian Studies and the Chinese University Press.

HUO RENZHI (ED.) 1994: "HuangHe WenHua (The Culture of the Yellow River)"; BeiJing: BeiJing HuaYi Publishing House.

JI TONGFANG (ED.) 1997: "ZhongWai WenHua GaiLun (An Outline of Chinese Culture)"; BeiJing: Arms University Publishing House.

JIA YUXIN 1997: "Kua WenHua JiaoJi Xue (Cross-Cultural Communication)"; ShangHai: ShangHai Foreign Language Education Publishing House.

JIAN BOZHAN 1983: "Qin Han Shi (The History of the Qin and Han Dynasties)"; BeiJing: Peking University Press.

JIANG ZUYAN (ED.) 1999: "RuShi JiaoDian (The Focus of Entering WTO)"; BeiJing: Economy and Science Publishing House.

JIN CHONGJI (ED.) 1999: "ErShi ShiJi ZhongGuo De JueQi (The Rise of China in the 20th Century)"; ShangHai: ShangHai People's University Press.

JIN YIMING 1999: "ZhongGuo JiaoYu JieGuo He LeiBie Yan Jiou (A Study on China's Education Structure and Classification)"; ShangHai: ShangHai Education Publishing House.

JIN YUANPU / TAN HAOZHE (ED.) 1999: "ZhongGuo WenHua GaiLun (A Brief Introduction to Chinese Culture)"; BeiJing: Capital University Publishing House.

KE JIANZHONG (ED.) 1998: "ZhongGuo GuDai LiShi GaiLun (An Introduction to Ancient Chinese History)"; ChengDu: SiChuan University Publishing House.

DE KEIJZER, ARNE J. 1992: "China Business Strategies for the 90s"; California: Pacific View Press.

VON KELLER, EUGEN 1982: "Management in fremden Kulturen"; Bern, Stuttgart: Verlag Paul Haupt.

LAFAYETTE DE MENTE, BOYE 1994: "Chinese Etiquette & Ethics in Business"; Illinois: NTC Business Books.

LAI YONGHAI (ED.) 1999: "ZhongGuo FoJiao WenHua (Chinese Buddhism)"; BeiJing: China Youth Publishing House.

LANE, KELLEY / YADONG LUO 1999: "China 2000: Emerging Business Issues"; London, New York, California: SAGE Publication, Inc..

LAO ZI, SHENGLI (ED.) 1995: "Ru Dao Fo BaiKeQuanShu (An Encyclopedia of Confucianism, Taoism and Buddhism)"; GuiLin: LiJiang Publishing House.

THE LEGAL BUREAU OF THE PEOPLE'S REPUBLIC OF CHINA 1995: "ZhongHua RenMin GongHeGong SheWai FaGui HuiBian (The Collection of the Foreign-Related Laws of the People's Republic of China)"; BeiJing: China Legal System Publishing House.

LEI QI (ED.) 1999: "XinBian ZhongGuo GuDai Shi (A New Edition of China's Ancient History)"; HaErBin: Northeast Normal University Publishing House.

LEI YIQUN / SHI TIEJING (ED.) 1999: "ZhongGuo GuDai Shi (Ancient History of China)"; BeiJing: Higher Learning Education Publishing House.

LI BUYUN (ED.) 1998: "ZhongGuo LiFa De JiBen JingShen He ZhiDu (The Basic Theory and System of Chinese Legislation)"; BeiJing: China Legal System Publishing House.

LI BUYUN (ED.) 1999: "ZhongGuo TeSe SheHui ZhuYi FaZhi TongLun (On Socialist Legal System with Chinese Characteristics)"; Bei-

Jing: Social Science and Historic Document Publishing House.

LI DEBAO (ED.) 1994: "The China Investment Guide"; HongKong: Pearson Professional Asia-Pacific.

LI HAIJIAN 1999: "ZuoXiang PingHengShi KaiFang-ZhongGuo DuiWai JingJi KaiFang JieGou YanJiou (Heading for Balanced Opening - A Study of the Structure of China's Economic Opening to the Outside)"; BeiJing: Social Science and Historic Document Publishing House.

LI JINGWEN (ED.) 2000: "ZhongGuo QuYu JingJi JiaoCheng (Course of China's Regional Economy)"; NanNing: GuangXi People's Publishing House.

LI JINGWEN (ED.) 1999: "ZuoXiang 21 ShiJi De ZhongGuo QuYu JingJi (China's Regional Economy Heading for the 21st Century)"; NanNing: GuangXi People's Publishing House.

LI QINGSHAN 1996: "ZhongGuoRen XinLun: Cong MingYan Kan MinXin (New Comment on Chinese: Read Chinese People through Proverbs)"; BeiJing: China Social Science Publishing House.

LI SHOUCHU (ED.) 1997: "ZhongGuo ZhengFu ZhiDu (The Government Policy of China)"; BeiJing: China Central Nationality University Press.

LI XIA 1996: "DaoJia Yu ChanZong (Taoism and Chan Sect)"; HeFei: AnHui University Publishing House.

LI XIANGHAI / WANG YUEBING (ED.) 1999: "RiBen WenHua YanJiou - Yi ZhongRi WenHua BiJiao Wei ZhongGuo (The Study of Japanese Culture - Centered on the Comparison of Chinese and Japanese Culture)"; BeiJing: China Social Science Publishing House.

LI XUEQIN 1997: "ShiLuo De WenMing (The Lost Civilisation)"; ShangHai: ShangHai Culture and Art Publishing House.

LI YINGNING (ED.) 2000: "QunYu FaChan XinSiLu-ZhongGuo SheHui FaZhan Bu PingHeng Dui XianDaiHua JinCheng De YingXiang Yu DuiCe (New Thinking on Regional Development - The Influence of the Imbalanced Social Development in China on the Modernization and the Countermove)"; BeiJing: Economics Daily Publishing House.

LIAN YONGJIE (ED.) 1999: "ZhongGuo ChuanTong WenHua GaiLun (General Introduction to Traditional Culture)"; XiAn: ShangXi People's Publishing House.

LIN GUANGPIN (ED.) 1999: "ChuShi ZhiHui ShouCe - XianDai GongGua JiaoShi (Philosophy of Life - Modern Public Relations Classroom)"; ChangChun: JiLin Culture and History Publishing House.

LIN JINZHOU / DENG LIPING (ED.) 1999: "ZhongGuo DuiWai MaoYiyu JingJi De (The Operation and Management of China's Foreign Economy and Trade)"; XiaMen: XiaMen University Publishing House.

LIU CHUNZHI / LIU SIQI (ED.) 1994: "SunZi BingFa JiaoBen (A Course of SunZi's Arts of War)"; BeiJing: State Defense University Publishing House.

LIU GUODANG 1998: "QianQi RuJia WenHua YanJiou (A Study of Early Stage Confucianism)"; GuiLin: GuangXi Teacher's University Publishing House.

LIU GUOGUANG / WANG LUOLIN (ED.) 2000: "2000 Nian ZhongGuo JingJi (China's Economy 2000)"; BeiJing: Social Science Publishing House.

LIU GUOXIN (ED.) 1995: "ZhongGuo Xiao TongShi (General History of China)"; BeiJing: China Youth Publishing House.

LIU HUAQING 1999: "ZouXiang ShiJie - XinZhongGuo DuiWai KaFang De Li-Cheng (Head for the World - The Opening Process of the New China)"; ChangSha: HuNan Normal University Publishing House.

LIU JINHUA (ED.) 1998: "FaLu JiChu (The Foundation of Law)"; ShengYan: Northeast Finance and Economics Publishing House.

LIU XIANGDONG (ED.) 1998: "ZhongGuo DuiWai JingJi MaoYi ZhengCe Yu GaiGe ZongLan (China's Foreign Economic and Trade Policy and the Reform)"; BeiJing: China Foreign Economy and Trade Publishing House.

LIU YUAN (ED.) 1999: "GuoJi ShangWu TanPan (International Business Negotiation)"; BeiJing: China Foreign Economy and Trade Publishing House.

LONG GUOQIANG (ED.) 1995: "ZhongGuo DuiWai MaoYi FuWu FangLue (The Strategy of Chinese Service Trade)"; BeiJing: China Honesty Publishing House.

LU RENFA 2000: "SheWai ShuiWu (Foreign Related Tax)"; *Foreign Related Tax*; BeiJing: Foreign Related Tax Editing Publishing House.

LU TAO (ED.) 1999: "ZhongHua WenMingShi (History of Chinese Civilisation)"; ShiJiaZhuang: HeBei Education Publishing House.

LU ZHENG (ED.) 1999: "ZhongGuo GongYe FaZhan BaoGao (China Industrial Economic Development Report)"; BeiJing: Business Management Publishing House.

LUO MUSHENG 1999: "Tequ FaZhan ShiGao (The History of the Special Economic Zones)"; GuangZhou: GuangDong People's Publishing House.

LUO YULIE / ZHANG ZHIGANG (ED.) 1998: "ZhongWai WenHua JiaoLiuShi (Sino-Foreign Religious Exchange)"; ChangSha: HunNan Education Publishing House.

LUO ZHENGKAI (ED.) 1999: "ZhongGuo GeMing Shi (A History of China's Revolution)"; Beijing: Economics and Science Publishing House.

MA HONG (ED.) 1999: "ZhongGuo ShiChang FaZhan BaoGao (Report on China's Market Development)"; BeiJing: China Development Publishing House.

MA YANG (ED.) 2000: "ZhongGuo JingJi JiShu HeZuo ZhiNan (A Guidebook of Chinese Economy and Technological Co-operation)"; BeiJing: Economy and Science Publishing House.

MOSER, MICHAEL J. / WINSTON K. ZEE 1999: "China Tax Guide"; HongKong: Oxford University Press Ltd. (China).

PAN SHUZHI (ED.) 2000: "GuoShi GaiYao (An Introduction to the History of China)"; ShangHai: FuDan University Publishing House.

PANG PU (ED.) 1994: "ZhongWai WenHua GaiLun (China's Traditional Cultural Spirit and the 30 Books Representing Chinese Traditional Culture)"; ShanXi: LiaoNing University Publishing House.

PENG XINGLU 2000: "ShiChang YingXiao Xue (On Marketing)"; BeiJing: China Financial and Economics Publishing House.

PU XINGZU (ED.) 1999: "DangDai ZhongGuo ZhengZhi ZhiDu (The Modern Political System of China)"; ShangHai: FuDan University Publishing House.

QIAN ZHIQI (ED.) 1999: "WaiShang TouZi Xin JinHui (The New Opportunity of Foreign Investment in China)"; *International Economic Co-operation*; BeiJing: International Co-operation Publishing House. No 10 166.

QITAO (ED.) 1999: "ZhongGuo TongShi JiaoCheng (The Course of Chinese History)"; JiNan: ShanDong University Press.

SCHUCHARDT, CHRISTIAN A. 1994: "Deutsch-chinesische Joint-ventures - Erfolg und Partnerbeziehung"; München: R. Oldenbourg Verlag GmbH.

SEITZ, KONRAD 2000: "China im 21. Jahrhundert"; Frankfurt: Alfred Herrhausen Gesellschaft für internationalen Dialog.

SHAO BINGREN 1999: "GaiGe ZhiShi ShouCe KeJiao GaiGe FenCe (A Handbook of Reform - Book of Education)"; BeiJing: Reform Publishing House.

SHAO BINGREN (ED.) 1999: "GaiGe ZhiShi ShouCe FaLu ZhiDu FenCe (A Handbook of Reform - Law Book)"; BeiJing: Reform Publishing House.

SHENG LIQUN (ED.) 1998: "ZhongGuo GaiGe KaFang De ShiJian Yu TanShou (The Practice and Exploration of China's Reform and Opening-up)"; NanJing: JiangSu People's Publishing House.

SHENG QIWEN (ED.) 1997: "HuaXia WuQian Nian (5000 Years of HuaXia)"; ShangHai: ShangHai Dictionary Publishing House.

SHIYUANQI (ED.) 1999: "ZhongGuo XianDaiHua LiCheng (The Modernization of China)"; BeiJing: The School of the Central Committee of the Communist Party Publishing House.

SHOUYONG (ED.) 1999: "ZhongGuo ChuanTong WenHua GaiLun (General Introduction to Traditional Culture)"; ShangHai: ShangHai Education Publishing House.

SHU YI (ED.) 1999: "ZhongGuo 21ShiJi JingJi FaZhan Da QuShi (China's Economic Development Tendency Towards the 21st Century)"; BeiJing: China Honesty Publishing House.

SONG KAIZHI 1999: "ZhongWai WenHua GaiLun (An Introduction to Chinese and Foreign Culture)"; NanJing: HeHai University Publishing House.

SONG ZHIMING (ED.) / DING YAN 2000: article in *Journal of Investment and Co-operation*; BeiJing, 8.

STRANGE, ROGER / JIM SLATER / LIMIN WANG 1998: "Trade and Investment in China"; London, New York: Routledge.

SUN GUOBIN / ZHANG XIOUE (ED.) 1997: "ZhongGuo DuiWai JingJi FaZhan ZhanLue (China's Foreign Economic and Trade Development Strategies)"; JinLin: JinLin People's Publishing House.

TAN QILIANG (ED.) 1996: "ZhongGuo LiShi CiDian-LiShi DiLi Juan (Dictionary of China's History - Volume of Geography and History)"; ShangHai: ShangHai Dictionary Publishing House.

TANG CHUANFENG / ZHAO XIOUCHEN / SUN XIOUFENG (ED.) 1999: "ZhongGuo DuiWai MaoYi JiguoJi JingJi JiShu ShiChang HeZuo ZhiNan (China's Foreign Trade and International Economic and Technological Co-operation Market)"; WuHan: HuBei People's Publishing House.

TAO QU / MILFORD B. GREEN 1997: "Chinese Foreign Direct Investment"; England: Ashgate Publishing Limited.

THOMM, RAINER 2000: "China: Mission impossible?"; BeiJing: World Affairs Press.

TIAN GUANGLIN (ED.) 1999: "General Introduction to Traditional Culture (ZhongGuo ChuanTong WenHua GaiLun)"; BeiJing: Higher Learning Education Publishing House.

TIAN GUANGQI 1998: "HeXieLun (On Harmony)"; BeiJing: China Overseas Chinese Publishing House.

TROMPENAARS, FONS 1994: "L'entreprise multiculturelle (Riding the waves of culture. Understanding Cultural Diversity in Business.)"; Paris: Maxima.

USUNIER, JEAN-CLAUDE 1992a: "Commerces entre cultures, tome 1"; Paris: Presses Universitaires de France.

USUNIER, JEAN-CLAUDE 1992b: "Commerces entre cultures, tome 2"; Paris: Presses Universitaires de France.

WANG CHENGGUANG (ED.) 1997: "Introduction to Chinese Law"; HongKong: Sweet & Maxwell Asia.

WANG GUIGUO / WEI ZHENGYI 1996: "Modernization, Market Economy and Law"; HongKong: Sweet & Maxwell Asia.

WANG JUHAO (ED.) 1999: "MianXiang 21 ShiJi De ZhongGuo ShiChang YingXiao YanJiou (Marketing Study of the Chinese Market in the 21st Century)"; HangZhou: ZheJiang University Publishing House.

WANG LIWEN (ED.) 1999: "ZhongGuo GeMing Shi (A History of China's Revolution)"; BeiJing: BeiJing Science and Engineering University Publishing House.

WANG LUOLIN / PAN WEIMING / JIANG XIAOJUAN / WANG JUN (ED.) 1999: "LiYong WaiZi Yu ZhongGuo JinRong TiZhi GaiGe (The Use of Foreign Capital and the Reform of China's Financial System)"; XiaMen: FuJiang Publishing House.

WANG RUIPU / SUN QISHOU (ED.) 1999: "ZhongHua RenMing GongHeGuo GuoShi TongJian (An Appreciation of the History of the

People's Republic of China)"; BeiJing: Modern Publishing House.

WANG XINTING (ED.) 1997: "ZhongGuo ChuanTong WenHua GaiLun (General Introduction to Traditional Culture)"; BeiJing: China Forestry Publishing House.

WANG YIMING (ED.) 1998: "ZhongGuo QuYu JingJi ZhengCe YanJiou (Study of China's Regional Economic Policies)"; BeiJing: China Plan Publishing House.

WANG ZHONGFANG / SUN WANFANG (ED.) 1999: "ZhongGuo FaLu NianJian (China's Law Yearbook)"; BeiJing: China Law Yearbook Press.

WEI XINGDONG / CAO BING (ED.) 1998: "ZhongGuo GuDai WenHuaShi (Ancient Cultural History of China)"; SuZhou: SuZhou University Publishing House.

WIENEN, INGMAR 1999: " Impact of Religion on Business Ethics in Europe and the Muslim World"; Frankfurt, Berlin, Bern, New York et al.: Peter Lang Verlag GmbH.

WU NANGONG 1994: "SongMing LiXue (Neo-confuicianism in Song and Ming Dynasty)"; ChuangChun: JiLin Culture and History Publishing House.

XIN CHUNYING 1999: "YiFa ZhiGuo Yu SiFa GaiGe (Rule of Law and Judicial Reform)"; BeiJing: China Legal System Publishing House.

XIN CHUNYING 1999: "ZhongGuo FaLu ZhiDu JiQi GaiGe (Chinese Legal System and the Reform)"; BeiJing: Law Publishing House.

XING HE 2000: article in *China Advertising Journal*; BeiJing: China Advertising Journal Publishing House. 83, 12-13.

YANG CHAOMING 2000: "RuJia WenHua MianMian Guan (Overall Survey of Confucianism)"; JiNan: QiLu Publishing House.

YANG SHENGMING (ED.) 1999: "FuWu MaoYi: ZhongGuo Yu ShiJie (Service Trade: China and World)"; Beijing: Democracy and Construction Publishing House.

YANG SHUWEN / CHENG ZHENGFANG (ED.) 1997: "ZhongWai JingJi ZhiWu FanZui ShiLu (A Faithful Record of the Criminals of China and Foreign Post and Economic)"; BeiJing: The Law Publishing House.

YANG XIANCAI / ZHU LING (ED.) 1993: "ZhongGuo GeMing Shi (A History of China's Revolution)"; BeiJing: Higher Learning Education Publishing House.

YANG ZENGWEN (ED.) 1999: "ZhongGuo FoJiao JiBen ZhiShi (Basic Knowledge on Chinese Buddhism)"; BeiJing: Religion and Culture Publishing House.

YI SONGZHI / PENG JINQING (ED.) 1998: "ShangWu TanPan Xue (Business Negotiation)"; ChangSha: HuNan Science and Technology Publishing House.

YIN CHENGLIN (ED.) 1994: "ZhongGuo GuDai Shi (Ancient History of China)"; KunMing: YunNan University Publishing House.

YOU LIN / ZHENG XILI / WANG RUIPU (ED.) 1998: "GuoShi TongJian (An Appreciation of Chinese History)"; BeiJing: Modern Publishing House.

YU MINGSHENG (ED.) 1997: "ZhongGuo FaZhi De LiShi JinCheng (The Historical Progress of Chinese Rule of Law)"; HeFei: AnHui People's Publishing House.

YU WEIQING / JIANG FUQU (ED.) 1999: "ZhongGuo XinXi ShiChang (China's Information Market)"; WuHan: HuBei People's Publishing House.

YU YANMING (ED.) 1999: "CIS MingPai ZhanLue De WangPai (The Key of CIS Brand Strategy)"; WuHan: WuHan University Publishing House.

YU YUDING / ZHENG BINGWEI (ED.) 2000: "ZhongGuo RuShi YanJiou BaoGao (Research Report on China 's Entry into WTO"; BeiJing: Social Science Publishing House.

YUAN QIGANG 1995: "GuoJi ShangWu TanPan (International Business Negotiation)"; JiNan: Yellow River Publishing House.

YUAN WANG / XIN SHENGZHANG 1998: "Business Culture in China"; Singapore: Butterworth-Heinemann Asia.

YUAN XINGPEI (ED.) ET AL. 1998: "ZhongHua WenMing ZhiGuang (Chinese Civilisation)"; BeiJing: Peking University Press.

YUAN YONGSONG (ED.) 1998: "ZhongGuo ZhengFu KuaShiJi ShiZheng FangLue (The Policy of the Chinese Government for the Next Century)"; BeiJing: Red Banner Publishing House.

ZENG KUNSHENG 1998: "Lun-ShiChang JingJi Yu ZhongGuo QuYu JingJi FaZhan (On China's Regional Economy - Market Economy and the Development of China's Regional Economy)"; ChangSha: HuNan People's Publishing House.

ZHAI XUEWEI (ED.) 1994: "RenQing, MianZi, GuangXiWang, ZhongGuo SheHui XinLi He XingWen TeZheng (Face, Human Sympathy and Relationship Net - Characteristics of Chinese Social Psychology and Behavior)"; ZhenZhou: HeNan People's Publishing House.

ZHAN JINFAN 1997: "ZhongGuo FaLu De ChuanTong Yu JinDai ZhuanXing (The Traditions of Chinese Law and the Transformation in Modern Times)"; BeiJing: Law Publishing House.

ZHAN JINGAO (ED.) 1999: "QiYe RenLi ZiYuan GuanLi (Enterprises Human Resource Management)"; WuHan: WuHan Geology University Publishing House.

ZHAN XIMING (ED.) 1995: "LaoDongLi ShiChang De YuZuo Yu GuanLi (Operation and Management of the Labor Market)"; NanChang: JiangXi Higher Learning Publishing House.

ZHANG DE / WU JIANPING 2000: "QiYe WenHua yu CI CeHua (Enterprise Culture and CI Strategy)"; BeiJing: QingHua University Publishing House.

ZHANG DUNHOU / LI LIPING (ED.) 1998: "TouZi HuanJing PingJia Yu TouZi JueCe (Evaluation of Investment Environment and Investment Strategy)"; BeiJing: China People's University Publishing House.

ZHANG PINGZHI / YAN JINGLUN 1998: "ZhongGuo Ren XinLun (The Shortcomings of Chinese)"; BeiJing: China Social Science Publishing House.

ZHANG SHUNQING / LI JINSHANG (ED.) 1992: "ZhongHuaRenMin GongHeGong WenHuaShi (The Cultural History of the People's Republic of China)"; HeiLongJiang: HeiLongJiang Education Publishing House.

ZHANG YUEQUN / QIAN YUCAI (ED.) 1997: "Deng XiaPing LiLun (The Theory of Deng XiaoPing)"; NanJing: NanJing University Publishing House.

ZHANG ZHUSHENG (ED.) 1997: "ZhongGuo SheWai JingJi FaLu (China's Foreign Related Economic Laws)"; BeiJing: Foreign Trade and Economic University Publishing House.

ZHAO DEYU 1998: "XiFang WenHua DongLai Yu ZhongRi LiangGuo De FanYing (The Introduction of the Western Culture and the Reflection of China and Japan)"; BeiJing: China Social Science Publishing House.

ZHAO RUQI (ED.) 1999: "SiChouZhiLu XiDuan LiShiYanJiou JianLun YanTu MinZu QianXi Ji GuoJia GuanXi (Study of the History of the Western Silk Road and the Nationality Migration and Country Relations)"; GanSu: LanZhou Publishing House.

ZHAO SHUMING 1995: "ZhongGuo QiYe RenLi ZiYuan GuanLi (Chinese Enterprises' Human Resource Management)"; NanJing: NanJing University Publishing House.

ZHENG JIFANG 1995: "QiYe XingXiang SheJi Yu WenHua YingXiao (CIS: Enterprise Image Design and Culture Marketing)"; BeiJing: Petroleum Industry Publishing House.

ZHENG LIWEN (ED.) 1998: "ZhongWai RuXue BiJiao YanJiou (A comparative Study of Chinese and Overseas Confucianism)"; BeiJing: Eastern Publishing House.

ZHENG PING 1998: "ZhongGuo DiLi, ZiRan, JingJi, RenWei (China's Geography, Nature, Economy and People)"; BeiJing: Asia Disseminating Publishing House.

ZHENG QIN (ED.) 1999: "ZhongGuo FaZhi History (Study of China's Legal System)"; BeiJing: Law Publishing House.

ZHENG SHUSHANG (ED.) 1998: "ZhongGuo JiaoYu NianJian (China's Education Yearbook)"; BeiJing: People's Education Publishing House.

ZHENG XIAOJIANG ET AL. 1998: "XianDai DaoDe Yu DangDai ZhongGuo (Modern Morality and Modern China)"; HeFei: AnHui Education Publishing House.

ZHI YUAN 1998: "Ren Zhi Chu (The Beginning of Human Beings)"; ChengDu: SiChuang Education Publishing House.

ZHOU DIAN KUN 1997: "ZhongGuo ShiChang FaZhan BaoGao ZhongGuo ShiChang FaZhan BaoGao (The Relationships of the Eastern and Western Market of China and Co-ordinating Development)"; ChengDu: Southwest Financial and Economics Publishing House.

ZHOU GAODE 1999: "DaoJiao WenHua Yu ShengHou (Taoist Culture and Life)"; BeiJing: Religion and Culture Publishing House.

ZHOU WENZHANG 1997: "TeQu DaoLun (An Introduction to Special Economic Zones)"; HaiNan: HaiNan Publishing House.

ZHU DAWEI ET AL. 1998: "WeiJinNanBei SheHui ShengHuo Shi (Societal Life History of WeiJinNanBei Dynasty)"; BeiJing: China Social Science Publishing House.

ZHU YOUXIN 1999: "WenWu Yu LiShi (Cultural Relics and History)"; BeiJing: Eastern Publishing House.

ZOU YONGXIAN (ED.) 1993: "ZhuXi Thoughts Exploration (A Forum of ZhuXi's Thoughts)"; XiaMen: XiaMen University Publishing House.

Peter Lang · Europäischer Verlag der Wissenschaften

Tadeusz Rachwał

Labours of the Mind

Labour in the Culture of Production

Frankfurt/M., Berlin, Bern, Bruxelles, New York, Oxford, Wien, 2001. 165 pp.
Literary and Cultural Theory. Edited by Wojciech H. Kalaga. Vol. 8
ISBN 3-631-36950-6 · pb. € 27.60*
US-ISBN 0-8204-4839-8

The main concern of the book is the way in which such seemingly obvious notions as labour and production have contributed to the formation of human subject in European culture. What is offered to the reader is a reading, and a re-reading, of a number of conceptualisations of culture, of a number of such "labours of the mind" in which labour and production, either explicitly or implicitly, become principles in the evaluation of cultures as well as powerful tools for the ideological constitution and reconstruction of social space. What the book also addresses is the question of the ways culture is related to nature, and hence the question of the reality of culture which, inevitably, hinges on questioning the reality of reality itself.

Contents: Labour · Culture · Production · Alienation · Utopia · Nature

Frankfurt/M · Berlin · Bern · Bruxelles · New York · Oxford · Wien
Auslieferung: Verlag Peter Lang AG
Jupiterstr. 15, CH-3000 Bern 15
Telefax (004131) 9402131

*incl. value added tax
Prices are subject to change without notice

Homepage http://www.peterlang.de